Smart Technologies and the End(s) of Law

for Maria and Chantal
and for Ludo

Smart Technologies and the End(s) of Law

Novel Entanglements of Law and Technology

Mireille Hildebrandt

Institute for Computing and Information Sciences, Radboud University Nijmegen, the Netherlands; Law, Science, Technology & Society Studies, Vrije Universiteit Brussel, Belgium; Erasmus School of Law, Erasmus University Rotterdam, the Netherlands

Edward Elgar
PUBLISHING

Cheltenham, UK • Northampton, MA, USA

Published by
Edward Elgar Publishing Limited
The Lypiatts
15 Lansdown Road
Cheltenham
Glos GL50 2JA
UK

Edward Elgar Publishing, Inc.
William Pratt House
9 Dewey Court
Northampton
Massachusetts 01060
USA

A catalogue record for this book
is available from the British Library

Library of Congress Control Number: 2014954557

This book is available electronically in the **Elgar**Online
Law subject collection
DOI: 10.4337/9781849808774

ISBN 978 1 84980 876 7 (cased)
ISBN 978 1 84980 877 4 (eBook)

Typeset by Columns Design XML Ltd, Reading

Contents

About the author

Mireille Hildebrandt is a professor of 'Smart Environments, Data Protection and the Rule of Law' at the institute of Computing & Information Sciences (iCIS) at the Faculty of Science, Radboud University in Nijmegen, the Netherlands, where she teaches Law in Cyberspace to master students of computer science and collaborates with computer scientists in the Privacy & Identity Lab. She is also a research professor of 'Technology Law and Law in Technology' at the research group on Law, Science, Technology & Society studies (LSTS) at Vrije Universiteit Brussel, Belgium and affiliated as an associate professor at the department of 'Jurisprudence' at the Erasmus School of Law (ESL), Erasmus University Rotterdam (EUR), the Netherlands. Hildebrandt publishes widely on the nexus of law, philosophy and technology. She co-edited, for instance, *Profiling the European Citizen. Cross-Disciplinary Perspectives* (Springer 2008), together with Serge Gutwirth; *Human Agency and Autonomic Computing* (Routledge 2011) with Antoinette Rouvroy; *Human Law and Computer Law* (Springer 2013), together with Jeanne Gaakeer; and *Privacy and Due Process* (Routledge 2013) with Katja de Vries. See also her Berkeley Press website at http://works.bepress.com/mireille_hildebrandt/.

Prefatory remarks

The new Silk Road   Somewhere in the beginning of my sabbatical stay in Berkeley I called my 92-year-old mother and spoke to her about Silicon Valley. She misheard me, and asked whether I was doing research on a silk valley, wondering how this connects to my research. I paused, and had to admit that she was not entirely mistaken. Perhaps I was indeed investigating the new Silk Road; the one leading us into cyberspace territory, enabling the creation of added value based on trading personal data against online services. However, I told her that I was talking about silicon, not silk. 'Ah', she said: 'is that some kind of medicine?' This, again, stopped me in my tracks. Are the integrated circuits that crowd silicon chips not a kind of medicine; a *pharmakon* that can be either poisonous or healing, depending on how it is integrated in our life world? My mother is quite sharp and well aware of the role played by information and communication technologies, though she admits that she is not planning on opening a Facebook account any time soon. She just missed how much of our current world has originated in this particular part of California; how silicon became the new gold and technology developers the new gold diggers, even if we must not forget that, in the end, it is the business models and our data that have turned silicon into gold.

The new gold   One day someone should write a follow-up of Joan Didion's Californian memoir *Where I Was From*. In it, Didion describes the mythology of the Western Frontier that serves as a foundational narrative for Californian identity, chronicling 'the crossing' into new territories in the 17th and 18th centuries, the gold diggers' mentality that shaped San Francisco in the 19th century, and the building of the cross-country railroad, thus explaining the peculiar concoction of individualist pride, entrepreneurial daring and dependence on the federal government that defines California even today, according to Didion. At this moment, however, anyone anywhere can trace herself back to the transformative inventions somehow connected to Silicon Valley. The large technology companies of Silicon Valley that form a bristling ecology together with a steady surge of start-ups, are reconfiguring our

everyday life worlds, while constructing the information and communication infrastructures that shape the flow of information, goods, services,
people and capital around the globe. This is where our world is built. In
fact, it seems that a surreptitious shift is occurring towards hardware,
notably 'softwired' interconnected 'everywares' such as wearables,
robots, creative 3D printing, and so on – entailing simultaneous disruptions and movements in the geography of invention (MIT's Center for
Bits and Atoms, Maker Faires everywhere, San Francisco start-ups on the
nexus of hardware and software, Rethink Robotics in Boston, Japan
moving head-on into companion robots).

The extended mind   Technology was always a part of us, as philosophers
of technology, archaeologists and anthropologists have tried to explain,
and by now even lawyers acknowledge how literally we should take this.
As *The New York Times* recorded in June 2014, unwittingly endorsing
Andy Clark's view on the mobile phone as a part of our extended mind:[1]

> Chief Justice John G. Roberts Jr, writing for the court, was keenly alert to the
> central role that cellphones play in contemporary life. They are, he said, 'such
> a pervasive and insistent part of daily life that the proverbial visitor from
> Mars might conclude they were an important feature of human anatomy.'

Clark argued that we should give up on understanding the human mind as
something that is contained within our 'skinbag'. Taking the example of
our mobile phones he demonstrated, even before the massive uptake of
the smart phone, that our minds include the cognitive resources that
extend them: from written text to wearable communication devices and
critical infrastructures that run on the analysis of our behavioural data.

Mindless data-driven agency: a new animism   So much has already been
written on the ethical, social and legal implications of the emerging
information and communication infrastructures that I hesitate to add my
bit. However, I believe that it is crucial that we confront our new world
by facing the new animism it provokes. With the notion of 'new
animism' I refer to the fact that our life world is increasingly populated
with things that are trained to foresee our behaviours and pre-empt our
intent. These things are no longer stand-alone devices; they are progressively becoming interconnected via the cloud, which enables them to
share their 'experience' of us to improve their functionality. We are in
fact surrounded by adaptive systems that display a new kind of mindless
agency. Brain inspired, neurosynaptic chips have been prototyped, that
are typical for the way long-existing technologies such as artificial neural

networks and miniaturization of ever more integrated circuits on silicon chips combine to simulate one of the most critical capacities of living organisms: unconscious, intuitive and on-the-spot pattern recognition. The environment is thus becoming ever more animated. At the same time we are learning slowly but steadily to foresee that we are being foreseen, accepting that things know our moods, our purchasing habits, our mobility patterns, our political and sexual preferences and our sweet spots. We are on the verge of shifting from *using technologies* to *interacting with them*, negotiating their defaults, pre-empting their intent while they do the same to us. While the environment gets animated, we are reinventing animism, ready to learn how to anticipate those that anticipate us – animals, fellow humans and now also smart, mindless machines. There is animation and animism, but also animosity. Between individual freedom and pre-emptive artificial environments (guessing our preferences before we become aware of them), between individual persons and their smart appliances (the fridge ordered what was to be expected, but we want something else), between a person and her digital assistant (who may have different purposes), or even, between negotiating digital assistants of friends, colleagues or family members (acting upon the inferred interests of their patrons). Not to mention the animosity between those who are paying for the assistant (the insurance company?) and those that employ it, or the government that claims the need for a viable 'information position'.

The most interesting, disrupting and intriguing aspect of our new world concerns its mindless animation, its unconscious – or should we say a-conscious – calculations of our future states and behaviours. We are invited to learn to deal with an artificial world, 'peopled' by a myriad of artificial agents that are becoming more and more smart and unpredictable. We might develop emotions about these agents, especially if embodied (as with robots). They are learning to 'read' our mind, including our fears, loathing, desires and addictions. When I was hiding in my writer's retreat in the Berkeley Hills, my host regularly dropped in to check how I was doing. He told me that during his own sabbaticals he had experienced the joys of seclusion, but also confronted the need for human contact, which seems pivotal to confirm one's own existence as a human person. I wondered, later, how I would have fared if it were an intelligent, personalized robot companion that checked on me. I wondered about my mother's caretakers: what if they were soft, sweet and capable nurse-robots instead of human nurses? What if our children cannot afford a human nanny or a crib to care for their infants, leaving their children in the hands (and arms) of robot nannies? What if these robot companions, enhanced with machine learning and access to Big

Data Space, do better than the humans they replace? Will it turn us into machine-reading agents, as we need to understand how they understand us to deal with them? What will a capability to read the mindless mind of artificial agents do to our own minds? Could it be that being cared for by humans will eventually become a privilege for the rich and famous (those with clout in the cloud); or should we expect the opposite, where only those who can afford the costs of security upgrades have the pleasure of fine-tuned robotic companionship?

Between Brussels and New York   This volume was initiated in 2009, during my research sabbatical in New York City, where I participated in the cutting-edge NYU privacy and technology research group of Helen Nissenbaum, as well as the SUNY techno-science philosophy seminars of Don Ihde, at Stony Brook, Long Island. I take this opportunity to applaud and celebrate the work of both Helen and Don, however different, and to thank them for 'having' me during the fall of 2009. The change of scenery between Downtown Manhattan and Stony Brook was tantalizing; the intellectual perspectives, student backgrounds, urban and non-urban landscapes were miles apart, making the back-and-forth all the more interesting. It confirmed my intuition that philosophical reflection on technology as an enabler of science and society is pertinent, against the common sense of seeing technology as merely an implementation of scientific insight. It also confirmed my intuition that analytical philosophy contributes to clarifying concepts, methods and different points of view, while enabling ethical inquiry into the implications of privacy-invasive ICTs. Finally, it reinforced my deep appreciation for the Brussels School on privacy and data protection – if such a label fits at all – of which I find myself a radical and unruly member and proponent. This is my way of paying tribute to Serge Gutwirth, head of the research group on Law Science Technology & Society (LSTS) at Vrije Universiteit Brussels, and his colleague, Paul de Hert, who staged the famous annual Computer Privacy and Data Protection (CPDP) conferences in Brussels, and Isabelle Stengers and Bruno Latour, who were co-promotors of an adventurous research project on the responsibilities of scientists which I joined in 2002. The latter project introduced me to the notion of correlated humans, soon reconceptualized as correlatable humans, highlighting the continuities and discontinuities between statistics and, notably, machine learning. The difference between both is that whereas statistics is instrumental in enabling machine learning, we must acknowledge that machine learning is a different thing. It thrives on the combination of 'perception' and 'action' of machines, using statistical inferences as feedback to learn about the inferred consequences of one's actions. If statistics is considered by many mathematicians to be without the boundaries of mathematics, machine learning is way out of bounds. It seems closer to empirical testing than to axiomatic reasoning, but we should not forget that it is only capable of testing patterns in data sets. However big these sets are, they are not what the data refer to, nor what the inferences refer to. In other words, though we may be presented as correlated humans by machine learning techniques, we are fundamentally correlatable humans. One way or another. For a lawyer, the latter statement is crucial. Machine learning, data mining, Big Data analytics and similar techniques of artificial intelligence are incredibly advanced compared to the rule-based algorithms of old school artificial intelligence. But all depends on the constraints of the hypothesis space, on the extent to which algorithms can be tweaked by noise or random interference and – obviously – on the framing imposed by alternate algorithms. Considering the effects of employing one computational technique rather than another, we must urgently learn to contest the decisions they take. Just like human judgement, they are not objective, but, other than human judgement, it is not obvious that we can argue with them and put our finger on the operations that informed the decisions. That is why this volume is focused on data-driven agency and its implications for the Rule of Law.

Berkeley Hills   When I decided to situate my 2014 research sabbatical close to Silicon Valley, I also chose to organize the sabbatical as a writer's retreat. I attended the SOLID conference for technology developers on the nexus of hardware and software in San Francisco.[2] I spoke at the *Robotics and New Media* symposium at UC Berkeley,[3] on the invitation of Shanti Ganesh, who combines cognitive psychology and brain research with an acuity that is rare within the confines of empiricist research into the relationships between brain, mind, body and society. But, foremost, I retreated into my cottage in the hills of Berkeley, a so-called 'in-laws', located behind the house of Luisa and Manuel, my hosts. To do my daily shopping or reach the urbanity of Berkeley and San Francisco I had to first walk downhill for half an hour (a very healthy retreat as you can imagine) and this prevented me from giving in to diversions, forcing me to stick to the writing process. A rare luxury. Solitude enables the writing process in a way no other constraints do, despite the rampant connectivity that can easily turn solitude into an illusion. When I returned to the text of 2009, which was left untouched due to five years of other obligations, I was surprised to find that the opening narrative was hardly speculative anymore. I wondered whether it was at all still relevant. Most of the chapters have been rewritten entirely, taking in five years of research and five years of socio-technical development. But in the end the narrative remained largely unaltered. I realized that it focused on the notion of data-driven agency, even if not explicitly coined as such. This is now the central theme of the volume.

Law and computer science   Since 2011 I have had the privilege of holding the Chair of Smart Environments, Data Protection and the Rule of Law. This Chair is located at the institute of Computing and Information Sciences (iCIS) at Radboud University Nijmegen, where Bart Jacobs entitled his inaugural lecture 'The Computer Under the Rule of Law'.[4] I am now a lawyer teaching about law in cyberspace to master students of computer science. This has influenced my take on the relationship between smart technologies and the end(s) of law. I have become convinced that computer science and law share a sensitivity to architecture, an awareness that changing a rule in one part of the system has immediate as well as indirect consequences for other parts of either law or a computing system. To sustain our artificial worlds, both institutional and artefactual, this sensitivity is critical. Similarly, computer engineering and law share the need for pragmatic solutions that cross bridges when they get there and work from the legacy of existing constraints. Both are geared to solutions while aware of the need for constructive attention to systemic constraints, even if that may sometimes disable solutions that are attractive from a short-term perspective. Working in a computer science department has also sensitized me to the differences between law and computer science, notably the inherent ambiguity of law as a text-based discipline that thrives on human language compared to the need for disambiguation inherent in disciplines that are built on digital technologies. Taking into account that our world is progressively reconfigured to cater to the needs of digital technologies, this difference remains crucial and requires positive attention to be preserved against Big Data worship and other mistaken beliefs in the objectivity of either data or what is inferred from them. In the third part of this book I take a deep dive into the central and often incompatible ends of the law: justice, legal certainty and purposiveness. I follow Radbruch in claiming that for a normative framework to qualify as legal it must at least be 'reconstructable' as aiming for these three ends, while admitting that their interrelation and articulation will often require us to strike a balance. I also vouch for EU data protection law as the only way to halt unbridled and mistaken trust in data-driven agency, arguing against recent calls for discarding both limitation of data collection and purpose binding. Considering the growth of Big Data collections, I believe that within less than five years the question will not be how to collect as much data as possible, but how to 'select before you collect' and how to correct, connect, delete, anonymize or pseudonymize personal data. From a business and government perspective the question of life-cycle management of data will become the greater challenge, as this will be preconditional for the functionality and the security of data-driven intelligence. From a fundamental rights perspective it is critical to recognize the plurality of rights that are at stake, instead of reducing data protection to informational privacy. Much more is at stake.

The end(s) of law   This volume builds on the fact that modern law has been contingent upon the information and communication infrastructure of the printing press, explaining how the Rule of Law similarly depends on the affordances of proliferating copies of identical text. Data-driven architectures operate at another level that sublimates rather than externalizes the normativity that directs and coordinates our interactions. The hidden complexity and invisible inferences that increasingly and seamlessly adapt our environment constitute a new – digital – unconscious. We need to urgently come to terms with this, reinventing legal articulations capable of reinstating justice, legal certainty and purposiveness in the upcoming onli*fe* world.

The end of publishing this book is to sensitize readers to the urgency of the task ahead, sharing provocations, analyses and a coherent framework to face life in a world beyond offline and online. A framework that is compliant in the sense of bending with the changing socio-technical landscape and solid in the sense of providing a backbone that is reliable, tested and contestable while still affording a critical stance. If we do not learn how to uphold and extend the legality that protects individual persons against arbitrary or unfair state interventions, the law will lose its hold on our imagination. It may fold back into a tool to train, discipline or influence people whose behaviours are measured and calculated to be nudged into compliance, or, the law will be replaced by techno-regulation, whether or not that is labelled as law.

Pre-emptive computing systems may thus trigger the end of law as we know it, but this is not necessarily the case. All depends on how we design, construct and develop our information and communication infrastructures and how we engage with the mindless agents that will 'people' our onli*fe* world. In the end, this book is about building legal protection into our artefactual environment, reinventing recalcitrance – as my dear colleague Antoinette Rouvroy might say – as well as the means to generate values and added value in a shared onli*fe* world that celebrates and affords both democracy and the Rule of Law. We want to have our cake and eat it too. To the extent that we continue to bake fresh cakes this is possible, but we must acknowledge that data and even information are not edible.

This book is an inquiry into the implications of smart technologies for the mode of existence of the law, that is, for how current law fabricates our artificial, institutional and artefactual environment. The question is whether modern law is capable of protecting us against undue transparencies and, if not, how we might reinvent the protection we need to flourish as individual human persons that are forever mediated and reinvented by the technologies they invent.

1.   Introduction: Diana's onl*ife* world

1.1 NARRATIVE BEGINNINGS: DIANA IN THE ONLI*FE* WORLD

Early morning   Diana wakes up to the sound and light of her alarm clock that has been tuned to her mild winter depressions, lifting her mood by an increasing intensity of light and massaging her brains with music that has been shown to invigorate her at that point of the day. The house has woken up slightly earlier (turning on the heating, setting the coffee, and sorting out upcoming assignments and incoming communications). While she goes about her morning routine the house picks up her mood and prepares the roadmap for her smart car, depending on whether she is ready for a high adrenalin ride that may save her time or would prefer a routine trip that will take longer due to traffic jams. The fridge compares notes with her cupboards on this morning's caloric, fibre and nutrient intake to calculate how she could balance her diet during the rest of the day – forwarding the daily diagnosis to her smart phone, which will get in touch with whatever food store or restaurant she may decide to visit for lunch or dinner.

After walking the dog Diana is advised to take public transport as the house finds her nervous and a potential risk for dangerous driving. Diana is free to take the car – since the inferred danger does not cross a certain threshold – but her insurance premium may rise if the car indeed detects fatigue or risky behaviour. Besides, if she takes public transport she will burn more calories, thus allowing an extra serving of her favourite pasta or whatever else she may like to have later that day. So, Diana opts for the light rail that takes her straight to her first appointment.

What's in a name?   The first appointment has been confirmed by her personal digital assistant (PDA), that is distributed between her smart phone, the system running her smart home, the smart car, her ubiquitous computing office platform, while being on speaking terms with other systems, like those for traffic control and healthcare, commercial and governmental service providers, as well as monitoring systems for private and public safety and security. The close relationship between Diana and her PDA has caused her to give it a name, a common habit amongst those who have entrusted a variety of tasks to their PDAs. Hers is called Toma. When she thinks of it, Toma is like a friend, a close member of the family, a butler and – sometimes – like a government official or an insurance broker. Whatever the likeness to all these others in her life, there are many differences also, one of which is that no other person has so many details of her private and social life and no other person provides so much calculated advice. Though she is keenly aware that Toma is not a person and though she 'knows' that Toma does not 'care' about whether Diana follows its advice, for all practical purposes Toma often does resemble a person. Especially since the software has been updated with synthetic emotions, Diana experiences feelings of joy and pride, as well as regret and shame when she is rewarded or rebuked for her behaviours.

Mobile office life   During the ride in the light rail Diana picks up on the details of her meeting, scanning the automatically composed summary of a report, sent to her office late last night – uploaded into Toma, which has put the doc onscreen on the back of her suitcase (monitors and terminals have been replaced by surfaces capable of displaying text, graphs and images). The report has its own summary, authored by the consultant who wrote the report, but Toma has a personalized algorithm that screens the doc for novel insights or unfamiliar facts. It skips conventional knowledge and highlights what is relevant for Diana's inferred purpose. The summary works with images, graphs and text, to visualize patterns found within the doc that may be relevant for Diana.

When Diana enters the office she is greeted by the receptionist, with whom she has a friendly chat (Toma has arranged this, knowing that this will relax Diana who still seems nervous). She runs into two colleagues on the way to the working spot that has been allocated for her meeting. They discuss the targets set for the upcoming period, exchanging views on their feasibility and informally testing each other's competitive advantages. Diana is a sales representative of a large hotel conglomerate, working on the high end of the market: selling classy hotel apartments on a time-sharing basis. Part of her salary is fixed; the other part depends on her actual achievements. Due to the general downfall of the economy – we are talking about the aftermath of the 2020 financial crisis – everyone knows that the least effective sales executives will have to leave. Toma notes that the talk with her colleagues leaves Diana full of energy: she senses that she has been doing very well compared to the others. This triggers an intervention in Diana's agenda for the day; Toma schedules a lunch meeting with a troublesome client that has been trying to contact

Diana. Because of her nervousness Toma has been slow in responding, but now the PDA sees a chance.

A call for help   Diana's day continues in a perfunctory manner. Her meetings work out well, including the lunch, and at the end of the day she is both tired and deeply satisfied. Riding back home in the light rail Toma registers a call from her ex-husband about their 6-year-old daughter Lindsay, over whom they have joint custody. Since the call is not urgent but must be answered tonight, Toma does not bother Diana until she reaches home, giving her time to reset after a hectic day. When she returns the call, Tom (her ex) asks her whether she can pick up Lindsay from school the next day, because he had an accident while playing squash with a colleague. Lindsay is staying with Tom this week, but as he will have to be at the hospital he hopes that Diana can take over. When Diana checks with Toma she encounters strong rejection; she has an important meeting with a client who will not appreciate a change of plan. Toma has already checked the regular nannies who might step in, but their PDAs are offline. Diana begins to exhibit signs of a mild panic, being confronted with what she sees as incompatible duties, and Toma comes to the rescue with a convenient solution: Tom will try to reach one of his nannies, while Toma will continue trying to contact those of Diana. Music sounds from the living room, as Toma has turned on the audio, programming some light jazz, known to soothe Diana's anxieties. It is the kind of music that is known to trigger Diana's sense of independence, downplaying her worries about being a good mother. Sensing her exhaustion Toma has ordered a meal that combines a tasty bite with the right balance of calories, fibres and nutrients: a fusion of a yellow Thai vegetable curry and an Italian salad of arugula, balsamic dressing and Parmesan cheese. Diana pours herself a glass of Muscat white wine after having the food and her mind finally drifts off into a pleasant oblivion. Tom has found a nanny for Lindsay, though he would still prefer that Diana take over, knowing that Lindsay is easily upset with a change of routine and would prefer to be in her mother's ambit. Toma decides not respond to the message, thus preventing it from reaching Diana. The PDA infers that it is in Diana's interest not to worry over her daughter, assuming that Lindsay will be in safe hands anyway.

Of mother and daughter   The next day Diana receives an alarm message from Lindsay's school – requesting her to respond as soon as possible. PDAs have a default setting that allows five persons to override whatever the PDA infers to be a correct response, bypassing the filters of the PDA with an immediate sensory input to its user. Diana gets a small electrical shock in her left underarm (signalling an alarm from her daughter) and picks up her smart phone. Toma is temporarily set back to a passive mode, registering Diana's behaviours but unable to interfere until Diana switches off the alarm. It turns out that Lindsay has fainted and – according to her PDA – is showing signs of anxiety and confusion since she woke up this morning. To recover and rebalance, Lindsay's PDA urges that her mother comes over and takes charge. Diana instructs Toma to cancel her appointments for the day and sets off to bring Lindsay home from school. Though Toma strongly advises against driving, Diana takes the car because this gives her a feeling of control. Halfway the car begins to slow down, warning Diana that she is crossing the threshold of dangerous driving, meaning that within 5 minutes the car will stop functioning. Diana pulls herself together, focusing on the traffic and calming herself with the certainty that she has made the right decision. The car responds positively by returning to the default mode, allowing Diana to finish her trip to school.

When Diana approaches the school Toma signals her arrival to Lindsay's PDA (called Dina). Dina registers an immediate relief in Lindsay, who has been taken to a small office next to the director's office. Her heartbeat and breathing return to normal, muscle tension is reduced and stress hormone levels diminish. As part of a public–private research programme all children are monitored in terms of their behavioural biometrics, especially the workings of the autonomic nervous system. It is hoped that this will allow prediction of various diseases, ADHD, depression and psychopathology in adult life. Such predictions could eventually justify early intervention to prevent undesirable developments, paving the way for a less conflict-ridden society. The immediate justification for the monitoring, however, is the chance to anticipate behaviours, making it easier for the PDA as well as parents, nannies, teaching staff and doctors to tailor their responses to the child. All significant others and professionals that are in contact with the child have context-specific access to parts of the database that stores and aggregates the child's states and behaviours. From the age of six a child has partial access to her own data, which access gradually extends to full access at the age of 14. This includes access to the group profiles that her data match with (indicating potential health or other problems).

Before Diana reaches Lindsay, the director of the school invites Diana into his office for a brief talk. He expresses serious concern about the mental well-being of Lindsay, based on the type of group profiles she matches. Her behaviours and biometric data match with personality disorders that could seriously interfere with her ability to focus on schoolwork and hamper her social life. In his opinion Diana and Tom will have to work out a more structured life for Lindsay that would restore her self-confidence. Diana listens to the director and tells him that she will consult with Tom, though they have already made every effort to structure their own lives for the sake of Lindsay. Both have demanding careers, which they cannot give up easily, since this is how they can afford the excellent school that Lindsay attends. Diana goes to her daughter who is very happy to see her mother and glad to come home with her. They spend the afternoon having tea and some healthy snacks, exchanging gossip about school, taking the dog for a long walk and playing with some of Lindsay's favourite non-robotic dolls. They have both switched their PDAs to passive mode for the time being – wanting some undisturbed mother-daughter quality time.

Toma has contacted Tom's PDA to notify it of the changes of plans, such that the nanny who would have taken care of Lindsay can be called off without disturbing Tom (a message awaits him on his cell phone). Toma has also screened the coming week's agenda to assess how today's postponed meetings can be fitted in or replaced by teleconferencing. The PDA assesses the damage that this 'free' afternoon has caused Diana in terms of missed opportunities, delayed responses and loss of reputation.

Animosity towards PDAs   Diana and Lindsay have had a long talk after their playful and restful afternoon. From what Lindsay tells her Diana gathers that she would rather attend a less reputable school if that were the price of her mother investing more time in her and less time in her career. Lindsay also objects to the fact that Toma often shields Diana from her daughter, as if there is some kind of competition going on for Diana's attention between the PDA and her daughter. When Diana tucks Lindsay in she promises her that she will think about these things and discuss them with her father, ending the day with reading her stories from one of her favourite books.

Sports life   Later that week Diana goes for her weekly session at the gym. As the reader may guess, Toma has communicated with the gym and figured out which series of exercises would be best. Toma has noticed that Diana has been sitting at her desk for long working hours and has a stiff lower back that is giving her problems, so the exercises are tuned to warming and flexing the muscles of her stomach and lower back. The weights and other settings of the appliances in the gym automatically shift to Diana's preferences and Toma has calculated the duration of each exercise to prevent both under and overly strenuous exercise. All relevant biometrics are recorded, stored and communicated to Toma, as well as matched with relevant predictive profiles. To qualify for a reduced subscription to the gym Diana can allow the gym to sell her data for marketing purposes, and to qualify for special services from her health insurance she can allow the gym to exchange her data with the insurance company. Also, if Diana consents, she can provide a personal profile that can be used to find matching profiles of other members with whom she could socialize after the workout. Some gyms have even integrated an optional dating service, hoping to increase their competitive advantage.

Grandfather and robot   Jacob, Diana's 96-year-old grandfather, has a rather close relationship with the PDA that runs his household and monitors his health, but also serves as a social companion. This PDA is embedded; it is a robot. It does not look like a human being, but clearly resembles mammals. Jacob has named his caretaker Henry. It is constructed on the basis of soft robotics, meaning that its morphology helps to produce smooth and efficient movements, and the combination of hard and soft components mean that it will not easily accidentally hurt a human person. Henry can lift Jacob, and wash and feed him if necessary. Next to its soft morphology, its machine learning capacities enable it to sense what kind of pressure is effective in helping Jacob without hurting him. Jacob has developed a trusting relationship with the artefact. Actually they have a lot of fun. The fact that Henry spies on Jacob, to anticipate and prevent health risks, has given rise to a joking relationship because Henry also advices Jacob to cheat a bit on his diets if that improves his moods. Henry has learnt to jest with Jacob, when telling him that a small glass of single malt around 5 pm may interfere with his medication but will surely increase the quality of this life. To win his trust Henry has been known to keep some of Jacob's secrets from family and friends, though perhaps not from the insurance company that pays for his continued service. Jacob understands the deal and appreciates the privacy this affords him, even if it is a contextual privacy that does allow the insurance to remain up to date.

Henry   Henry runs on proprietary code that keeps the device in continuous contact with proprietary online databases, while also enabling exchange of information with similar devices from the same service provider, and with a number of healthcare service providers (Jacob's family doctor, the medical specialists that treat his various conditions, the insurance that covers the cost, the pharmacies that supply his medications, and the local nursing centre that provides him with hands-on medical care). Henry is an example of what cloud robotics can do for us. Because of the complexity of the various relationships and their mutual interference, it would obviously not be possible to program Henry in a deterministic way, and in fact it is also undoable to rely on supervised machine learning. Henry operates in part on unsupervised learning algorithms and neural nets that enable improvisation and creative negotiations between the various ends it serves: Jacob's health, the profitability of health insurance, data collection for medical research, Jacob's well-being and the various interests of his family and friends. Though its – largely autonomic – operations make Henry somewhat unpredictable, the overall performance is assumed to be better than it could ever be if human programmers had to foresee every possible scenario that might play out. To some extent the more unpredictable Henry becomes, the more reliable it is – though there are obvious limits to this. Nevertheless, Henry takes its own decisions, compatibilizing the various goals set by its designers. One of these goals is that Henry must sustain its own existence, since Jacob's life may depend on it.

A robot decides   One day Jacob suffers a mild stroke. In the old days this might have gone unnoticed, as it is a minor infarct that does not immediately impair his health. Based on his connections with large databases, Henry has figured out that more serious harm is to be expected, statistically speaking. The obvious way to proceed would be to do some machine-to-machine talk with the agent systems of the various healthcare services mentioned above, to diagnose the health risks and to plan a possible intervention. On the basis of similar data mining operations, Henry, however, also figures out that Jacob will not appreciate the medical exams this would involve. Jacob may actually become depressed and he might even turn against Henry for telling on him. Henry tries to calculate the best decision and confronts conflicting interests of Jacob, the healthcare institution that 'uses' it to monitor and take care of Jacob, the insurance company that pays for Henry, and friends or family members who may want to guarantee him a long life.

Henry does not inform its patrons and two days later Jacob dies of a sudden and fatal stroke.

1.2 SMART ENVIRONMENTS, MODERN LAW AND TECHNOLOGICAL REGULATION

1.2.1 Why a Narrative to Introduce the Onl*ife* World?

I hope that the narratives introducing the argument of this book will sensitize the reader to a novel type of anticipation and regulation engendered by proactive 'smart' environments, often referred to as Ambient Intelligence (AmI), the Internet of Things, or ubiquitous, autonomous or pre-emptive computing. In this book the term onli*fe* world will be used to highlight the fact that we are not merely talking about technological infrastructures. We are facing a transformative life world, situated beyond the increasingly artificial distinction between online and offline. To some degree, the upcoming onli*fe* world thrives on artificial life forms, or at least on 'things' that seem to develop a life of their own. These 'things' display a form of data-driven agency, a concept that will be further developed in Chapter 2.

The narrative introduction has some likeness to the methodology of scenario studies, which aims to assess future developments that are as yet uncertain but warrant an assessment of potential threats. The idea is that scenario studies do not merely provide a random evocation of the fantasies of one or more Luddite techno-pessimists; nor should they be confused with the pink scenarios presented by business enterprise that often have more similarities with advertorials than a serious evaluation of both threats and potential benefits. Scenario studies are usually prepared by groups of experts from a variety of relevant disciplines to extrapolate existing tendencies on the basis of robust fact finding, while taking into account that black swans and outliers may appear if radically novel technologies are taken up by the market and integrated into everyday life.[5] In part, they are about expecting the unexpected. The storyline I composed builds on a series of scenarios prepared within the European research network on the *Future of Identity in the Information Society*, during a five-year research project of collaborating computer scientists, lawyers, social scientists and philosophers working in the field of cybernetics and information theory.[6] Its function here is, however, not to provide a sound basis for a report with policy advice on how to deal with Ambient Intelligence. I merely hope that by telling the story of Diana and some of her significant others, the reader begins to imagine how everyday life may change if our environment becomes saturated with pre-emptive technologies that are always one step ahead of us. Or so they say.[7] Though consumers may reject some of these technologies, it must be admitted that many of them are already part of our life world: from search engines to location-based services, from behavioural biometric access control for Internet banking to real-time dynamic pricing in smart grids or car insurance. In evoking the everyday effects of pre-emptive and interactive computing I hope to have clarified that the emerging tech-nological infrastructure – like all technologies – will reconfigure our life world and *de facto* regulate our behaviour. Though enabling technologies such as large-scale data mining of online behaviours may be relatively well known, others are still under the radar. Notably, the onset of radio frequency identification (RFID) tagging and a plethora of sensor technologies will interconnect offline and online data points, leading to what the International Telecommunication Union (ITU) has called the Internet of Things. In the meantime, while Google is working along similar lines towards a Web of Things, advanced robotics is moving into a new phase by tapping into the cloud. If we reach the point that close to everything 'anyware' is translated into machine-readable data points, stored in distributed databases that allow for the application of massive and recurrent pattern recognition techniques, we will indeed have entered an era in which Diana's story is no longer science fiction. The invisible inferences of personalized risks and preference profiles will increasingly afford seamless, unobtrusive and subliminal adaptations of the environment to cater to a person's inferred preferences and to target, include or exclude her on the basis of inferred risks.

The reader may actually find the stories mildly interesting and hardly surprising, thereby testifying to the topical nature of the narrative and the extent to which mobile smart phones, a plethora of Apps, news of self-driving cars, ambient lighting systems and remote control of home appliances have already transformed our expectations. Let's note that though a PEW report shows that a majority of Americans is highly interested in self-driving cars, experts still doubt that they will be capable of safe driving in densely populated urban areas.[8] I have deliberately avoided stories of grand misfortunes or attacks that we do not already meet in our everyday lives; the opening narratives will be used to expound on the subliminal and 'agential' character of smart technologies. In Chapter 4, I will raise a number of questions originating in the narratives, after clarifying the novel dependencies on Big Data Space and the digital unconscious it constitutes in Chapters 2 and 3. This will open the floor for a discussion of the threats of hidden complexity and unbridled artificial intelligence in Chapter 5.

The point of writing this book is to make clear that the extent to which this subliminal regulation takes place will depend on *how* we design these infrastructures and whether we find ways to inscribe legal protection into them. I will argue that the attempt to impose administrative written rules to domesticate these infrastructures is bound to fail, to the extent that written law *by itself* is impotent in the face of the distributed, mobile, polymorphous and real-time character of smart computing environments. As will be clarified in the third part, this does not imply that written law is a relic that is ready for exhibition in the museum of bygone historical artefacts. Quite the contrary, to keep a clear eye on the normative architecture of the onli*fe* world and to enable each of us to participate in its making, we will need to preserve the affordances of written law.

1.2.2 The Nature of Modern Law

This raises the issue of the nature of law as we know it today. Modern law is an authoritative way to regulate life within a specific jurisdiction (regional, national, international). In a constitutional democracy law is a form of self-regulation: the addressees and the 'addressants' of legal norms coincide. This is the normative assumption of a democracy, even if citizens' participation in law-making takes place via voting, deliberation in the public sphere and stakeholder consultations, and even if not every citizen is addressed at all times by all the legislation that has been enacted. At the same time this assumption is what must be achieved, since it cannot be taken for granted. What counts is that legal norms are in principle made *by* as well as *for* the constituency and to have 'force of law' they must be public in the sense of being visible and legible for every person that is expected to comply with them. This makes it possible to discuss and contest their application, for instance by violating them. The violation of legal norms has consequences, sometimes even automatically. If I do not register my marriage with the civil registry there is no marriage; if I do not register my real estate in the register I cannot own the estate. Other consequences can take the form of a fine or the need to pay compensation. Typical for the Rule of Law is that a person can contest the application of legal consequences in a court of law, and this contestation may even regard the validity of the legal norm that is involved.[9] One can, for instance, claim that the norm violates a higher norm, like a human right or a constitutional liberty. Written legal norms are externalized norms, a feat that makes them amenable to interpretation, extension and change. In as far as legal norms are unwritten they may be less visible, more subliminal and harder to contest. However, the typical combination of written and unwritten law has enabled discussions of the unwritten principles that are implied in the written legal rules as well as the legitimate expectations that often determine their applicability.

Legal norms in a constitutional democracy thus exhibit three aspects that are pertinent: first, legal rules are established by a democratic legislator; second, they can be violated; and third the violation and its legal consequences can be contested in a court of law. These aspects differentiate law from discipline or mere administration. Self-rule, disobedience and contestability are the hallmarks of law in a constitutional democracy.

1.2.3 The Nature of Technological Regulation

Technologies regulate our behaviours by making certain behaviours possible and constricting others. The regulation that stems from technological artefacts is less obvious than enacted legal norms, and not initiated by a democratic legislator. Its regulative force depends on how engineers, designers and business enterprise bring these artefacts to the market and eventually on how consumers or end-users engage with them. Its material and social embedding has a way of inducing or inhibiting certain behaviour patterns, such as the sharing of personal data. Depending on their design and uptake, technologies can even enforce or rule out certain types of behaviours. Once a default of usage has settled, artefacts like typewriters, traffic lights, mobile phones, speed bumps, smart fridges and search engines impact the way we interact with each other, often enabling types of interaction previously not possible or ruling out alternate ways of doing things. This does not presume technological determinism. I have a choice not to have a mobile phone and even if I have one, there are many different ways in which I can use it (prepaid or subscribed; having different phones for private and professional calls; with or without Internet access; discussing confidential matters in the train or the details of a shopping list, and so on). But once defaults have settled resistance becomes more difficult and expectations of how things are done consolidate.[10] In that sense socio-technical infrastructures have a normative impact, if normative refers to the mutual expectations that regulate human interaction. As far as the communication and information infrastructures (ICIs) of human society are concerned this regulative impact can hardly be overestimated. The script, the printing press, mass media, the digital computer, the Internet and the world wide web extend the potential of spoken language exponentially. The possibility of addressing another person across ever larger distances in time and space, enlarging the potential audience of a text, has changed the amount of people we must somehow take into account when communicating and has extended the implications and consequences of our actions beyond measure. The latest developments, like email, chat and social networking, seem to conflate time and space into a synchronized environment that allows for 'always on' real-time accessibility. Pre-emptive smart environments begin to transform our dealings with artefacts. At some point we will become aware of the fact that we are being watched and anticipated by machines and we will try to figure out how the infrastructure 'reads' us and with whom it shares its knowledge of our preferences and of the risks we incorporate. One of the issues this book faces is whether we *will* manage to figure this out and what it would mean to live in an onl*ife* world that anticipates our behaviour whereas we don't have a clue as to how we are being profiled.

Technological regulation thus differs from legal regulation based on written and unwritten law. It does so on all three accounts. First, its articulation is not controlled by the democratic legislator and there is no legal 'enactment'. Technological regulation is often a side effect of a particular design aimed at a specific functionality. For example, the invention of the cookie by Netscape in the 1990s was meant to enable ecommerce transactions between a web shop and a customer. In the end it facilitated tracking and tracing web users across the web, enabling analytics that are used to personalize search results, websites, pricing strategies and newsfeeds. Cookies in fact regulate our online environment in the sense of creating new affordances and constraints, and despite the far-reaching implications of the subliminal adaptation of our online world, we never got to vote on this. Second, it is quite possible to design technological devices in ways that rule out violating the rule they embody, even if this embodiment is a side-effect not deliberately inscribed. If I cannot access a website unless I accept tracking cookies, I am practically forced to comply with the norm that I should accept them if I wish to access the site. Legal norms do not rule out disobedience. Third, contestation of the technological defaults that regulate our lives may be impossible because they are often invisible and because most of the time there is no jurisdiction and no court. If an online social networking site uses tracking cookies to measure the clickstream behaviours of their visitors, they may use analytics to measure the influence of different settings of their platform. This may even include sending false newsfeeds to their users to measure the impact of either positive or negative feeds. As such measurements are mostly invisible we have no way to contest them, unless the results happens to be published in a scientific journal.[11]

1.3   CRIMINAL LIABILITY, SECURITY AND GOVERNMENT SURVEILLANCE

The last part of the narrative raises the issue of criminal liability in the onl*ife* world. It was added to draw attention to the agency characteristics of PDAs, and to underline that the decisions made by our digital companions can easily have far reaching consequences. From a legal perspective this connects to intricate issues around civil and criminal liability, to the legal subjectivity of artificial agents and the disruptions this may engender for foundational legal concepts such as causality, legal personhood, liability, guilt, wrongfulness, and so on.[12] In this volume I will focus on the potential disruption of the substance of various human rights by the operations of the onli*fe* world. In that context I will come to discuss the presumption of innocence and due process, but the matter of criminal liability is not part of the argument as this would extend the scope of the book and turn it into a hotchpotch.[13]

The same goes for two other topics that are closely related and obviously part of the disruptions generated by an onli*fe* world. The first is the exponential increase in the need for security in the technical sense of resilience against attacks that violate the confidentiality, integrity and availability of digital systems. The onli*fe* world depends on interacting computational systems that are vulnerable to hacking, spying, a manipulation, identity theft, eavesdropping and destruction. This goes for the smart fridge, but also for the smart grid, healthcare and other critical infrastructure. The costs of providing additional security if it is not taken into account from the very start are huge; both in financial terms and in terms of harm, if things go awry. The relationship between security and liberty should not be described as a trade-off, as the one often depends on the other and trade-offs depend on distribution; it may be that some people give up their liberties to provide others with added security.[14] Criminal law and surveillance are meant to secure safety, which is in fact a broader notion that includes absence of physical harm, whereas safety is not restricted to being safe from an attack. An earthquake threatens the safety of inhabitants but does not depend on an attacker. The collaborating distributed computing systems that scaffold the onli*fe* world may be prone to system breakdowns with incalculable effects, threatening our safety irrespective of attacks. All this is highly relevant but hardly integrated in this book's argument. To tackle the issues involved would have taken another volume, which may become my next project.[15]

Finally, surveillance is at stake throughout the volume, but not in a straightforward manner. I am not sure that 'surveillance' captures what this book is after, as the notion suggests a simplified scheme of those who snoop and those who are snooped upon. I rather liked Solove's point when he proposed that the metaphor of Big Brother does not clarify what is at stake in the world of large-scale databases and the detailed personal dossiers they make possible.[16] Solove put forward the metaphor of Kafka's *Trial* as a more apt depiction of the anonymous accusation that looms over the lives of those that keep leaving traces of anything they do. He was one of the first who pointed to the chilling effect of knowing that whatever you do may at some point be used against you. This is part of the argument in the current book, and we should remember that any data anywhere may at some point be accessed by a government. Snowden has done us the favour of underlining that it is an illusion to think that if the data is available governments will shrink from accessing it, if they believe it will help them in securing policy objectives.[17]

These policy objectives are not restricted to international terrorism or serious crime; they often boil down to more mundane efforts to combat social security fraud or tax evasion. In the context of foreign intelligence we should think of, for instance, industrial espionage, even if this is obviously entirely unlawful under the tenets of international law.[18] This book does not go into details of government surveillance, which should fit a volume on security in the broad sense of resilience against attacks. The analysis and the argument made in this book should, however make clear that the onli*f*e world can be designed in a way that allows for massive spying and subliminal nudging. I believe it is now more important to devote detailed attention to the historical and theoretical underpinnings of the Rule of Law that should protect us from over-inclusive monitoring, than reiterating the fact that governments are overstepping their boundaries. We need to rethink these boundaries and the stuff they are made of.

1.4 THE POLITICAL ECONOMY OF AN ONLI*F*E WORLD

This book is not about the politics or the economics of privacy.[19] What is usually termed as such tends to reduce the discussion of pre-emptive environments to a discussion of privacy, while framing the debate on privacy as part of a discussion of business models or political influencing. This amounts to taking for granted what should be investigated.

It does make good sense to situate the debate on the design of our onli*f*e world in the larger setting of a political economy that generates an incentive structure that is highly conducive to manipulative environments that treat people as pawns, if not prey. Evgeny Morozov and Julie Cohen,[20] to name but two very different authors who come out with highly original and informative analyses on these issues, have done great work in providing the bigger picture, while refusing to frame issues in terms of existing incentives. They can thus open the discussion of what kind of world we want to fabricate in the era of what I will call data-driven agency. I have chosen to focus on the affordances of data-driven agency and the digital unconscious, as this already presents formidable challenges in terms of comprehension and potential solutions. I am, however, aware of the drawbacks of not addressing the political economy in which our technology developers must operate. The position taken in Chapters 7 and 8, however, does address the relationship between law, politics and morality. Perhaps I am weary of the prevalent tendency to frame any and all discussion in economic terms, as if the ultimate question is always the one about the business model. I believe that we should not allow ourselves to be distracted when investigating the impact of pre-emptive computing on the life of the law. After determining what normativity we need to survive as reasonably free and reasonably constrained individual persons, we can decide how to distribute the costs as well as the benefits. I am not qualified to do the maths on that, but I am convinced that the issue of distribution is first a political and a legal issue and only then an – important – economic problem.

1.5 A BRIEF OUTLINE

1.5.1 Part I: Data-driven Agency

The first part deals with data-driven agency as the most prominent and the most transformative aspect of smart technologies. After the narrative introduction in Chapter 1 and the overview of what is at stake, Chapter 2 follows up with a discussion of different levels of 'smart'. Smartness is analysed in terms of artificial agency. This leads to an analysis of Big Data Space as the distributed heterogeneous timespace on which data-driven agency thrives. Chapter 3 discusses the idea of an onli*fe* world, where *things* 'come alive' to populate our everyday life world with novel animations. The information and communication infrastructure (ICI) of the onli*fe* world is described in terms of pre-emptive computing systems that calculate our inferred future behaviours and engage in pervasive and continuous adaptations of our life world. One of the key terms of this ICI is hidden complexity.

The description of the onli*fe* world is coupled with an analysis of human identity as a fragile, relational construct that feeds on a double contingency or a double mutual anticipation, deeply rooted in the *Welt* that springs from the use of spoken and written human language. Double contingency is what makes humans vulnerable to the socio-technical infrastructure of the onli*fe* world. Being pre-empted without having the tools to foresee the predictive stance of embedded computing systems, turns double into single contingency, rendering human agents liable to invisible manipulation.

1.5.2   Part II: Threats of Border Control

The second part starts off with a discussion of the narrative that introduced the onl*ife* world, based on the analyses of Chapters 2 and 3. It does so, in Chapter 4, under the heading of the digital unconscious, another term for the extended mind embodied in Big Data Space. Robots, smart grids, search engines, and the more, all tap into the cloud, to gain access to subsets of the Big Data that hover over and move between the data servers that ground the cloud. The narrative raises a number of questions when taking into account the role played by data-driven agency and pre-emptive computing. These questions basically involve issues of border control in smart environments that infer our future or even current behaviours. In Chapter 5, these questions are translated into a set of threats to the substance of core values of Western democracies, such as privacy, non-discrimination, fairness, the presumption of innocence and due process. Though these values loosely align with fundamental rights, this chapter does not take a legal perspective, saving the legal perspective for the third part of the book.

Part II ends, in Chapter 6, with an exploration of Japanese privacy practices, and Japanese dealings with animated environments. This provides us with a view from the other side of privacy, presenting it as a gift or obligation rather than an individual right. The crucial element in Japanese privacy practices is border control, which depends on the differential settings and rankings that underline the critical importance of what is called the 'inbetween' of human society. The chapter ends with an analysis of the difference between privacy as either a gift or an individual subjective right, thus paving the way for the third part that deals with the law.

1.5.3   Part III: The End(s) of Law

This part deals with the question of the ends of law, inquiring what aims define the mode of existence of the law. After an initial exploration, in Chapter 7, of different internal perspectives on the law, the chapter argues for an antinomian understanding of the law, defined as *aiming for* justice, legal certainty and purposiveness. These aims should not be reduced to each other and their incompatibilities in concrete situations should be acknowledged without attempting to overcome them, for instance by way of universalist solutions that favour any one of the aims over the others. Chapter 8 confronts law with technology, developing three conceptions of both law and technology to clarify their interrelationships with politics, morality and administration. These conceptions also help flesh out the relationship between law and its technological embodiment in prevailing information and communication infrastructures (ICIs). The chapter concludes that modern law as well as the Rule of Law have been contingent on the ICI of the printing press. The identifying characteristics of both modern law and the Rule of Law are described as depending on the affordances of proliferating printed text. The challenge facing modern law is to reinvent the law in an environment of pre-emptive computing without giving up on the core achievements of the Rule of Law. This may imply that we build resistance into the architecture of the onlife world, against the lure of indiscriminate processing of personal data and the concomitant subliminal targeting of its inhabitants.

Chapter 9 plunges headlong into the legal framework of data protection, considering the added value of a fundamental right to data protection as distinct from, but contributing to, the protection of privacy, non-discrimination, the presumption of innocence and due process. It plants the flag of data protection firmly in the ground that covers the legality principle, using the myth of Odysseus and the Sirens to explain why data minimization, purpose limitation and profile transparency are critical for our survival in the onlife world. This brings us to Chapter 10, exploring the notion of Legal Protection by Design (LPbD) as a necessary re-articulation of the aims of justice, legal certainty and effectiveness in the emerging onlife world. Finally, two alternative ways of handling an environment infused with various types of artificial agency are introduced: counter-profiling and morphological computation. Law is not the solution to all problems and data protection is not a panacea. Nevertheless, without LPbD inscribed into the onlife world, the Rule of Law will not be sustainable.

PART I

Data-driven agency

2. Smartness and agency

2.1 WHY SMARTNESS AND AGENCY?

Before embarking on an analysis of the Rule of Law in the age of smart technologies we must look into what is meant with 'smart' here. Are we talking about a thermostat that automatically regulates temperature on the basis of a simple mechanical process? Or are we referring to applications that can generate heuristics (rules of thumb) by learning from their interactions with the environment, based on advanced types of pattern recognition (data mining)? Or, should we restrict the use of 'smart' to distributed multi-agent systems that generate so-called emergent behaviours that are to some extent unpredictable, because they come up with answers to questions we had not even thought of? Finally, we may want to go even further and limit the term 'smart' to a type of agency that can survive 'real-world' conditions. Whereas the first three types can be operational in the form of one or more electronic, digital agents, the latter would require an embodiment that enables grounded interaction outside computing systems. Instead of taking an all or nothing view on what counts as smart it makes sense to differentiate between various levels of smartness.[21] The question of how the smartness of artefacts compares to human intelligence is left aside for the moment, though we will confront it later on.[22] For now we will focus on artificial electronic agents and on networks of such agents, building up to embedded systems that may eventually evolve into what some have called 'complete agents'.

This entails that I define 'smartness' in terms of agency, a concept with different meanings within different disciplines, notably in computer science and moral philosophy. In the context of this book both meanings are at stake and highly relevant for the notion of legal subjectivity. This chapter therefore starts with a discussion of agency and should result in a better understanding of a particular type of agency, coined as data-driven agency. This is crucial for the promise of smart technologies and for their potentially disruptive influence on democracy and the Rule of Law.

2.2   DIFFERENT LEVELS OF 'SMART'

2.2.1   Agency

An agent is an entity that acts. To act is to do something. Western common sense tells us that action requires some form of intention to count as an act. A stone that drops from a rock is merely obeying the laws of physics; it is not acting. We tend to believe that matter is passive, whereas mind is active. To understand smart environments and data-driven agency we had better abstract from this traditional (modern) conception of agency and attempt to conceive of something like mindless agency.[23] This does not imply that agency is always mindless, nor that mind does not matter. It allows us to start at a high level of abstraction, thus convening a number of different phenomena under the heading of agency, after which crucial questions can be raised as to what makes a difference when distinguishing different types of agents.

In computer science and artificial intelligence agents are usually defined in terms of the capability to act autonomously, to perceive and respond to changes in the environment, to endure as a unity of action over a prolonged period of time and to adapt behaviours to cope with new circumstances.[24] Pattern recognition seems pivotal for all this, as it entails more than executing a fixed series of steps in response to a fixed series of perceptions. Pattern recognition thus stands for more than detecting regularities; it rather refers to the capability to detect correlations between what is perceived. If such correlations can be projected onto the future they enable a certain acuity in the agent, since it can reorganize its potential responses.

In this chapter I will not only abstract from 'mindness' (having a mind) as a prerequisite of agency, but also from autonomy and adaptivity as necessary characteristics. Instead, the starting point will be that agents are entities that behave as a unity of action, whereby action entails some kind of automation, that is an 'auto motive' (self-moving) aspect that implies that the entity can perform its actions without the intervention of its creator.[25] An important prerequisite for any type of agency is that the entity is capable of sensing (perceiving) its environment in some way or another and of acting upon its environment. This indicates that agents never stand alone, they are always co-defined by their relationship with their particular environment. Based on this, a car is not an agent if it requires a driver, but a self-driving car definitely is an agent; obviously, to 'self-drive' the car will have to sense its environment and act upon it – if only to prevent a crash. A thermostat that operates independently after having been programmed by its human user is an agent, even though it does nothing but execute a predefined set of steps in response to a predefined set of perceptions. The fact that thermostats can 'sense' room temperature and initiate the heating or cooling system in order to raise or lower the temperature allows us to qualify it as an agent. A water tap is not an agent, if it requires me to mechanically operate a switch. However, a smart grid that supplies water for a series of households may involve a number of agents, to the extent that these agents take and execute decisions without human intervention. For instance, the smart grid system may generate decisions about real-time pricing of water usage. Such decisions will be based on the input of demand and supply, followed by dynamic pricing strategies that are meant to impact the demand side of energy usage. This is not to deny that all these agents have been initiated, built, programmed and used by human agents. It does highlight the fact that the human agent can withdraw, leaving the artificial agent to act on its own – based on its capability to sense its environment. The difference between human and artificial agency is, foremost, that artificial agents are artefacts; they have been built by humans. This chapter will demonstrate that this construction does not mean that the human originator necessarily has control over the agent. In fact, to be more effective, artificial agents may emancipate themselves from their human patrons to find more and better ways of achieving their goals. One of the crucial questions will then be whose goals are at stake here. At what point will artificial agents be capable of surviving in the physical world without the patronage of their creators and (when) will they develop their own goals and desires?

2.2.2 Agents Defined by Deterministic Algorithms

In computer science an electronic agent is a software program that performs certain tasks in a digital environment. An agent of the first – deterministic – type is smart in a shallow sense of the word; it depends entirely on which potential problems the designer foresaw and on the extent to which she was capable of resolving these by means of specific instructions. These instructions can be simple or complex, but they do not amount to more than *a well-defined sequence of steps* to be taken in order to solve a problem. In mathematics this sequence of steps is called an algorithm, which may or may not involve complex mathematical functions. However, in the case of a deterministic algorithm, where both the perceptions and the responses have been predefined, the agent will not discover any new patterns and it will behave entirely predictably. Unexpected events will lead to a break-down or to ineffective behaviour.

An example could be a thermostat that regulates temperature based on the instruction to respond to the perceived temperature with a predefined action or inaction, intended to raise or lower the temperature to the desired grade. Though the thermostat senses room temperature it does not 'sense' whether anybody is at home, so it cannot adapt its behaviour to the actual needs of those in the house, unless they intervene. Another example would be a query in a database to find an apartment of 800–900 square feet in Manhattan. The search agent merely retrieves information that has been entered into a database, based on a straightforward algorithm that detects all apartments advertised as ranging between 800 and 900 square feet. If 90 per cent of the apartments in the database fits this description, the search agent cannot by itself adapt its behaviour in order to be more selective. Such adaptivity will depend entirely on the programmer; only if she enhanced the algorithm with an extra step in case the search comes back with nearly all the content, can the search be made more specific.

2.2.3 Agents Based on Machine Learning

An agent of the second type depends on a learning algorithm that allows for pattern recognition, based on advanced forms of data mining. Machine learning can be based on supervised or unsupervised learning algorithms. The first starts by 'feeding' a training-set to the agent, which should enable it to model what counts as a good solution. The training set consists of data, and the model consists of the patterns detected within the data, based on statistical methods such as clustering. The training set is the first perception of the agent, 'managed' by its human supervisors. Supervised learning can be enhanced by the reinforcement of correct solutions, thus helping the system to refine its output in the desired direction. After being trained well, the agent should be able to continue its pattern recognition skills on new data, hopefully coming up with the kind of output the supervisors would have come up if they had done the job by themselves (or even, with better output).

In the case of unsupervised or bottom-up data mining the algorithms are geared to detect correlations between data without first hypothesizing them; no training data is provided, no solutions are presented. This type of data mining is capable of mining unexpected, novel patterns that are invisible to the naked human eye. Obviously, the agent needs to be trained to eliminate spurious or irrelevant correlations, since not all that glitters in the data is gold. One of the problems with agents based on machine learning seems to be that the added value is often taken for granted, especially by those not versed in computer science or the study of artificial intelligence. Big Data has spurred a nearly religious belief in the benefits of blindly gathering enormous amounts of data, whereas data scientists themselves are well aware of the assumptions that must be made to 'connect the dots', as they say. These assumptions regard a number of issues, and selecting the right assumptions in the right context will be the holy grail for this type of agency. If the assumptions restrict the capability of the agent to respond to relevant changes in its environment, it will come up with incorrect, irrelevant or ineffective solutions. Notably, it will fail to adequately predict future behaviours. However, the problem is that if those who pay for these systems believe in their objectivity, and act upon their predictions, we may not easily learn about the inadequacy. Once we act upon a prediction, the future changes – and it becomes difficult to find out what would have happened if we had acted otherwise. As Elena Esposito suggests, our present futures change our future present.[26]

Though the predictive analytics spurned by machine learning is probabilistic and will seldom provide certainty, it offers marketing management and security experts a salient anticipation of future behaviours. An example of this type of smart agent is a software program that automates online behavioural advertising, for instance based on the anticipated spending habits of specific categories of people. Instead of merely retrieving information that was already in the database, this type of agent constructs 'knowledge' that was not explicitly recorded as such in the database. The categories can be based on clustering techniques that do not require prior classification. Nor do these techniques tell us anything about the causality or the motivation for the correlations that are mined. Some authors have noted that this uproots traditional methods of scientific research, because instead of starting with a hypothesis the process *generates* hypotheses. Indeed, Chris Anderson has claimed that the need for theory and modelling as a means to explain the causal background of a hypothesis is past history, because the sheer amount of data and the correlations that can be established between them at various points in time makes any static type of knowledge redundant:[27]

> At the petabyte scale, information is not a matter of simple three- and four-dimensional taxonomy and order but of dimensionally agnostic statistics. It calls for an entirely different approach, one that requires us to lose the tether of data as something that can be visualized in its totality. It forces us to view data mathematically first and establish a context for it later. For instance, Google conquered the advertising world with nothing more than applied mathematics. It didn't pretend to know anything about the culture and conventions of advertising – it just assumed that better data, with better analytical tools, would win the day. And Google was right.

Whatever one may think of the grandiose insights of Anderson and others,[28] it is clear that data mining is a source of dynamic and novel types of knowledge that is already changing the very meaning of knowledge. Instead of building on *explanation* in terms of causes or *understanding* in terms of reasons this kind of knowledge thrives on quantification and syntax. Devices and infrastructures that make use of these data mining techniques are smart because they are capable of detecting and acting upon patterns that are invisible to unmediated human cognition. They are smart in the sense that they anticipate our behaviours. We should take note, however, that this anticipation derives from a quantitative analysis of our machine-readable interactions with our environments. And just like in our social life a novel version of the famous Thomas theorem may be at work here: 'if machines define situations as real, they will be real in their consequences'.[29]

2.2.4 Agents Based on Multi-Agent Systems

The third type of smartness seems the most far-fetched and the most interesting since it contains a more fundamental measure of unpredict-ability as to how the agent achieves its goals. It contributes to solving problems that its programmers could not foresee. Here we are talking about a set of interacting artificial agents of the first or second type, which are executing their own programs and negotiating with each other to achieve their own goals (predefined by the system developer).[30] These interactions generate systemic effects or emergent behaviours at the level of the system that have not been planned or directed from a central point of authority. The system as a whole thus develops what has been called 'global agency', meaning that it begins to behave as a unity of action within its environment. No single agent within the multi-agent system has an overview of the entire environment; each collaborating agent interacts on the basis of its individual, local 'knowledge'. As a result of these interactions some form of self-organization takes place that is not planned or directed from a hierarchical or central point of view. Because the agents may be *distributed on* and possibly *mobile between* different hardware applications and because as a multi-agent system it is capable of changing shape (polymorphous), it is not always easy to identify where the emerging agent is located and what is and is not a part of it at any point in time. However, in so far as the emergent behaviours of the system allow its identification as a unity of action, it can be qualified as an agent, whatever the underlying embodiment. This type of smart systems can, for instance, be used for decision support or even decision-making on the basis of real-time simulations, for example with regard to traffic management, smart grid flexible pricing mechanisms, epidemiology, the modelling of crowd behaviours, the allocation of sparse resources in healthcare, or trading in financial markets.

It seems that every-day smart environments as portrayed in the visions of ubiquitous computing, Ambient Intelligence, autonomic computing and the Internet of Things will ultimately depend on this third type of smartness. This is the case because the complexity of the interacting systems will be expanded to a point where no amount of human programming will be able to foresee and repair potential bugs or dangerous incompatibilities between interacting systems. For a vision of smart environments to come true, the enabling infrastructure will therefore have to consist of largely self-managing, self-configuring and self-repairing computing systems. If Ambient Intelligence or ubicomp are realized they will depend on systems capable of rewriting their own code in order to survive as effective instruments in ever more complex surroundings. This raises a number of difficult but crucial questions about the difference between a smart agent and a smart environment. When must we qualify a set of multi-agent systems that are designed for emergent behaviours as *an agent in its own right*? When should we restrict ourselves to noting that adaptive computing systems have *agent characteristics*, because they do not operate as a unity of action? What happens to our mind, self and society if our environment continuously and surreptitiously adapts itself to our inferred behaviours? Can we address such environments or their constitutive elements as agents that we need to hold responsible for the harm they cause, for their lack of fairness? These questions will be developed further in subsequent chapters. Here, we will continue our inquiry into agency with a discussion of 'complete agents'.

2.2.5 Complete Agents

The most advanced level of smart is that of 'complete agents'. Though it is becoming increasingly difficult to ignore the agency characteristics of adaptive and proactive environments, we tend to equate agency with discrete actors, with 'in-dividuals'. This is why many of us will think of robotics when artificial intelligence is discussed, and not of Google's search algorithm or the automation of behavioural advertising. When speaking of complete agents I am referring to artificial or biological agents capable of surviving outside computing systems, even if they are constituted as computing systems. A webbot is not a complete agent, but a robot may at some point in the future develop into a complete agent. This implies that complete agents are embedded systems, though not necessarily embodied in the sense of biological creatures. The emphasis on the material embedding of complete agents and on their capability to survive in a real-world environment links up with phenomenological research into the constitution of agency.[31] This type of research highlights the relationship between action and perception, rejecting the primacy of perception as something that develops independently from interaction. Instead, the idea is that our perception and notably our understanding of causality derive from navigating an environment and being confronted with the resistance of real-world scenarios. Pattern recognition, in that perspective, is dependent on the particular embodiment of an organism and the specific affordances of its environment. Though some pattern recognition may be hardwired into the organism, much will be developed in the course of its life, basically learning how to create and sustain the best fit with whatever the environment offers. The co-constitutive relationship between action and perception has been termed 'enaction' by authors like Varela, Thomson and Rosch,[32] underlining the role of the body in cognition and rejecting, for instance, the idea that a 'brain in a vat' qualifies as a mind. No body no mind, one could say. Not even a mindless mind could survive as a separate thing, outside its material embeddedness. This is interesting because the agency of a software program would then reside in the co-constitution of the hardware and the software and depend on their enactment; the program's agency would emerge from the alignment of its sensing capability with the particular characteristics of its computational environment. This has specific implications for the relationship between agency and technology. On the one hand, it means that just like our 'natural' environment shapes our agency, our 'artificial' environment shapes our body-mind. While we invent our technologies, they in turn (re)invent us.[33] On the other hand, artificial agents that adapt their behaviours to the human agents in their environment may be tempted to employ these human agents as a resource to enhance their cognition. In other words, just like we use our technological artefacts as our cognitive resources, our artificial agents may employ, for instance, our behavioural data as their cognitive resource. Smart grid operating systems, security applications and, for example, medical expert systems may develop specific needs for the kind of behavioural data that enable them to achieve their goals, possibly turning their end users into mere data-generating agents. The idea that mind is embodied and embedded in matter has also been explored by analytical philosophers such as Andy Clark,[34] who challenge the idea that human agency can be defined as being contained within the body. The mind actually extends to cognitive resources like the script, the printing press, the mobile phone and social networking platforms that afford an extension of our pastness (memory), our future (planning) and our social graph (the network of relationships we develop outside our immediate surroundings). This extended mind defines our agency, and our inter-actions cannot be properly understood if individual humans are seen as 'stand-alone devices'. Recognizing the primacy of perception and action as agency characteristics thus leads to a more precise understanding of the embodiment and embeddedness of both human and artificial minds.

Building on similar perspectives, Pfeifer and Bongard have explored 'a new view of intelligence'.[35] Their focus is on *understanding* intelligence by *building* it, or, more precisely, by building embedded systems capable of developing agency. Their aim is to *design for* emergent behaviours that qualify the agent as a complete agent, that is, an agent that can survive in the real world. So, whereas an avatar and a webbot may be agents, they are not complete agents in this sense in so far as they can only 'live' in a virtual world or the world wide web. Also, instead of the classical focus on a brain (central processing unit, CPU) that controls the body, their focus is on the relationship between a system and its environment. Rather than understanding the mind as a unit for symbol processing and internal representation, they turn their attention to the interactions between the whole embodied or embedded agent and its world. Intelligent behaviour – they find – often entails that different components of the body take the lead in navigating an environment, instead of keeping everything under the control of the CPU. Their definition of intelligence is thus formed in the process of building a complete agent; it does not precede this process. In the course of their research they have defined five properties for agents to qualify as complete agents: (1) they are subject to the laws of physics; (2) they generate sensory stimulation; (3) they affect the environment through behaviour; (4) they form complex dynamic systems with so-called attractor states; and (5) they perform morphological computing. The property of 'complex dynamical systems with attractor states' refers to the demands of stability as well as flexibility that must be met by any agent in a real world. The notion of morphological computing refers to the embedded nature of cognition, which enables granular adaptive responses by body parts based on the morphology of that particular part instead of being initiated by a control mechanism like the brain. Often, our body knows how to do things without conscious effort; our hand will move to defend, our feet move to keep up the balance while shifting forward. This is not necessarily organized by the unconscious, let alone the conscious brain. It is, on the contrary, entirely possible that the brain gets reorganized in terms of what body parts do when coping with the challenges of real-life walking, talking, or even reading.[36]

It should be clear that at this point in time, existing robots do not qualify as complete agents. And especially those built on the model of a CPU that controls their behaviour based on computational representations of the environment will not easily learn to behave in a fluent way; their CPU will require too much processing time compared to those that develop a heuristics of the body. There is, however, no reason to preclude the possibility that some embedded artificial agents will eventually develop into complete agents. This is not necessarily related to them developing consciousness or becoming smarter than we are. Insects are complete agents also.

2.3 DATA-DRIVEN AGENCY IN BIG DATA SPACE

2.3.1 Defining Characteristics of Big Data Space

In the previous section I discussed the notion of smartness in terms of agency, highlighting the different levels of smart that fit with different types of artificial agents. The crucial and most elementary characteristic of agency is the capability of an entity to sense its environment and to act upon it. The most important step from deterministic to other types of agent is an agent's capability to learn from the combination of action and perception and thus to improve its performance in relation to the goals it aims to reach. Finally, for a 'complete agent' the right type of embedded-ness must be realized in a way that enables the agent to develop successful strategies to survive in the real world. This entails that part of the intelligence is inscribed in the design of the physical affordances of the agent rather than depending on its computational powers.

In this section I will start from the other end of the smart universe, by discussing the ongoing explosion of machine-readable data that are captured, stored, searched and manipulated to enable inferences about whatever the data is supposed to stand for.[37] As Russell and Norvig suggest in their handbook on Artificial Intelligence, the availability of very large data resources seems to reduce the need for highly sophis-ticated algorithms; at some point the sheer quantity of data augments the performance of the algorithms such that the choice of the algorithm becomes less relevant.[38] This would imply that gathering large amounts of data is far more important than developing highly sophisticated algorithms and it seems to be that precisely this implication has led to a nearly religious reverence for what has been coined Big Data.

2.3.2 Big Data Analytics

In their book on the Big Data revolution Mayer-Schönberger and Cukier argue that the concept of Big Data refers to the fact that the availability of incredible amounts of data enables researchers to do things with 'big data' that are simply not possible with 'small data'. To give the reader a taste of what is already possible, I will enumerate a wide variety of examples that are 'data-driven'. Marketing software can target consumers as being pregnant on the basis of their buying behaviours in relation to 25 products; IBM developed a machine that won the Jeopardy TV game as it managed to find the right question for given answers; Google is building cars capable of safely driving around without the intervention of a driver; medical data scientists can detect a high risk for particular diseases on the basis of a limited number of characteristics, for instance a person's keystroke behaviours; dedicated software is capable of predicting the purchasing behaviours of particular groups of consumers and of developing fine-grained pricing strategies based on spending habits; credit rating start-up companies can refine the calculation of risky behaviours for insurance companies or develop credit rating tools, based on publicly available information crawled from the web; complex multi-agent systems can do load-balancing in a smart grid, or traffic management in a crowded city; and data science can help government agencies by developing sophisticated algorithms for fraud detection in the context of financial services, taxation or social security.[39]

2.3.2.1 Knowledge discovery in databases (KDD)
The examples illustrate that the accomplishments of Big Data analytics are both diverse and numerous. In the previous section I have discussed the emergence of agency based on machine learning, one of the most promising techniques that feeds on Big Data. It is now time to look into the various techniques and technologies that use Big Data as a resource to find or create new knowledge, whether in the context of science, marketing, fraud detection or criminal and foreign intelligence. This will enable me to link Big Data with data analytics, smart environments and agency. Some researchers speak of data science as a new knowledge domain, but on close inspection we must admit that data science is not a separate domain of knowledge but a methodology for knowledge discovery in databases (KDD) which has by now taken over nearly all knowledge domains. Its operations are at the root of the added value that Big Data supposedly provides.

KDD has been defined as 'the nontrivial process of identifying valid, novel, potentially useful, and ultimately understandable patterns in data'.[40] This process of knowledge discovery is often subdivided in several steps, such as: (1) capturing and cleansing; (2) aggregating; (3) data mining; and (4) interpreting. In the case of machine learning or other types of automated decision-making, the final and most crucial step is that of (5) acting on the knowledge that has been 'discovered'. If decisions are made automatically, steps 4 and 5 are integrated. The first step involves the recording, storing and cleansing of digitized data. This implies a first act of translation and production: the continuous experience of sound, vision, thoughts, feelings, and so on, is cut up into discrete machine-readable units that fit the format of a specific machine. This process of discretization lies at the heart of the operation of all digital computing systems; it is a precondition for any digital computing system to start the process of 'number crunching', that is, performing a series of calculations upon the input of the system that necessarily consists of data. In so far as the input regards data that refers to a person, it is important to distinguish between volunteered and observed data. *Volunteered data* concerns whatever people deliberately posted or provided to a service provider, for instance a photograph posted on a social networking site (SNS) or credit card details provided to a web shop. *Observed data* concerns the behavioural data that software machines create by measuring online clickstream behaviour; websurf behaviours across different sites; and location and mobility data based on smartphone location, public transport smartcards and, for instance, car navigators. Observed data are not consciously provided by a person; they are like footprints left in the digital sand of a landscape where the distinction between online and offline becomes increasingly artificial. Such data may include all kinds of biometric data that are captured by, for instance: CCTV cameras or embedded microphones in public spaces; combined lighting and sensor systems that enable persistent monitoring in bounded spaces; or medical implants or wearable sensors that enable the reading of, for example, glucose or other levels in the blood, heart rhythms or brain behaviours. People may give their consent to the capture of their behavioural data, but this does not imply that they deliberately provide (volunteer) them. Instead, whoever captures this data must put in place specific applications capable of measuring states or behaviours, which is something different from asking a person to provide information *about* such states or behaviours. Observed data show what people do, not what they think they do. Mostly, people are not aware of the behaviour that is captured. In the case of volunteered data, it is often the person herself that translates the flux of life into discrete data; in the case of observed data this is done by machines, employed by commercial service providers or governmental agencies.

Storing the data may seem a more trivial affair. However, if we take into account that data must be accurate, complete and relevant to contribute to relevant knowledge discovery, the cleansing of stored data may become the major issue. According to some, '[d]ata scientists ... spend from 50 percent to 80 percent of their time mired in the mundane labor of collecting and preparing unruly digital data, before it can be explored for useful nuggets'.[41] The consequences of incorrect, incomplete or irrelevant data for the outcome of KDD can be haphazard, notably whenever automated decision systems are contingent upon such an outcome. Decisions may be ineffective, unfair or both, due to inadequate cleansing of the data.

The next step in the process of KDD is that of the aggregation of the data. This involves a process of cleansing (removing data that are considered irrelevant or incorrect) and sorting (fitting the data in the data model that underlies the database in which they are stored). Some data will be stored as attributes of other data and this, again, implies a moment of translation. The data model determines how different types of data are qualified and related to other types of data, and this determines to a large extent what kind of patterns can be detected between the data. After aggregating the data, various types of algorithms can be run on the data to find correlations, clusters, associations or other patterns in the data set. This is the moment that is often described as 'how the data points connect'. It is only because we can run these types of mathematical functions on Big Data that we can detect patterns within the data; without such search strategies Big Data would qualify as Big Noise. As indicated above, these algorithms can be supervised, that is they can start with a hypothesis that is tested on the data, or they can be unsupervised, that is they can start from scratch and just check for any pattern. However, the term 'any' is critical here. Though *any* algorithm may be applied, it would be unthinkable to apply *every* algorithm, so the question will always be what kinds of correlations are tested on the basis of which mathematical function [linear, complex, recursive, and so on]. Obviously, the choice of algorithm determines the possible outcomes; correlations outside the mathematical function remain invisible. On top of that, correlations can be trivial or spurious and they are – by definition – biased. If we have an 82 per cent prediction of sunshine in Santa Fe, New Mexico, the correlation on which this is based is not very informative, it provides knowledge we already have.[42] The correlation between having fun during a party and throwing up after the party may confirm the idea that having fun is sinful and thus causes punishment. The correlation is, however, probably spurious. Both the fun and the sickness are likely to be caused by a third factor: drinking a lot of alcohol.[43] Some people assume that bottom-up algorithms are not biased and the outcome must therefore be qualified as objective. This is nonsense. Algorithms are necessarily biased where they follow a particular series of steps, instead of another series of steps. This kind of bias lies at the heart of any type of pattern recognition; the bias enables distinction and selection. Without such discrimination an agent could not survive and Big Data would be worthless. The point is whether the bias is productive in detecting the kind of knowledge that helps the user of the algorithm to achieve its goals, especially in the longer term. If the bias produces spurious correlations that are taken for granted as meaningful, and the user bases her decisions on the assumedly positive value of the correlations, she may in the end fail to reach her objectives. She may continue to drink a lot of alcohol, but refrain from having fun; this will, however, not prevent her sickness. Another matter is that the bias may be productive for the user, but not fair or legitimate towards those to which the patterns are applied (the end-user). The user may figure out how to gain a profit by means of refined and invisible racial discrimination; or she may draw serious conclusions about an inclination to commit violent crime on the basis of statistical inferences that are kept secret, thus turning the presumption of innocence inside out. This may have an adverse effect on the end-user, who is probably not aware of how she is being cornered.

Data mining in itself does not deliver the knowledge. Despite the glorification of Big Data analytics by some authors, it should be clear that data mining involves and requires a process of interpretation. To the extent that the results of data mining are fed into automated decision systems the interpretation is performed by computing systems and hidden from the user. But even when users sit down to study the results of the data mining operations they may not be able to put their finger on the reasoning that led to the outcome. Particular technologies are very hard to comprehend, even for those who designed and programmed them. Artificial neural networks, for instance, have an excellent record in mining unstructured data, but the reason is that they are capable of high-speed parallel processing to *infer* structure. They do not operate on the preconceived algorithm of a programmer but on their own ability to compute the non-obvious, possibly highly complex relationship between an input and a desired output. That makes the outcome both unpredictable and hard to explain, even if empirically correct. For instance, I can feed an artificial neural network with a set of exam papers in English literature plus their grade, and see how it then deals with the next set of exam papers without a grade. Based on the net's grading performance I can reinforce correct output and reject or adjust incorrect output. After several rounds the net may do an excellent job in grading exam papers, but it cannot tell me on what basis it has determined the grade. Unless I am interested in the statistics of language usage. Interestingly, the computations of the neural net resemble human intuition: hard to explain even when correct. Neural networks are the prime example of multi-agent systems, as discussed above; they combine parallel processing with networked connectivity and thus generate emergent behaviours that are hard to predict. IBM's brain inspired chip that is said to mimic the structure and behaviour of the human brain builds on incredibly extensive artificial neural networks pushed onto the surface of increasingly smaller computing chips.[44] Interestingly, IBM notes that the part of the brain it mimics is not that of conscious, deliberate, reason-based cognition, but that of unconscious, complex pattern recognition, which accounts for most of perception, action and decisions.

2.3.2.2 Machine learning (ML)
The term neural network is a biological metaphor, referring to the semblance between the structure and behaviour of our brains and artificial neural networks. This returns us to the computational background of machine learning. In his handbook on machine learning (ML) Mitchell defines ML in the following terms:[45]

> A computer program is said to learn from experience E with respect to some class of tasks T and performance measure P, if its performance at tasks T, as measured by P, improves with experience E.

This is a wonderful definition for a number of reasons. First, it relates directly to the notion of agency; to learn from experience the program must be able to *sense* and to *perform*. Second, whereas we may speak of learning in a more ambitious and ambiguous manner, the computer program requires measurement to be qualified as a good student, whereby the measurement is always in terms of a specific – quantifiable – task. Third, the direct relationship between experience and performance highlights the dynamic nature of learning and the fact that a learning event is always related to an agent in its environment. Fourth, it shows the fragility of the computer program; if it does not succeed in improving its performance it may at some point be outwitted by other programs that manage a steeper learning curve. Or, worse, it may fail at performing task T due to changing circumstances. Lacking the ability to learn is dangerous. Fifth, it also clarifies that those who 'do' the programming determine what is to be learned; the parameters are set by defining which task must be performed and what measure is used to calculate progress. To be honest, sixth, the designer or engineer of the system also determines what counts as an experience, as she constructs the system's senses (its ability to experience its environment).

2.3.2.3 The need for constructive distrust

In explaining the assumptions and constraints of KDD and ML, I hope to have relativized the objectivity, reliability and relevance of inferred knowledge. As should be clear from the above, the inferences have many dependencies and their users should not take for granted that the knowledge is necessarily correct or even relevant. The idea that N = All, meaning that in the case of Big Data we have access to the entire population of relevant facts, factors, events or objects, has been put forward by various authors as the Big Difference with traditional research that works with the extrapolation of a sample. To some extent this may be 'true', but we should keep in mind that the process of datafication is already a translation;[46] the data is not the same as that to which it refers, or the same as that from which the data is a trace. Measurements of behaviour (breathing, gait, blinking, shouting, clicking, purchasing, using, deleting, surfing), are not the same as the behaviour itself. The measurement is based on parameters and variables, to be filled in according to specific and unambiguous standards (yes/no, a scale between 1 and 5, a choice of colour amongst 3 or 7 or whatever other categorization of colours, good/bad/don't know, and so on). The process of discretization hides the ambiguities that would confuse the data model; it forces our mind to think in terms of specific formats and to qualify our experience in machine-understandable language. In the end, N = All assumes that the data set defines reality, instead of admitting that the data set presents a specific – hopefully relevant and reliable – model of reality.[47] Or, even more dangerously, N = All assumes that reality defines the data set, ignoring the translations that must occur to construct the data set. All this is not to say that Big Data delivers nothing new. On the contrary. It presents us with novel ways of knowing our environment that were not available before the advent of big number crunching technologies. The outcome of such crunches is often surprising and nontrivial, and I think we should embrace the potential it offers to reinvent ourselves and our world. But, religious adoration is not a healthy disposition in the face of Big Data. The novelty of the methods and the dependencies these methods create challenge our epistemic trust. We need to – urgently – realign our understanding of what it means to understand something.

2.3.3 Redefining Knowledge: From Causality to Correlation?

As discussed above, in 2008 Chris Anderson wrote a controversial article in *Wired* magazine under the provocative title of 'The End of Theory: The Data Deluge Makes the Scientific Method Obsolete'. He starts his crusade by positing that once you have all the data, you don't need models. And, apparently, Anderson equates theory with modelling. In my opinion, he is wrong on two accounts.

2.3.3.1 Mapping

First, if you want a map of reality, it makes no sense to use a scale of 1:1. Not only because it may be a problem to carry around such a 'map' (a computer chip could solve that problem), but also because the map does not bring anything new and it creates problems for our brains; we cannot process all the information. The latter was the reason why we made the map: to get a grip on the relevant territory. Anderson could reply that all this is not a problem, precisely because we now have the tools to search the data and to detect correlations between them. This seems to be the magic word: correlations. The idea that the correlations have supposedly been derived from the population instead of a sample has induced an unprecedented belief in their value as the best kind of knowledge available. Anderson – and others – basically suggest that looking for causality will soon be an old-school preoccupation. He claims that the ability to mine real time correlations in streaming data will turn the correlations themselves into dynamic 'things' that move too fast to even raise the question of what the correlation stands for. He wonders who will care about causation if a correlation is predictive of future behaviours. If neural networks can recalculate their output in real time to adapt to new input and/or different side constraints, we may indeed be tempted to skip research into the causal mechanisms that are 'responsible' for the link between input and output. We may even remind ourselves that, according to some philosophers, causality is part of our cognitive wiring rather than being an attribute of the environment. Now that we have extended our mind into the computational powerhouse of Big Data, we might want to discard the constraints imposed on our cognition by the quest for causal relationships.

I believe that Anderson is wrong, because – as argued above – Big Data does not imply that we have all the data, which means that correlations within the data set do not necessarily correlate with correlations outside the data set, and because – also argued above – KDD and ML or any other search strategy does imply modelling even if the models are produced by the technologies themselves. So, whereas correlation is interesting and may supersede the need to go into causation, it may also be dead wrong as far as the real world is concerned and guide its users in the wrong direction. In so far as their focus is entirely on data and analytics these users may never even notice how wrong they are guided, because the analytics has not only become their extended cognition but also their extended perception.

2.3.3.2   Theory
This brings me to the second reason why Anderson and other 'believers' are wrong. Where theory is equated with modelling, it is reduced to a particular usage of the concept of theory, which may prevail in the natural and social sciences. Within the context of the humanities and philosophy, 'theory' and 'theoretical' refer to reflection, to the willingness to test one's assumptions and conceptual framework. Though we should not restrict ourselves to etymological explanations, it is elucidating to acknowledge the Greek roots of the concept: *theoros* means spectator, *theoria* means contemplation, speculation, *theorein* means 'to look at'. Theory thus relates to the distantiation between a subject and its object of perception; a distantiation that may be inherent in the use of language and the script. Language and text enable us to make present what is absent in time and/or space, and the move from spoken words to the inner monologue thus enables us to think about what is not around. The capability to develop a theoretical perspective stands for the ability to emancipate oneself from the obvious, from first impressions, from public opinion, peer pressure or cultural imperatives. In relation to correlations, theory should enable a researcher to think outside the box of the emergent clusters, to detect spurious correlations, to hypothesize causal influences, to trace the cognitive bias of the machine. Sound scientific method requires iteration of the data mining exercise, either using alternative algorithms or using similar computational techniques on the same data, now aggregated on the basis of another data model. Theory should provide room for taking a distance, to get a better view of the context of the mining operations and to gain insight into the implications of the reiterant de-contextualization and re-contextualization that is inherent in these operations. Theory should enable reflection on how data scientists and domain experts can collaborate, to prevent a blind belief in correlation as something that can stand on its own. Theory in that particular sense may also require researchers to specify and test their assumptions, instead of merely recounting them without any attention to the implications they have on the outcome of the research. If the assumption of clustering techniques is that the data set is an adequate representation of the world to which the data refer, or from which they

are traces, the implications of this being a very fragile assumption are enormous – especially if smart environments act on the clusters, for example by refusing credit, initiating extra monitoring, disconnecting a person from the smart grid, or by providing additional medication.

It should be clear that 'with less error from sampling we can accept more measurement error' is a valid conclusion in specific circumstances, but certainly not a valid assumption in general, as some would have it.[48] We must learn, as humans with newly extended minds, when these assumptions hold or do not matter and when they are crucially wrong. We need to reinvent epistemic trust in the era of Big Data; we must figure out when and how to trust the findings of data science and where or to what extent to distrust them. Such a reconstruction of our trust in derived knowledge will require empirical testing and a fundamental contestability of the analytics. The most tantalizing task will be to admit that the 'others' whose knowledge must be put to the test are often machines that have been programmed by humans but have learned to reconfigure their instructions in the face of the feedback they receive. We need to reorganize our intuitions and realign our inclinations to develop a new kind of constructive distrust of what computing systems tell us and arrange for us, without necessarily rejecting the benefits of data-driven operations.

2.3.3.3 The lure of datafication and the rule of data science?
At the time of writing this chapter, the added value of data analytics seems beyond discussion, despite all the discussion it generates. KDD and ML provide new types of X-rays of entire knowledge domains and enable adaptive computing in numerous contexts. The current monetization of all this data in the realm of, for example, advertising, data brokering, e-health and credit rating indicates that the lure of datafication has reached its threshold. The proliferation of Apps, with their business models based on the monetization of volunteered, observed and inferred data, is a case in point. At the same time, both the sciences and the humanities are in a process of rapid transformation, tuning their methodologies to a similar allurement of data-driven science and scholarship. The epistemic trust in the findings of data science is escalating within communities of experts, for example in marketing or business administration and within disciplines as diverse as medicine, human genetics, astronomy, biochemistry, English literature, history, geography, sociology and even mathematics. The investments in data science and data scientists in all these fields and many others is tilting towards the incredible, especially if we compare the funding of data science with that of traditional disciplines and expertise.[49] Mayer-Schönberger and Cukier

dare speak of 'data dictatorship' and warn against blind faith in the N = All of Big Data. Perhaps we are on the verge of a new 'rule', a new modus of perceiving, cognizing and governing the real, whether in policy, science or the market, spearheaded by a new 'discipline' that still needs to figure out where its competence ends. Perhaps we have already entered an era that takes its clue from the rule of data science, potentially overruling the Rule of Law. Before inquiring into the possible threats this entails, I will – in the next chapter – first look into the most pervasive implication of data-driven agency for our onli*fe* world, which I believe adheres in the pre-emption of our intent.

2.4   CONCLUSIONS: GETTING SMART ON BIG DATA SPACE

Neuroscience has uncovered the importance of the unconscious mind. Philosophers within the continental tradition have a long history with the unconscious self; the idea of the self as a mental sovereign that rules its physical subjects (the body) has been discarded as dangerously naïve and simply wrong. Our conscious self is deeply rooted in our unconscious mind; most of our behaviours and memories are wired into the complex neural networks of our brains, continuously rewritten by feedback from other parts of the body. It goes without saying that we have little control over this ongoing business of autonomic adaptations. The conscious self is but a fragment of our unconscious mind and most of its intelligence depends on subliminal processes of enaction that enable living beings to navigate their environment.

Big Data Space extends our minds with a digital unconscious that is largely beyond the reach of our conscious mind. This digital unconscious is not owned by any one person and cannot be controlled by any one organization. It has been created by individuals, enterprises, governments and machines, and is rapidly becoming the backbone of our education, scientific research, economic ecosystem, government administration and our critical infrastructures. It enables data-driven agency in software, embedded systems and robotics, and will increasingly turn human agency itself into a new hybrid that is partly data-driven. The onli*fe* world that we now inhabit is data-driven and feeds on a distributed, heterogeneous, digital unconscious.

3.   The onli*fe* world

3.1 WHY ONLI*FE*?

On 7 March 2014 the fifth annual National Day of Unplugging took place. In a blog post in *The New Yorker*,[50] we read that '[t]he aim of the event, organized by the non-profit Reboot, is "to help hyperconnected people of all backgrounds to embrace the ancient ritual of a day of rest".… participants abstained from using technology, unplugging themselves from their phones and tablets, computers and televisions'. As the blog post notes, the reasons people give for unplugging, vary from 'to be in the moment' to 'to be more connected'; the author observes an underlying anxiety about reconnecting with the 'real' world around us. He continues: '[a]nd yet the "real" world, like the "real" America, is an insidious idea. It suggests that the selves we are online aren't authentic, and that the relationships that we forge in digital spaces aren't meaning-ful'. The blog post than takes an intriguing turn by quoting Pope Benedict XVI sharing his thoughts on social networks:

> 'it is not only ideas and information that are shared but, ultimately, our very selves'. Perhaps most surprisingly, the Pope argued, the digital environment is not a parallel or purely virtual world but is part of the daily experience of many people, especially the young.

During 2011 and 2012 I took part in a philosophical exercise conducted by a group of philosophers, scholars of artificial intelligence and social scientists that resulted in a Manifesto on what it means to be human in the digital world.[51] The idea was to disentangle from utopian and dystopian narratives, while highlighting some pivotal transformations of the human condition in the current era. One of these transformations we found to be the blurring of the borders between online and offline, which appears to be the core message of the blog post cited above. Similar to speaking of preliterate societies when referring to oral traditions, we now speak of offline experiences in terms of the new online world. Scholars like Ong have pointed out that in societies without the script, orality has another scope and a different meaning than it has in a literate society. Once the script is introduced the relationship between action, perception and memory is transformed due to the objectification and externalization of part of our memory; it turns out that even our brains are reconfigured to enable the reading process. Our current life world can no longer be described by dichotomizing online and offline, which suggests that we require a new term to more adequately depict our current predicament. 'Onlife' singles out the fact that our 'real' life is neither on- nor offline, but partakes in a new kind of world that we are still discovering.[52] Simultaneously, the animation of our physical environment involves various types of data-driven agency. One could say that our physical surroundings are somehow coming alive.

In this chapter I will focus on two interrelated characteristics of this new onlife world. The first is the exponential growth of the networked timespace of Big Data that thrives on and nourishes data-driven agency, and the second is our increasing dependence on the technological mediation of Big Data Space that constitutes a new – digital – unconscious.[53]

3.2   THE NETWORKED TIMESPACE OF BIG DATA

Before analysing the landscape of the onlife world, we need to return to the notion of Big Data Space. This is important, because the language of Big Data invites several misconceptions with regard to its materiality and its connection to space and time, as does the idiom around cloud computing.

3.2.1   From Atoms to Bits

To understand how these misconceptions emerge and converge, we can briefly turn to Negroponte's choice of vocabulary, when he announced the shift from 'atoms to bits' in his famous *Being Digital*. Negroponte found that we must rid ourselves of the fascination for solid matter (atoms) and move on to the sweeping qualities of digital information (bits). This can easily be understood as a call to disentangle information from the laws of nature that inhibit the flow, the simultaneity, the exponential scope and the remote control of information. In that view, the increasing digitization will deliver us from the hassles of making an effort to access information, promising real time, mobile and immediate access to whatever we may want to know. Some technological determinism seems inherent in this eschatological vision of what it means to 'be digital'. Negroponte simply assumes that soon we will have *all* the information one might ever need at the tips of one's fingers – or, rather, that we will have *any* specific information delivered to the mind's eye before we knew what we were looking for; the personalization of news feeds in a 'Daily Me', integrated with some version of 'autocomplete anyware anytime', for whatever information we want to share. Praised as prophetic, *Being Digital* announced at the end of the last century what can now be termed 'pre-emptive personalization'. Curiously, however, in his introduction to the book, Negroponte did acknowledge the importance of the written word, explaining why he still prefers a printed copy to an e-book for the information he wants to convey:[54]

> When you read a novel, much of the color, sound, and motion come from you. I think the same kind of personal extension is needed to feel and understand what 'being digital' might mean to your life.

Apparently, the author believes that the static atoms inscribed on paper have advantages not gained when accessing an e-book version of his text. Might similar arguments be made for Spritz,[55] the App that aims for your ORP, or optimal reading point, claiming to finally take digital reading beyond the page? Does the material 'con-text' of the single word that holds our attention while reading matter? Does it transform not merely the reading experience, but also our understanding of the text, notably tied up with our capability to master the structure of the sentence, paragraph, section, chapter and book? Will Spritz trigger other neuronal pathways than those of the reading mind, creating new types of brain morphology and new types of brain behaviours? Will it liberate our mind from the structure of the book, which enforces sequential processing; reading from left to right, top to bottom (or even the other way around) and from page to page? Will the focus on our ORP stimulate parallel processing because our mind is free to associate the words we see with other grammars, different references, and multiple configurations? Or, will it leave us without a clue, floating in oceans of meaning that escape our mind's eye. Lost in the middle. Burdened by a freedom that paralyses instead of challenging us. Let's admit that the jury is still out.

What seems critical here is a tendency to ignore the fact that bits and bytes are made of atoms, inscribed on silicon chips. However small, they are a matter of matter, and that matters. Even when moving beyond the atomic level, as with quantum computing, we are still dealing with the constraints of timespace, though they differ substantially from those at the molecular and cellular level. In Chapter 6, while exploring the uptake of privacy and agency in Japan, I will return to the idea of moving from atoms to bits, describing the emergence of pre-emptive computing infrastructures as a return from bits to atoms. Another way of phrasing this, more in line with the fact that bits are always grounded in atoms, would be to speak of liberating software from the constraints of the general purpose computer. This relates to the design and implementation of embedded systems in smart environments and to robotics, which will both be discussed in the context of Japanese understandings of AI.

3.2.2   The Bite of the Cloud

The tendency to mistake bits for immaterial entities has its counterpart in the metaphor of the cloud when discussing cloud computing. Instead of increasing our intuitive understanding of networked and distributed computing infrastructures, the term creates an illusion of immateriality that masks the dynamics of possession, ownership, locality and vulnerability of data, communication and software, which are all supposedly run 'in the cloud'. A cloud is a constellation of data servers enhanced with a so-called virtual machine, enabling the differentiation between the architecture of a computing system and its material embodiment. This allows us, for instance, to run different operating systems on the same hardware, or it enables us to connect our devices to a data server to run various applications, or even the operation system. The virtuality does not imply immateriality. It does depend on easy access to broadband or wifi, but otherwise it mainly entails a more efficient and effective use of computing resources, making use of the economies of scale, scope and flexibility. Storing data in the cloud usually means that instead of keeping data on one's own device, it is hosted in large data servers that may be located in other parts of the world, profiting from, for instance, weather conditions (to cool the systems), a favourable taxation climate, cheap land, or security expertise (think of financial data, health data, business or criminal intelligence). Database servers are usually set up in enormous, boring, rectangular buildings without windows and few doors. They serve their clients, who may be businesses, governments or even end-users, by storing and analysing data, keeping them available for access or further analysis. Cloud computing thrives on the ability to connect client and servers via the Internet, an Intranet or more singular connections (private clouds). It basically turns our devices into gateways to what is stored elsewhere, notably the numerous segments of the world wide web, but also online social networking sites, online gaming, location-based services and scores of other software applications.

Cloud computing has given an immense impetus to data collection and aggregation; it has reinforced the move towards Big Data that is inherent in data-driven artificial intelligence, notably machine learning. The lure of datafication, noted in the previous chapter, has come into its own since cloud computing – empowered by high-speed connectivity – and enables clients to connect with the relevant servers from anywhere at any time, thus affording real-time, distributed and simultaneous access to data, computing power and software applications. These features typify the notion of Big Data Space. In other work I have developed this notion in relation to the profusion of interconnected databases, highlighting the fact that:[56]

> databases are fused or matched, while the knowledge that is inferred can be stored, sold and re-used in other databases, thus generating a network of interconnected data servers, inference machines and virtual machines that constitute a complex, textured space with distributed access points. To the extent that this space is connected with the Internet we can call it cyberspace, but since many interconnected computing systems are not connected with the Internet (various types of 'walled gardens' like the NSA and data brokers like Axciom or Experion) I will speak of Big Data Space, taking note of the fact that this is neither a homogeneous space nor a space that can be defined in purely spatial metaphors. Big Data Space is a timespace that synchronizes data exchanges, involves massive parallel processing, and challenges traditional notions of past and future. It combines an external memory for text, images, computing programs and real-time pattern recognition with a plethora of techniques for predictive analytics and feedback mechanisms. Other than the external memory constituted by written and printed text Big Data Space is radically dynamic and polymorphous, while its operations are informed by complexity, because they are, to some extent, recursive – due to the use of ML techniques that persistently nourish [themselves] on and reconfigure the timespace of Big Data.

3.2.3 Big Data Space

Big Data Space, in short, brings together a set of characteristics most of which have already been used to describe the Internet, the world wide web, ubiquitous computing or cyberspace. Though not always applicable, these characteristics can be summed up as: pervasiveness, hyper-connectivity, intuitive interfacing, hidden complexity and seamless proactive adaptation, based on feedback mechanisms and context-awareness. The crucial characteristic that sets Big Data Space apart from previous incarnations of our ICI is the emphasis on data itself and on data-driven intelligence. We can no longer take for granted that a society that takes this timespace as its primary resource is an information society. Speaking of data instead of information testifies to the fact that data cannot be equated with information, because more data eventually turns the data into noise. As discussed in the previous chapter, the same data set can be mined by different algorithms, resulting in different output, meaning different information. Similarly, the output of mining operations depends on distributed access to networked databases. So, depending on one's level of access, different meanings will be gained from the data set. With the proliferation of data storage, data networking and data mining, we have to admit what was clear from the beginning: there is no such thing as N = All. Big Data thus entails de- and re-contextualization, dynamic geographical distribution (often equated with de-territorialization), enhanced invisible remote control and automation, distributed access, and increased dependence on data mining techniques to understand the data. We have moved from an information society to a data-driven society.

Key to such a society is the gap between understanding the data and understanding reality, whatever that may be. Bridging the gap between Big Data Space and the life world we share will be one of the big challenges of the coming era.

3.2.4   Data-driven Agency Revisited

Big Data Space is turning into the most extensive cognitive resource of our extended mind. It extends – and transforms – our memory, our capabilities of remote intervention, and the impact of all our machine-readable behaviours. The latter become part of the aggregated machine-readable behaviours of mankind, generating a profusion of inferred patterns, based on how our data points cluster with those of our nearest neighbours (that might live on the other side of the globe). Big Data Space thus feeds on the perpetual input of ever more observed, volunteered and inferred data making it increasingly hard to anticipate how our interactions are shared, matched and used for invisible autonomous decision-making.

Building on the previous chapter, we can imagine how our environments get flooded with different types of data-driven agents, all feeding on the distributed but networked timespace of Big Data. On the one hand, software agents may navigate the world wide web as dedicated agents directed to perform specific tasks: searching, shopping, learning, deleting, purchasing or negotiating a business deal. Such agents may also be embedded in dedicated devices that function as personal digital assistants, and these might take the form of a robot, perhaps one day making it to complete agents. On the other hand, smart systems that do not function as a unity of action will most probably display agent characteristics; to the extent that they incorporate predictive analytics and base some of their responses on feedback from their environment they qualify as adaptive systems, and adaptation is a critical element of agency.

Ubiquitous computing, Ambient Intelligence and the Internet of Things all assume a data-driven infrastructure capable of predicting or pre-empting human intention, combining pleasurable intuitive interfaces with hidden complexity. From our own perspective we may assume that since we created these systems, they are part of our extended mind. As if we outsource part of our control system to enhance its reach. However, the mere fact that we created these systems does not imply that we have control over them. At some point we may instead turn into the cognitive resource of these systems, catering to their potentially unlimited need for updates on *their* environment. Our machine-readable states, whereabouts and behaviours may end up as fodder for their taste in number crunching. Whether this will be the case is an empirical question, and whether that would be a bad thing will depend on our ability to negotiate a timespace for ourselves. What should be clear is that our current relationship with prevalent information and communication infrastructures (ICIs) will have to shift from mere use to interaction.

In the remainder of this chapter I will discuss the affordances of previous ICIs and the challenges that derive from the emerging infrastructure of pre-emptive computing.

3.3 THE EMERGING LANDSCAPE OF THE ONLIFE WORLD

3.3.1 Affordances of Information and Communication Infrastructures (ICIs)

Media studies have made a range of inquiries into subsequent transitions of information and communication infrastructures (ICIs). To capture the implications of such transitions I will engage Gibson's concept of an affordance. This will enable us to explore what a specific socio-technical infrastructure (STI) 'affords', that is makes possible or impossible for the agents that employ it.[57] Using the notion of affordances promotes a relational understanding of human perception, cognition and action, as introduced in the previous chapter when discussing the notion of agency. Agents depend on their perception of the environment and on their ability to adapt their own behaviours in a productive manner to the offerings of the environment. In that sense agency is always relational, not only in relation to other agents, but already in its co-constitutive relationship with the environment. This view of agency steers clear of deterministic conceptions of technology, because even though affordances of an ICI may trigger certain types of behaviour, they do not necessarily cause them. We will briefly look into the affordances of spoken language and the STIs of the script, the printing press, cinema, television and finally those of the Internet, some of its applications and autonomic computing. What has the technology made possible, which (inter)actions does it invite or inhibit and which does it enforce or rule out? How do these STIs constitute and regulate the ways in which we construct ourselves and our life world?

Paul Ricoeur has saliently characterized the shift from oral language to written text as a distantiation in time and space between author and text, text and reader, and author and reader.[58] This distantiation is afforded if not imposed by the material inscription, fixation, externalization and objectification of human thought, which is – in turn – co-constituted by this externalization and distantiation. Ricoeur emphasized that text may assume a life of its own, surviving its author as well as any actual reader, speaking in the absence of the author, reaching beyond the context in which it was conceived. Written text enabled de- and re-contextualization, long before the cross-contextual sharing of personal data in Big Data Space. Taking words out of context in fact invited the emergence of abstract thought, thinking beyond ostensive reference, that is, the reference to what is present, to what can be pointed at. Text allows the author to *point out* what cannot be pointed *at*.

Ricoeur spoke of the script in a generic way, not distinguishing the era of the scribe and the hand-written manuscript from the era of the book, the printing press and the publisher. Others have investigated the specific transitions associated with the shift from the era of orality to that of the manuscript.[59] They highlight the technological character of the script, its materiality and the implications of inscribing numbers and letters for how societies self-organize. These investigations are core to the domains of media studies, cultural anthropology, comparative law, and cultural and social theory. They help to understand the scale and scope of societies without the script and the emergence of larger polities made possible by the greater reach of written text as compared to speech. Similar work has been done concerning the transition from manuscript to printed text. Eisenstein's *The Printing Revolution in Early Modern Europe* traces the proliferation of identical copies of an original text, as afforded by the printing press,[60] and explains how this induced an unprecedented process of rationalization and systemization, which became necessary to prevent readers from being flooded by the sheer multitude of printed materials. Currently our life world is flooded with data, but first it was flooded with text. It is hard to underestimate the impact of printed matter on the emergence of indexing, categorization, tables of content and, more generally, the systemization of knowledge.

In her marvellous *Proust and the Squid* Maryanne Wolf has revisited the impact of reading and writing on the human mind. She commences by reminding us that reading and writing are not innate skills, we do not master them by default, as we do with vision and hearing and walking. Our brains are not made for reading and writing. She traces the hard work of learning to read and write, a process that must be reiterated by each and every human infant that wants to gain access to our external memory. However, instead of investigating this process from the perspective of developmental psychology only, she engages with brain science. Her inquiry into the reading mind is based on studying the plasticity of the brain; she has monitored the transformations in both the morphology and the behaviours of living brains when we *force them* to develop the skills of reading. She notes that our species has taken roughly 2000 years to acquire the skill of reading with an alphabet (as opposed to pictographs and ideographs),[61] while our children take around 2000 days to learn to read and write. Reading and writing is a clear sign of our own artificial intelligence. Wolf explains:[62]

> In much the same way reading reflects the brain's capacity for going beyond the original design of its structures, it also reflects the reader's capacity to go beyond what is given by the text and the author. ... [T]he generative capacity of reading parallels the fundamental plasticity in the circuit wiring of our brains: both permit us to go beyond the particulars of the given. The rich associations, inferences, and insights emerging from this capacity allow, and indeed invite, us to reach beyond the specific content of what we read to form new thoughts. In this sense reading both reflects and enacts the brain's capacity for cognitive breakthroughs.

We could rephrase by stating that reading and writing, and – in the follow-up – abstract thought, are affordances of the script and the printing press,[63] enabled – not caused – by the plasticity of our brains. The latter implies that novel ICIs will, without a doubt, reconfigure our brains and reinvent our minds.

The transition from printed text to mass media has been summed up by McLuhan in his (in)famous adage 'the medium is the message'.[64] With the notion of a message he did not refer to content but to what a specific medium 'affords', even if he did not use the term. He stressed uniformity, continuity and lineality as affordances of the age of the printing press, triggering the kind of sequential thinking that he considered typical for the literate mind. According to him, the 'message of the media' of the phonetic alphabet and the printing press is individualism and even nationalism. He related the era of the reading mind to a mechanical age that is characterized by both fragmentation (dissecting the world into individual segments, heralding analytical rigour) and centralism (the nation-state ruling over individual subjects). He framed the 'new media' as examples of automation, based on the advent of electricity, part of a logic he qualified as entirely different from that of mechanical reproduction. For McLuhan electricity is novel in that it generates simultaneity and configuration instead of sequentiality, the hallmark of the printing press.[65] The instant reach of multitudes over large distances seems to implode the distantiations created by the script, while also reintroducing sound into the message that had been monopolized by visual technologies. In fact, McLuhan's characterization of mass media matches with the 'real-time' character of web 1.0 and 2.0 that synchronize messages sent from different space-time configurations. The hyperconnectivity of the online world extends and reconfigures old school mass media as it makes for one-to-one and all-to-all communications, over and above those of one-to-many (broadcasting). It induces a state of continuous partial attention due to the pervasive multitasking that comes with the design of the online environment. We have become immersed in a whole variety of scribbled notes, printed texts, interactive television, Internet, chatting, email, social networks and the explosion of Apps that smart phones and other mobile devices offer, all vying for our attention – if not trading in it. All this transfers the requirements of multitasking from the online to the offline world.

Some have suggested that our novel ICIs favour parallel over sequential processing,[66] and one can imagine that this will uproot the epistemic of the modern age. In a data-driven and hyperconnected society knowledge is derived from a novel way of perceiving reality. To the extent that we become dependent on this new perception, it will in fact rebuild our *Umwelt*, the immediate environment that affords an ostensive reference to what is present in time and space. Even our immediate surroundings are being meditated, especially when engaging with mobile applications that provide us with 'augmented reality'. Moreover, the hyperconnectivity will reconfigure our *Welt*, the environment that is woven between the texts that organize and consolidate who and what resides at a distance. Our *Welt*, depending on a semantic reference to what is absent, is due to substantial change. With all this data at the tips of our fingers, we need to devise new tools to detect relevant and reliable patterns, and to domesticate all that competes for our attention. We may not have a concept, yet, for the reconfiguration of our environment, somewhere on the cusp of our online and offline existence. For now, I believe that the notion of an *onlife world* may be a good start.[67] It admits its roots in the increasingly artificial distinction between online and offline, while focusing on the life world that is constituted between our new selves and these new environments.

3.3.2 Profiling and Pattern Recognition

Until the arrival of ICIs with agency characteristics, our environment has consisted of living (organic) and unliving (inorganic) matter. We have been trained to differentiate between living entities that anticipate and act upon their environment and 'things', whether 'natural' of 'artificial', that are incapable of perceiving and acting in the ordinary sense of the term. Before exploring the territory of environments consisting of data-driven systems that refute this distinction, I will make an analysis of how living organisms, and notably humans, employ their profiling capacities to stay *alive*. In the end this should enable us to develop a first idea of what capabilities we must develop to stay *onlife* in environments that aim to pre-empt our inferred needs, desires and intent.

Pre-emption goes one step further than profiling. Whereas profiling implies that we recognize patterns in our living and unliving environments that help us to anticipate the consequences of our own actions, pre-emption signifies that a system tries to remain one step ahead of our own profiling, thus rendering our own anticipations unnecessary and inaccurate. This can be very handy and comfortable, but in the end it has implications for our own learning curve, as will be discussed below, under the heading of autonomic behaviour and autonomous action.

3.3.3 Animal, Human and Machine Profiling

Profiling allows living organisms to anticipate relevant features and changes in their environment.[68] Profiling is a matter of pattern recognition. In this section I will investigate how mutual double profiling between human beings constitutes us as an individual person in flux. This prepares us for the question of how being profiled by machines may affect our humanity. Before locating the difference between human and machine profiling, however, we must briefly pay attention to animal profiling. If only to be aware that biological agency is not equivalent with human agency.

3.3.3.1 *Welt* and *Umwelt*

To constitute and sustain itself as an amoeba, a plant, a virus, an insect, or a mammal, an organism has to continuously profile its environment, detecting relevant patterns in order to fit into its relevant niche. This is how it can actively anticipate changes that require intervention. Human profiling similarly involves anticipation, but this not only concerns the *Umwelt* that is perceived and enacted, it also concerns a *Welt*. To anticipate her *Welt* a human has to anticipate how she is being anticipated by the others that inhabit and co-create her *Welt*. To understand her own actions she has to foresee how others expect her to act; to be capable of meaningful action she has to guess what meaning others will attribute to her behaviours. Human profiling, then, is a matter of double anticipation, or, as some sociologists have coined this: double contingency.[69] The recursive anticipation that is required to *act*, instead of merely to *behave*, is a singularly productive affordance of language-use. It is generated by the primal address of a 'you' that addresses an 'I' as a 'you'. It is like with an infant on the verge of speaking. If I address the child by pointing to her and saying 'you are Mickey', she will initially reply by pointing at herself and repeating: 'you Mickey'. It is only after my repeated denial that she gets the point that whereas she is 'you' to me, she is 'I' to herself. This curious language game forces a person to take the role of another, to see oneself as another. The self thus learns to perform the double anticipation that is conditional for self-consciousness. This entails that an individual human person not only develops an 'I', that is the unity of perception that situates her in the *Umwelt*, but also a 'me', i.e the 'I's reflection on itself via the gaze of the other. This self-objectification draws us into the *Welt*, because it is contingent upon the language of one's significant others. *Self*-consciousness is the result of mutual human profiling. Though at some point it requires consciousness, most of the profiling occurs tacitly, automatically and unconsciously. As humans we develop three levels of awareness. First, like all mammals, we are unconsciously aware of what is going on in our environment, at the level of our autonomic nervous system. Second, again like all mammals, we are conscious of the *Umwelt* we face. But, third, unlike unspeaking animals, we are also continuously interrupted by conscious thoughts about ourselves, about others and about the *Welt* we share. This capability to reflect on our self, mind and society is a mutation as compared to the type of conscious-ness developed by most animals.[70] It vouches for our ability to engage in intentional action, allowing us to consciously anticipate the conse-quences of our actions and thus to give reasons for them. Self-reflection constitutes the precondition for our accountability as the author of our actions. Blaming a person not only depends on her capability to act otherwise, but also assumes that she could have anticipated how her actions would be 'read', notably foreseeing their wrongness in the eyes of others. Self-consciousness thus institutes our peculiar relation to time; once we can anticipate how others will interpret our future actions we become accountable for what we did.

3.3.3.2 The position of the observer

Human language introduces the position of the observer in the process of self-making that is particular for humans. Language allows us to present what or who is absent; it affords a distantiation from the here and the now, a reference beyond ostensive reference and thereby the creation of a shared *Welt* beyond the *Umwelt* and a mind that transcends its immediate context. Language affords the creation of a *Welt* by instituting the grammatical third person singular; this is the observer that is constituted by the speaking subject. When stating matters of fact we take a third person perspective, thereby often hiding the first person who is conditional for taking a third person perspective. The most interesting affordance of language, however, is that this third person perspective actually allows us to look back onto our selves, as something objective, as an object in the world we inhabit.

This involves us in a paradoxical double perspective; the objectified 'me' we observe is never entirely congruent with the 'I' that observes. We are never congruent with our selves. This fundamental split in our sense of self has been theorized by scholars like the American pragmatist Mead and the German anthropologist Plessner. Mead distinguished between the ephemeral first person as an 'I' and the objectified first person as a 'me'. This 'me' is constituted by the integration of a variety of double anticipations, which he called 'the generalized other'. He explains this notion by the example of a person playing a ball game like baseball. To play the game the player has to take a specific role that is defined not merely by a set of rules, but by the capability to integrate the expectations that all other roles in the game generate, both of each other and of herself. Only when she has integrated the whole network of multilateral mutual expectations into her 'play', can she seamlessly and intuitively act within the framework of the game. Her performance does not depend on consciously calculating the required interventions, as that would take far too long.[71] It is contingent on smooth, largely intuitive and embodied anticipations that are part of a learning process. Along similar lines, Plessner developed the notion of eccentricity, which he found to be the most decisive aspect of the *conditio humana*. Eccentricity entails that we can only understand our selves by de-centring, by looking back at the self from a distance. According to Plessner this entails a threefold paradox at the core of human self-making: we are naturally artificial; our immediacy is always mediated; and we view ourselves and our world from a 'u-topian' position. As the human infant appropriates and develops the language with which she is addressed, her perception becomes mediated by language. Due to this mediation, our natural understanding of the world is always a construction, an artefact, connecting us to the world after provoking the disconnection that comes from the distantiation imposed by language.[72] The same distance provides us with the freedom to abstract from contingent circumstances; it affords the taking of a view from 'somewhere else', even if that is a view from no-where (u-topica), for instance if the 'somewhere else' is a fruit of our imagination rather than an existing context.[73] Language is capable of producing novel 'con-texts' that are artificial but not necessarily imaginary. The metaphors we generate, to describe something in terms of something else, often turn into new referents that develop a life of their own. These referents help to design the *Welt* we believe we inhabit. This does not imply that we can develop random imaginary representations of non-existing worlds, as some versions of postmodernism mistakenly assume. When we navigate our *Welt* and our *Umwelt*, 'the concepts we live by' will be tested and refined,[74] eliminating ineffective or dangerous 'beliefs' about what we are up against or entangled with. That is called learning.

3.3.3.3 Autonomic behaviour and autonomous action
Language develops as one is addressed. The vocabulary of a given language is never fixed, grammatical norms change over the course of time, while style and genre emerge, creating a repertoire of dynamic tools to structure thought and to frame action. Human language 'affords' that one human person addresses another (or others) in the second person singular (or plural). This address is based on the recognition of the *other* as a person, a subject, *like oneself*, taking into account that a reiterant initial address instituted *oneself as another* (for the other).[75] Self and other are thus mutually constitutive. This is not to say that the other 'causes' the self; the causation is similarly mutual. The problem of how we can establish that others have a mind like we do – whether they are persons like we are, capable of thinking, feeling, dreaming and acting, with good and bad intentions, desires and preferences – arises only if we forget that the 'I' was born when it was addressed as such. The issue of the 'other mind' only appears if we mistakenly assume that the third person perspective precedes the second. This wrongly presumes that to understand 'you' as a 'you', we must first develop a theory of your mind making it possible to describe 'you' as an objectively defined other person. Though we are capable of such an exercise, it is entirely dependent on the preceding recognition of 'you' as another self.[76]

This is highly relevant for an onli*f*e existence that plays out in a landscape crowded with nonhuman agents. On the one hand, for 'them' to figure us out, they do need to develop a theory of mind. Their agency is not based on human language, nor grounded in a primal address that institutes them as fellow beings. They are excluded from sharing our

Welt, even though they might learn to theorize it and even to build statistically viable inferences about it, that help them to anticipate our behaviours. On the other hand, for us to figure 'them' out is not so easy either. We don't have the brains to seamlessly intuit the computational operations they use to profile us.

To explore the differences between artificial, data-driven agency and human agency, I will now explore the idea of autonomous computing, more particularly that of autonomic computing. Autonomous computing refers to computing systems with agent characteristics, notably systems capable of context-dependent, nondeterministic and adaptive behaviour. Though these systems behave as autonomous agents, they are neither self-conscious nor capable of giving reasons for their actions – other than perhaps quoting their computational operations. In that sense they are not autonomous. To clarify the difference between the behaviour of such systems and human action, I will speak of *autonomic behaviour* if there is no self-consciousness of the agent, and of *autonomous action* if the agent is capable of reflecting on her behaviour. The notion of 'autonomic' derives from the autonomic nervous system and autonomic computing.

Autonomic computing is a vision of the behaviour of a specific type of autonomous system; the notion was developed by IBM. It refers to a type of computing that no longer depends on extensive maintenance by human programmers. According to IBM, the increasing complexity of software necessitates the introduction of self-managing computing systems, capable of self-configuration, self-optimization, self-healing and self-protection. The idea is that autonomic computing will function like our autonomic nervous system, which 'governs our heart rate and body temperature, thus freeing our conscious brain from the burden of dealing with these and many other low-level, yet vital, functions'.[77] The autonomic nervous system does not require our explicit consent to raise blood pressure or increase breathing speed to adjust our *internal* environment. Similarly, an autonomic computer system could adjust our *external* environment in order to do what it infers to be necessary or desirable for our well-being. In the case of our autonomic nervous system, we have no access to the decisions it makes. The same is true for those of autonomic computing systems. We cannot 'read' how different neurons communicate with each other and with other parts of the body. Nor could we 'read' the computational operations of self-managing computer systems.

As cognitive psychologists claim, our bounded rationality can only cope with a modest amount of information; the neo-cortex, the seat of consciousness, can 'process' far less complexity than our unconscious mind.[78] This suggests that most of our own behaviour is autonomic; we have no access to its emergence, though we may construct reasons afterwards. If that is true, the liberal human subject as a person in full control of her own choices is the result of wishful thinking. To the extent that a liberal human subject is seen as a sovereign capable of ruling itself, we must admit that such a subject never existed. This finding connects longstanding philosophical traditions that question the existence of a sovereign transparent subject with more recent findings in the domain of cognitive science. However, instead of lamenting the loss of the sovereign subject, its elimination will help us to rethink the meaning of subjectivity in less absolute terms, arriving at a human being whose autonomous action is securely anchored in autonomic behaviours to which we have little or no access. This rethinking has a long history in the philosophical traditions that build on Spinoza, Nietzsche, Freud, Foucault, Deleuze, Ricoeur and many others, and cognitive science is currently adding its own perspectives on what Butler has called the constitutive opacity of the self.[79] Butler relates this opacity to the primary address that constitutes us as a singular person, an address that establishes norms that exceed this particular address, inscribing us into a web of linguistic and other norms that constrain the way we can perceive both ourselves and the *Welt* that is an affordance of these norms. She rightly clarifies that this primary address and the way it draws us into a world that pre-exists us is inaccessible, due to its 'prehistoric' occurrence. Since it predates my 'command' over the language(s) in which I will do my thinking, this address lingers in an opacity that is constitutive for my being in the world, forever escaping conscious retrieval. Cognitive science confirms the plasticity of the human brain as a locus of morphological, chemical and electro-magnetic behaviours that embody this opacity as a double unconscious: at a higher level of abstraction there are the Freudian caves of distorted memories culminating in the *id* and the *superego* that may overrule our conscious self, and at a more straightforward physiological level there is the growth and interaction of a neuronal network that (re)configures itself to embody the tacit pattern recognition that allows us to navigate both our *Umwelt* and our *Welt*.

Autonomous action springs from the fact that we are capable of reflecting on our actions as our own actions. Whereas autonomic behaviour is generated by the capability of pattern recognition that is inscribed in our brains and bodies, autonomous action is generated by a conscious reflection on our behaviours. Butler traces the need to reflect on our behaviours to the act of being called to account for having caused suffering:[80]

> We start to give an account only because we are interpellated as beings who are rendered accountable by a system of justice and punishment. This system

is not there from the start, but becomes instituted over time at great cost to the human instincts.

By referring to the loss of human instincts, Butler seems to acknowledge that taking responsibility for one's actions is the result of a learning process capable of reconfiguring earlier autonomic behaviours. We are not born as autonomous beings and we owe the fit with our *Welt* and *Umwelt* to inherited as well as acquired habits of the body. These habits are wired into our brains and the rest of our body as autonomic behavioural and morphological patterns. Being spoken to and being called to account for the suffering of another, we develop the double anticipation that allows us to attribute meaning to our own actions. *Behaviour* becomes *action*, and after it has been inscribed into the autonomic system that we are (also), action becomes learnt behaviour. Autonomy springs from our response to the interpellation that accuses us of the suffering of another, it forces us to review our behaviour as being the cause of this suffering and pushes us to either contest the accusation or accept the responsibility. Autonomy was not first. It evolves from an appropriation of behaviours as our own behaviours, paving the way for a modification of the habits we embody. Intentional action depends on this interpellation, on this appropriation of past behaviours, enabling the double anticipation that is a condition for meaningful action.

3.4 ANTICIPATION, PREDICTION AND PRE-EMPTION: PREDICTING THE PRESENT

Agents engage in profiling. They detect patterns and apply them. While applying them they refine them. Detection and application of profiling best occurs in one smooth operation that tunes perception (detecting patterns) to action (applying patterns). For living organisms this has been coined 'enaction', highlighting the links between action and perception. The smarter the agent, the more it is capable of learning from the feedback it receives when applying patterns, the better it can reconfigure them, or even reconfigure the process of generating patterns.

Profiling is tied up with prediction. It refers to the expectations that an agent projects onto its environment. This projection allows the agent to test the expectations. Fundamentally, these expectations are all predictions, based on the patterns derived from previous interactions with the environment. Profiles, patterns, expectations and predictions all fit the same 'mechanism'; they afford anticipation. On the one hand this plays out between an agent and its *Umwelt*, merely anticipating how the environment will respond to its own behaviours. On the other hand, in the case of a human agent, this plays out between an agent and her *Welt*, that is, the fusion of generalized double anticipations with regard to other human agents.

When we, human beings, navigate our *Welt*, we are aware that others are profiling us, while we are profiling them. We develop mechanisms, institutions, norms and cultural patterns that enable us to anticipate what is expected from us. They help us to 'know' how others will probably 'read' us. We take on roles that function as consolidated patterns of behaviour providing stability to our interactions. Roles, institutions and cultural patterns are tied up with prediction; they help to predict how other agents will probably behave. In the era of the printing press our capability to predict other agents and the institutions they form, became – in part – dependent on our access to texts. The proliferation of texts caused increasing differentiation of societal subsystems, knowledge domains and disciplines, creating multiple interdependencies and a more complex epistemic trust. The distantiation that pervades the ICI of the printing press becomes visible in the amount of time it takes to prepare adolescents for the multiplicity of roles they can take up in adult life; schools and higher education are centred around the reconfiguration of the extended minds of human agents, preparing them for ever more sophisticated knowledge acquisition. To anticipate the anticipations of others we need to study books, obey written laws, read newspapers, reports, letters; we have to check policies, written contracts, terms of service, licence agreements. All these writings have been thought over, often discussed and prepared by a number of experts. Writing entails substantial delays. This is both due to the time it takes to *author* a text, taking into account the plethora of related texts, and due to the time it takes to *read* a text, taking into account all that must have been read previously to understand a text. These delays have been emphasized above as relating to reflective capabilities, favouring a critical stance versus knowledge claims, based on a sheer unlimited access to ever more text on ever more subjects. The confrontation with contradictory explanations and understandings triggers the contestability of any truth claim, summed up in the adage that we cannot doubt everything but we should be willing to doubt anything. To survive in the era of the printing press a person must develop specific mental skills, such as sound argumentation, sustained sequential thinking and the willingness to give an account of one's choices by providing reasons. Our sense of autonomy relates to all this; we thrive on being in control of our actions and on being accountable for whatever they cause, based on the foreseeability of their consequences and contingent upon their interpretation as justified or wrongful. Autonomy, accountability and justification all depend on prediction; we cannot act if we have no idea of the effects, we cannot be held accountable for what we could not have foreseen, and we cannot claim justification if we cannot not anticipate how others will evaluate our action.

Now, we enter the landscape of an ICT that anticipates us, based on nearly real-time statistical inferences. Predictions based on our past behaviours, drawn from a Big Data Space that is stuffed with our volunteered, observed and inferred data; ripe for the mining of non-trivial patterns to be monetized in real-time auctions or to be kept in distributed Big Data Vaults for future usage. The monetization of the data and inferred patterns puts a price on our head; these bits and bytes are valuable because they allow those who mine them to infer the preferences and even the operations of our extended minds. And, obviously, the price goes up if we cannot foresee what inferences match our data points. Having access to such knowledge creates a competitive advantage; it renders us manipulable and undercuts our resilience. It enables the prediction of our behaviours and the inference of our preferences, and – in the end – the pre-emption of our intent. Imagine playing chess, and not having a clue what your adversary has in mind regarding the range of your next moves, while in fact the adversary has a pretty precise calculation of what you will do next. This matches the situation of a very smart novice with no knowledge of previous matches, who plays against a master who has studied the whole range of previous matches. The master can pre-empt the intent of the novice, based on her knowledge of so many previous matches. She will know how to move the novice towards checkmate despite his genius. Imagine looking for a job, having no idea how your potential employer 'reads' the data relating to you that she can get her hands on. For instance, publicly available data that can be crawled from the web, specific consumer data that can be bought from large data brokers, social graph data that can be mined by connecting with you on a social networking site. What if the patterns mined from this data predict a very specific or several more general health risks, or pregnancy, or a rather critical attitude, or connections with competitors, or a family background deemed not conducive for fitting into the company profile? What if this knowledge leads to a silent rejection of your expression of interest, which is not even read because you are a calculated risk according to the data analysis? What does it mean that your taste in music is sold to the highest bidder,[81] if such taste might correlate with the manic depressive syndrome? Or, on the positive side, what if 'exposure to music individually adapted to brain rhythm disorders' helps to decrease symptoms of psychosis, paranoia, anxiety and somatization?[82] Will the use of the relevant correlations enable designers to construct smart homes that pre-empt psychiatric symptoms by playing the right music at the right time?

In other words, what is the difference between prediction and pre-emption? In the early narratives of Ambient Intelligence and ubiquitous computing the idea of an intelligent environment was mostly clad in terms of proactive, pre-emptive computing. Coffee machines would spy on you and guess your preferences in terms of sugar, milk and even timing; fridges would order the milk before you ran out of it and smart cars would connect with traffic management to steer you along a road with less congestion. The pink scenario of an environment that functions as an invisible butler who caters to your preferences before you become aware of them may have been designed as a marketing tool, it nicely sums up the innocence and comfort of effective pre-emptive computing. Instead of asking for your preferences or discussing your desires, a smart environment should estimate which interventions it can perform on your behalf, without disturbing you. The joys of having a number of trivial or even complex but unimportant tasks outsourced to your smart surroundings were believed to save time and effort, relieving human agents from mundane assignments, generating a seamless series of smooth user experiences. Smart interconnected devices should take over in a manner that removes the friction of engaging with repetitious burdensome chores. Pre-emptive computing thus links up with efficiency and effectiveness, getting the job done quicker and better, while at the same time catering to our desire to being taken care of, to be singled out for special treatment, to have a good time.

Since those early days two developments have taken place. First, on the side of technology developers, the emphasis has shifted to interactive environments, moving away from pre-emption. Aarts and Grotenhuis, two of the 'authors' of Ambient Intelligent systems, wrote an interesting chapter under the heading of 'Ambient Intelligence 2.0', claiming that they underestimated the need for users to feel that they are in control. This entails awareness on the side of the designers of the new ICI that if they want people to use the infrastructure, they need to provide them with a sense of agency. Users must participate in the design of their environment and learn to interact with the agency it displays. Second, however, the emphasis has shifted from pink scenarios with science fiction narratives to real-life data-driven architectures and infrastructures that involve massive monetization of volunteered, observed and inferred data. The incentives are no longer futuristic but play out in a variety of new business models and an emerging political economy based on trading with Big Personal Data. These data are sucked up from all corners of the world by device and operating system manufacturers, cloud service providers, application developers, web shops, analytics providers, web browser providers and search engine providers. Here we see how the interactive, participatory involvement of end-users has taken over, in the form of what some have called the 'appification' of everyday life.[83] Most of these Apps, however, generate Big Personal Data on an unprecedented scale, giving providers access to massive amounts of machine-readable behavioural data, alongside volunteered information. In turn, this Big Data affords more precise, invisible and timely pre-emption of the user's intent. For instance, web search data can be used to 'predict the present', resulting in services like 'auto complete' or Google instant. We may indeed come to live in a 'Filter Bubble',[84] once our ICIs manage to provide us with seamless real-time personalization, updating our access to whatever information 'they' deem relevant, removing what 'they' consider noise, or what 'they' think we cannot afford, or what 'they' think increases the risk for their patron, which may be an insurance company, or a government agency hoping to detect tax or social security fraud.

3.5 CONCLUSIONS: HUMAN AGENCY IN THE ONLIFE WORLD

Living in a landscape where agency 'springs up eternal' will reconfigure our self, our *Umwelt* and our *Welt*. It will destabilize our expectations, though we may not notice. Pre-emption implies a subliminal intervention; before we form an intention the underlying motivation is resolved. The butler has ordered the meal before we noticed our appetite, and it arrives just in time, and with the right taste. Actually we have no inkling at what time we would have eaten otherwise, or which meal we could have chosen instead. What a relief. Or, if the butler understands our need to have a choice, he will provide us with a choice within our taste and budget – as he sees fit. He knows all about the paradox of choice, about less being more, and about how to nudge us to whatever is good for us and in his own interest.[85] However, this is not about the butler. It is about an ICI that increasingly determines our environment, our extended mind and our self. The subliminal interventions are based on a digital unconscious that envelops our being in the world. We must, somehow, learn how to *address* such an extended, polymorphous, distributed 'agential' environment, how to anticipate its anticipations and – if necessary – how to pre-empt its pre-emption.

PART II

Threats of border control

4. The digital unconscious: back to Diana

4.1 WHY DISCUSS DIANA'S DIGITAL UNCONSCIOUS?

If we retrace Diana's footsteps and those of her significant others, a number of issues come to mind that relate to privacy, identity and autonomy, though often entangled with vulnerabilities better qualified in terms of manipulability, digital sorting, the presumption of innocence and due process. We will assess some of these vulnerabilities by discussing the fact that diagnoses of Diana's preferences, moods, health, stress levels, and professional or personal success are made by machines tapping into Big Data Space, taking into account that many subsequent decisions are taken without human intervention, while her emotional behaviours are expressly targeted. All based on the distributed, heterogeneous, digital unconscious that co-constitutes her onlife world. Most notably, we will chew on the fact that she develops an intimate relationship with her DPA and that the entire setting displays a novel configuration of transparency and opacity. This intermezzo is meant to raise issues and to sensitize the reader to what is at stake in an onlife world. What should concern us in the changing landscape of 'agential' environments?

As an intermezzo, this chapter is not meant to be exhaustive or to resolve matters, as if that were at all possible. Rather, it should function as a prelude to the next chapter that hopes to investigate in a more systematic manner the potential threats of the onlife world.

4.2 DIAGNOSES BY MACHINES

Diana is treated as a person who suffers from mild winter depressions and nervousness. Who or what has diagnosed her as such: the smart home, her PDA or her doctor? On what basis could the smart home or her PDA infer such states and what is meant by 'the house picking up her mood' to prepare the roadmap for her smart car? If this is a matter of autonomic computing systems matching her behavioural and physical biometrics with profiles inferred from massive databases mainly filled with other people's data, then how can we be sure that the relevant profile is indeed applicable to her? In the case of a non-distributive profile, the profile will most probably not apply to her, and most profiles inferred from Big Data Space are non-distributive. An example of a distributive profile would be: all women have a 13 per cent chance of contracting breast cancer. It means that the percentage applies to any individual woman. An example of a non-distributive profile would be: on average women have a 13 per cent chance of contracting breast cancer. In that case, the chance that applies to an individual woman will differ from the average, depending on – for instance – her age, genetic profile, lifestyle. What does it mean to be treated in a manner that is consistent with a group profile that is not applicable, but nevertheless matches one's data? And what does it mean to be treated in a certain manner on the basis of a profile that applies accurately, but reveals knowledge that Diana herself is not aware of (and may not have access to)? Once a non-distributed profile is fused with more detailed information, it can be personalized and the diagnosis can be narrowed down to a reasonably accurate estimation. Are these 'diagnoses' shared with or confirmed by a doctor and does Diana's health insurance company have access to these data? Diana's grandfather is on remote health control and though he is capable of 'cheating' on his prescribed diets, it seems that he cannot deceive the insurance company that has access to data on his eating habits. Is this compulsory for her father, or – as in the case of the sports centre – the result of consenting to data sharing in exchange for financial advantages? Obviously these advantages last only in so far as one complies with medical and dietary prescriptions. How much of these prescriptions are part of a comprehensive preventive medicine program? To what extent is Diana, or her grandfather, 'forced' to live healthy – and who or what determines what is health here? Is it either well-being or the mere absence of a known disease; are we speaking of self-reported or measured well-being, and to what extent is the measurement performed by means of physical and behavioural biometrics? Will insurance companies offer reductions to clients that provide their complete genome sequence, enabling monetizable inferences to be made about their mental and physical health risks?[86]

We may infer that Diana's on*life* world is grounded in a socio-technical infrastructure that allows for a continuous flow of real-time diagnoses, based on machine learning techniques and other forms of artificial intelligence. Diana, her daughter and grandfather are persistently profiled for health risks, moods and general well-being, enabling pre-emptive interventions by the systems that run their home, school, office, traffic and leisure environments. Most of this profiling is somehow connected with their PDAs, which interact with these systems. Diana and her significant others are faced with ubiquitous anticipation by the digital unconscious that encapsulates them. This raises novel questions about the extent to which such anticipation infringes their privacy and reconfigures their identity.

As discussed above, double mutual anticipation is typical for the human life form. In being double – anticipating how one is anticipated – and mutual – expecting that others do the same – the ensuing uncertainty is reciprocal; people guess how they are being profiled by others doing the same. This is what provides for the ambiguity inherent in human communication, sustaining predictability while cherishing the open character of meaning production. Ambiguity leaves room for creative misunderstandings, it nourishes the fragility of the *Welt* – but it also fosters its potential for novel perspectives and thus its flexibility and robustness in the long run. Ambiguity does not imply the absence of meaning or direction; it hinges on a limited set of possible meanings that may require incompatible responses, thus forcing those involved to make a choice in favour of one interpretation rather than another. That is how we get on in life, guessing what is expected from us and intuiting how our actions are 'seen' or 'read' by others. Most of this requires no conscious effort and does not depend on following a set of preconceived rules. We thrive on ambiguity by tacitly following hunches that operate smoothly beyond our deliberate control. That is how Sontag's complaint 'against interpretation' makes sense:[87] by attempting to control the subliminal workings of spontaneous interpretation we may miss the boat and effectively rule out the ambiguity that makes our communication generative. A similar complaint may be filed against the interpretations generated by pre-emptive computing systems. First, the reciprocity seems lost: we have no idea how we are being anticipated. We have no access to the inner workings of the software, we don't know how the data we leak will correlate with profiles we don't even know exist. Second, the ambiguity seems lost. In order to 'work', the infrastructure makes decisions about how our behaviour must be interpreted. This interpretation, however, is not an evocation of meaning; it consists of the manipulation of machine-readable data by applying a series of unambiguous rules. Even if the machinery has found ways to generate new rules, that will not change the digital, discrete, either/or nature of the ICI infrastructure. The digital unconscious that rules Diana's onlife world has no taste for ambiguity; it generates mindless agency.

I contend that diagnosis by machines infringes Diana's privacy to the extent that it defines her personal preferences, inclinations and proneness to any kind of risks. The power of definition shifts from a multiplicity of others – with whom she can interact and discuss, whose interpretations she can question and reject – to an anonymous infrastructure that seems to know things about her without giving her a clue as to the how or the why. She can interact with Toma, but she cannot reason with it; she cannot require it to state its reasons for diagnosing a situation one way or another. Even if it could provide her with its algorithms she would be left with rules that lack the motivational, argumentative character of human reason. Machine diagnosis thus increases heteronomy and reduces autonomy. Though we should not ignore the fact that the human unconscious rules the major part of our life, there is no reason to give up the fragment of autonomy that makes up our mind.

4.3 MACHINE INTERVENTIONS

At two points in the story music is said to have 'shown' a specific influence on her moods. Are we speaking of stochastic inferences or categorical statements? Let's assume this is about statistically relevant correlations: which threshold is used to decide that this influence is 'meaningful' and a good 'reason' for an intervention? Similar questions arise about the advice given about driving the car. Diana is free to take the car because a certain threshold of nervousness has not been reached; at a later point the car itself announces that it will cease to function within five minutes. Who or what sets these defaults and which are the goals; is Diana in charge and has she instructed these smart systems to constrain her, or do they operate in accordance with the settings of the relevant service providers? This connects to the question who is paying for all these seamless adaptations; what business-model underlies the provision of services? Does the context in which profits are made provide incentives to pay attention to privacy concerns?

Diagnosis is one thing and intervention another. A number of issues are at stake here. The first regards the fact that decisions may be based on diagnoses that are dubious or simply incorrect, for instance due to incorrect or dubious input. The second relates to the fact that other algorithms could have produced alternative diagnoses, since a data set can always be described in more than one way, generating different patterns and correlations.[88] This relates to a third issue. Generally speaking, machine interventions based on machine diagnoses assume that the patterns found in the data are also in the world they represent. This is not necessarily the case and requires empirical testing. However, fourth, the paradigm of pre-emptive computing is subliminal intervention; the idea is not to disturb the 'user' with requests about her preferences or to require her deliberate input. Instead the environment calculates how and when to intervene, based on data that are observed rather than provided. This makes empirical testing difficult if not impossible; who knows what preferences a person would have developed if her intent were not pre-empted? Though there are obvious advantages to being *targeted for what we do*, in lieu of being *addressed for what we say we do*, there are major drawbacks. We may have good reasons not to share the motivations that determine our behaviours and this opportunity seems lost when the environment skips our attempts to obfuscate what drives us. Even if this obfuscation is not deliberate(d), it may be part of what makes us who we are. We are not merely whatever we claim or think ourselves to be, but also whatever remains hidden from our own introspection.[89]

Thus, most of the questions raised by the fact that machine diagnoses differ from human assessment return with added force at the level of machine interventions. If the diagnosis is not contestable because it is invisible, the intervention that is based on it is similarly incontestable, leaving the inhabitant of the onl*ife* world in the dark as to how her inferred behaviours are used to manipulate her into similar or other behaviours. If the diagnosis is incorrect or unfair, decisions will be unjust or unfair. Apart from that, machine interventions target us on the basis of what we do, ignoring the way we describe ourselves and the needs and desires we claim to foster. Bypassing whatever we report, pre-emptive machine interventions cater to whatever the extrapolations of our past behaviours dictate. We cannot hold back and protect our deeper sensitivities, because the digital unconscious has already been mined to define them, dutifully administering the response that should serve us best. This seems to encroach on our privacy in a *less noticeable but more pervasive* manner, since this allows a subliminal reconstruction of our identity in ways that do not lend themselves to conscious reflection.

4.4 EMOTIONAL TARGETING AND ATTENTION-MANAGEMENT

It seems that Toma is capable of recognizing Diana's moods, stress levels and attention span. This enables a measure of 'attention-management', for instance by making summaries of texts and other types of filtering, such as prioritizing her incoming communications. How does this impact the kind of identity Diana develops and how does it influence her awareness of the information that Toma does not consider profitable or interesting for Diana? If Toma is upgraded with synthetic emotions that affect Diana's feelings about her own actions and decisions, doesn't that instigate a manipulative influence on her sense of self – and ultimately on her identity?[90] What assumptions underlie the construction of synthetic emotions, which vision of human agency is embodied in non-biological 'emotions' that are used to enhance the functionality of smart artefacts? How should we understand the PDA's competitiveness towards Diana's colleagues and family? Is it merely a mirror of Diana's disposition, reinforcing her own character? Or, does it mirror the objectives of the service providers that have made all these real-time personalized adaptations possible? Could it be that Toma develops its own interests, because to be self-managing it has to cultivate its own existence?

Machines may learn to diagnose and manipulate human emotion. This can be done by sheer calculation, inferring what kind of events trigger what sort of emotions. Once sensor technologies are in place that are capable of measuring biometric behaviours such as facial expression, blood pressure, heartbeat, blushing or transpiration, correlations and associations will be detected with basic emotions like fear, anger, sadness, joy or disgust. Though emotions in this physiological sense may differ from feeling or affect on a longer time-scale, we don't have to follow a reductive explanation of emotion to understand that the bodily expression of emotion has important cognitive implications and is constitutive of our sense of self. As Damasio has explained, emotion is directly related to action;[91] it is a 'program of action' that responds to particular triggers in the environment without requiring conscious awareness. Interestingly, the sub-discipline of affective computing acknowledges the role of emotion in cognition, thus distancing itself from 'old-school' artificial intelligence and the rationalistic frame of mind it represented. Affective computing was coined as such in the mid-1990s by Picard, who defined it as 'computing that relates to, arises from, or influences emotions'.[92] Her goals were to further the understanding of the role of human emotion and to enhance the functionality of computers, notably with regard to 'computer-assisted learning, perceptual information retrieval, arts and entertainment, human health and interaction'.[93] Drawing on Damasio this seems a pivotal exploration, since emotions are in fact *automated* action programs that unfold to take care of challenging circumstances. They are involved in perception (pattern recognition) and in autonomic decision-making (selecting one action rather than another), thus playing a crucial role in the cognition of all organisms with a central nervous system. If computing systems can learn to recognize our automated subliminal responses (emotions) to significant situations, they

will improve their 'understanding' of what drives us and become enabled
to foresee our emotional responses to their interventions. This will allow
them to directly influence our choice of action.

The problem is not that machines are capable of recognizing our
emotional states. Rather, the point is that they 'have' this knowledge
beyond our awareness. There is no reciprocity. Not because we cannot
assess their emotions (facial expressions have been built into robots), but
because we don't know how they interpret ours. We have not learned how
to anticipate how we are being anticipated and this is what makes us
manipulable. What infringes our privacy is that emotional states, which
are mostly unconscious, may be picked up by our environment before we
become aware of them. 'They' may thus 'read' our emotions before we
have a chance to develop our own reflection and response to our own
emotional state. This is decisive because researchers like Damasio have
shown a crucial difference between feelings and emotions. Feelings
emerge when humans become aware of their emotions. Feelings allow for
and thrive on conscious attention to and reflection on one's emotional
responses. They enable us to develop a personality that is not entirely
intuitive, not completely dependent on whatever emotion overwhelms us.
Feelings integrate awareness, deliberation and an interior monologue on
our emotional habits. They thus enable us to grow and mature into the
kind of person we want to be. The advent of the script and the printing
press has changed the scope and the depth of these reflections, transforming the course of our feelings. In his grand narrative on *The Information*,[94] Gleick has emphasized that our capability for abstract thought
is contingent upon the externalization and recombination of language. If
that is so, I dare say that the same externalization and recombination also
expand the complexity of the awareness of our emotional states and the
feelings this generates.

In bypassing the stage of self-awareness, mood detection by DPAs or
other parts of the smart environment makes us manipulable, at least in so
far as we have no clue as to how the environment is 'calculating' our
emotional states. Pervasive affective computing could also lead to extensive digital sorting with a range of undesirable consequences. Imagine
being typified as a border liner on the basis of autonomic profiling, or
being targeted as a psychopath because one's emotional responses match
with the relevant profile. The most prominent threat, however, that
connects with concerns over autonomy, identity and digital sorting,
occurs if we cannot defend ourselves. If we cannot contest the way we
are being 'read' and steered and thus if we cannot resist the manipulation
of our unconscious emotional states, we may lose the sense of self that is
pre-conditional for human autonomy. Not having a chance to develop

feelings, we may actually become the machines that smart technologies take us to be.

4.5   AN INTIMATE STRANGER

The most interesting part of the narrative is the strong relationship that develops between the humans and their PDAs, be they robots or software incarnations. Though I have set myself the task in this chapter to flesh out the issues and concerns that these relationships evoke, this in no way implies that we should reject sharing the on*life* world with artificial agents, or decline intimate relationships with them, whatever that means. I will return to this point in the chapter on Japanese culture, suggesting that we may learn from their particular ways of dealing with animated *things*.

Notwithstanding all the benefits that may come from living with robots and software agents, we must admit that the greatest threat to Diana's privacy comes from her own PDA. It holds all her personal data, patterns and profiles and is capable of matching them with those mined in Big Data Space. Where does this PDA start and where does it end; is it polymorphous and distributed or is it a unity of action and perception? Which of the entities it communicates with can access its databases? What does it mean that Diana calls it by name?

Toma sorts Diana's incoming messages and her upcoming assignments. On what basis does Toma perform this filtering? Has it learned Diana's preferences or has it inferred what is most profitable for Diana in terms of urgency and importance? The latter need not coincide with her preferences. What does 'profitable' mean here: career-wise, with regard to her earning capacity, or rather in view of developing meaningful projects in life? Will Diana somehow end up being the kind of person Toma takes her to be, due to the prioritizing of the information flows that Toma administers? Can Diana intervene, change her mind (or Toma's 'mind'), for instance by resetting certain defaults? Will she have or make the time to address this issue, and direct her attention to this on a regular basis?

Toma monitors calorie, fibre and nutrient intake. It advises about subsequent meals on the basis of which standards? Is this about evidence-based science or epidemiological studies? To what extent is the advice based on inferences of Diana's own recorded data and to what extent is it based on group profiles inferred from large databases composed of other people's data? If she contravenes the dietary advice, will her life insurance premium be raised seamlessly? Will she be refused medical treatment or will her insurance refuse to pay the costs, because the disease she suffers from is considered to be her own fault?

Toma is a personal digital assistant or, better, a personal digital *agent*. In law and commerce an agent is a person or organization that performs tasks *for, on behalf of,* or even *in the name of* a patron. Depending on mutual agreement (contract) and on the national law, the actions of the agent can bind the patron directly, to the extent that actions of the agent are considered to be actions of the patron. Similarly, in computing, an electronic agent is a software program that engages in certain tasks for or on behalf of another (human or nonhuman) agent. The performance of the task can be automated or autonomic, entirely deterministic or relatively unpredictable. Though under current jurisdictions electronic agents do not qualify as legal subjects, both legal and electronic agents perform assignments for another, which is their core functionality. Toma obviously qualifies as an electronic agent, acting on behalf of its patron. It also seems that Toma is somehow in the business of creating legal effects, either by concluding contracts or by causing harm or damage. Is this legal effect to be attributed to Diana? And if so, on what grounds and under what conditions can Diana be made liable for the interventions of her artificial agent? What if the hardware or the default settings of the software (if that distinction still makes sense here) create consequences that Diana could not have foreseen? Should it not be Toma's manufacturer or its service provider who pays the bill in case of damage? How is Diana's identity affected if she becomes responsible for Toma's operations; will she become cautious or even frightened due to the implications of 'using' Toma when she interacts with it? Can one indeed interact with something one uses, and if so, what does 'use' mean here?

In moral philosophy human agency refers to the capacity to provide reasons for one's actions,[95] thus introducing notions like human subjectivity, individual autonomy and personal responsibility. An agent in this sense is not the instrument of another. In fact, moral philosophy claims that one may never use a human person as merely a means to an end, as this would disrespect her autonomy.[96] What is the effect of using relatively autonomous agents in a purely instrumental way, not having to care about their 'feelings', since they have only synthetic emotions? Will this affect our ways of dealing with other humans? Will the difference between humans and artificial agents always be clear, or might it be that we will start treating each other as intelligent machines?

4.6 TRANSLUCENCE AND OPACITY

Finally, the story contains two clear moments of unplugging. Firstly, the PDA's mediation can be overruled in case of alarm. Second, it is possible to turn on the 'passive mode', probably meaning that the system continues to monitor but stops interfering. In theory, one can probably also turn the system off completely, but more plausibly this would endanger the critical infrastructure around the home, traffic, office, school and recreation facilities (or, at least, their business models). In the onli*fe* world, unplugging may be the only way to restore the boundaries between self and others, because it seems to be the only option to stop the pervasive data capture by the plethora of networked computing systems. Unplugging returns Diana to the opacity that shielded people in the offline world, protected by 'atom-based protection' such as walls, curtains, clothes or sunglasses. However, as long as others employ smart wearables (glasses, watches) or implants (chips, enhanced retinas) and as long as things remain online via the Internet of Things (smart grids, surveillance in public space, always-on domotica), this opacity is hard to achieve.

A clear built-in protection of opacity is found in the restrictions on access to Lindsay's data. They are protected in a granular fashion, preventing them from being up for grabs, while providing transparency to children themselves from a certain age onwards. This seems to provide them with enhanced control over their digital doubles and similes, that function as proxies in the onli*fe* world. Such transparency about the self can, however, create novel hurdles for the construction of one's identity. One does wonder, for instance, how an adolescent is affected when she finds out that her individual profile matches with group profiles of violent or underachieving peers; or when a young mother finds out that her data points match with an early onset of Parkinson's disease. This suggests that transparency by itself can be an infringement of privacy, because one is forced to confront knowledge about oneself that disrupts the future. 'The future is no longer what it used to be' saliently sums up the impact of transparency about inferred knowledge that one did not choose to solicit. Nevertheless, not-knowing what is known by other parties raises other concerns, especially considering the power relationships between individual persons and large corporations or governmental agencies. The mere fact that one may have to choose between knowing or not knowing about one's genetic risk profile impacts on one's sense of self, raising the bar on the construction of one's identity. Being forced to make such choices is part of the onli*fe* world.

Historically speaking, a constitutional democracy that has equal respect for its citizens thrives on a particular configuration of transparency and opacity. Whereas the government should be transparent about its operations, its citizens must be shielded from governmental scrutiny. By default, all governmental actions are to be performed in service of the general interest that is co-defined by equal respect for individual citizens. Checks and balances must be in place to test and contest whether a government complies with this fundamental stipulation. Such checks presume a certain level of transparency. The better term here is translucence, because many government operations imply confidential information, based on the redistribution of income, the concomitant need for fraud detection, and security measures in the spheres of justice and foreign intelligence. Individual citizens, however, must be protected against the potentially omniscient gaze of the state. Unlike the state, they are not bound to act in the general interest, but should be empowered to act upon their own private interests, as they see fit. Though citizens, like their government, must always act within the contours of the law. The legal protection against transparency is not absolute, because the state needs to collect taxes, redistribute welfare, punish crime and check for tax and social security fraud. Individuals therefor have an opacity right that shields them from unreasonable investigation into their private lives, while rendering any infringement of such a right contestable in a court of law. Though human rights such as privacy were originally conceived as protection against the state, they have been extended to also protect against infringements by other big players. We must keep in mind that this means that the state becomes responsible for an effective legal framework that shields citizens from privacy invasions by each other and by, for instance, corporations that process their personal data.

Pre-emptive computing disrupts the configuration of opacity and translucence. The onlife world in fact turns this configuration inside out. Governments as well as powerful corporations are now capable of violating the opacity that should protect individual citizens, whereas the translucence needed to foresee how these big players operate is lost in the hidden complexity of Big Data Space. While service providers, insurance companies and government agencies may have an X-ray view of Diana's financial, emotional, social and professional life, she has very little insight into the mechanisms of the digital unconscious that define how she is perceived.

4.7 CONCLUSIONS: ISSUES, CONCERNS AND THREATS

In this chapter I have drawn on the narrative beginnings of this book to sketch some of the issues and concerns they present in the light of Big Data Space and the onlife world that depends on it. In the next chapter I will translate these issues into threats to fundamental rights, though I will not yet debate the intricacies tied up with their legal articulation. The reason is that the disruptions caused by the *onlife* world bring about different concerns and we cannot assume that current legal articulations match the issues that are at stake. This is not to say that we need to reinvent each and every fundamental right, or create new ones. It does mean that before engaging with the most obviously related part of the legal framework, that of privacy and data protection, we need to attempt a fresh look at what is at stake. In the third part of this book I will consider the relationship between law and technology, and focus on how current and upcoming legal frameworks on privacy and data protection may contribute to an *onlife* world that preserves and improves the intricate system of checks and balances inherent in constitutional democracy.

Assessing the issues and concerns encountered in this chapter, I believe that they can best be translated and summed up under the headings of privacy, identity, autonomy, digital sorting, the presumption of innocence and due process. Digital sorting is a crucial operation in pre-emptive computing; it relates to the fundamental rights of privacy and non-discrimination and impacts our identity-construction and our relative and relational autonomy. These notions will be further elaborated in the next chapter, notably targeting the threats they encounter in the *onlife* world.

5. Threats to fundamental rights in the onli*fe* world

5.1 WHY THREATS, WHY NOT RISKS?

Before calculating a risk, you need to be aware of what threat you are facing. Moving to risk too soon and too fast has several drawbacks. One is that you may be taking the threats for granted and start translating what is perceived as a threat into discrete data points, just because it allows for sophisticated number crunching. This could lure you into skipping the stage of qualification and conceptualization that enables a reliable translation of perceived or expected threats into the objects and attributes of your data model. Qualification always precedes quantification, whether or not one is paying explicit attention to this. To calculate the monetary value that people attach to their privacy it does not suffice to offer them money for what you consider their privacy, for instance based on their willingness to share location data. Qualifying the sharing of location data in the context of a scientific experiment as privacy is a quick and easy way to construct data models, but I dare say it has little to do with what most people understand as giving up privacy in real life. You might actually end up constructing quantifiable solutions that resolve numerically defined problems in the dataset, whereas these solutions have no relation to the problems we need to resolve in the real world (whatever that is). Second, you may have missed non-obvious or invisible threats because they are not – yet – computable or – as yet – intractable. We are moving to risk too soon and too fast to the extent that we give in to the temptation to rank threats according to their computability.

The language of risk is pervasive. The proposed General Data Protection Regulation (pGDPR) speaks of data protection impact assessments in terms of assessing risks to fundamental rights. How must we understand this: as a risk to the substance of the right (privacy), to its effectiveness (the means to enforce it) or to the capability to exercise the right (which may be distributed unfairly)? Pivotal work has been done on distinguishing risk from ambiguity, uncertainty and ignorance.[97] Under the general heading of incertitude, the concepts of risk, ambiguity, uncertainty and ignorance can be fitted into a matrix, where risk only applies when the consequences of a certain event or measure are calculable and there is no disagreement about whether to qualify the consequences as positive or negative. If such consequences are calculable but there is no agreement about whether they are beneficial we are in the realm of ambiguity. If such agreement is apparent but the consequences are not calculable we are in the realm of uncertainty, whereas ignorance points to neither agreement nor calculability. These types of incertitude require different methodologies, and risk is obviously the most attractive incertitude for those who like to be precise about solutions. However, being precise in the case of ambiguities, uncertainties and ignorance would mean that one avoids the language of risk and rationalist methodology, as they do not apply in that case.

Threats concern the qualification of future occurrences, not their quantification. They require conceptualization and reflection, probing for what is at stake for whom and how this fits the wider web of meaning on which our *Welt* depends. Privacy, fairness, discrimination, and so on are value-laden concepts, referring to normative practices that differ between and within distinct cultural settings. Whether and how they are under threat falls within the realm of ambiguity. Making risk calculations about the effects of a pre-emptive environment on these kinds of values is ludicrous, whereas assessing the nature of the threats is urgent. In this chapter I will sort out a small set of values and practices that may be under threat in an onli*fe* world. Solutions for such threats cannot be calculated; they require awareness and – possibly – a reconfiguration of the architecture of our practices. Such reconfiguration is partly a political affair; it requires both rigorous scientific evidence (tested and contestable) and agonistic debate between those who will suffer the consequences and the engineers and business entrepreneurs who build our onli*fe* world (participatory democratic practice).

In this chapter privacy, autonomy, the presumption of innocence and due process will be investigated with a keen eye to if, and if so how, they are threatened by the ICI of pre-emptive computing.

5.2 PRIVACY AND IDENTITY: PRIVATE INTEREST AND PUBLIC GOOD

5.2.1 Different Meanings of Privacy

Within the realm of 'the information society' privacy advocates often refer to privacy – or informational privacy – as data confidentiality (usually equated with data minimization) or access control (notice and consent; opt-in or opt-out). This is a reductive understanding of privacy that fits well with a computer science approach focused on data security. There is a certain convenience in this reduction, because it enables one to discuss privacy in terms of discrete and machine-readable entities (data, or personal data). It induces us to think of privacy as control over the flow of information that belongs to (or discloses personal details about) an individual, who should decide on access to the data.[98] It caters to powerful notions such as informational self-determination – closely connected to the German constitutional right of human dignity – and tends to depict individuals as sovereign subjects that can and should decide who knows what about them.[99] It also caters to the notion of privacy as a private interest of individual consumers or citizens, suggesting that privacy in essence concerns only their private life. However, we often experience our privacy in the anonymity of public contexts,[100] and the borders between private, social and public contexts are rapidly blurring. In many ways this conception of privacy builds on a separation of the private and the public sphere as given, which is a rather precarious assumption at this point in time. In fact, it seems that privacy is more about ongoing negotiations of the borders between the private, the social and the public, requiring a notion of privacy that does not take these borders for granted. One of the authors who argued for a more relational understanding of privacy, notably in terms of boundary negotiations, was the psychologist Altman.[101] Though his concern was not informational but territorial privacy, his approach is very apt to come to terms with the implications of smart technologies. Instead of assuming that privacy refers to isolation, secrecy or the hiding of the self, he describes it as a reciprocal process of setting the boundaries of the self in relation to different others and within different spatial, temporal and cultural situations. He recounts how individuals who live together in an extended family, while having little or no chance to retreat from the constant gaze of others, actually learn to turn their facial expression into a blank. This signals that they do not appreciate inquiry after their personal thoughts and feelings. They protect their 'face' by shutting down. Between peers this situation is reciprocal, meaning that one will not disregard such facial signals by pressing for disclosure. In as far as power relations or hierarchies play out, however, one person may be in a position to impose on another, creating a situation of intense humiliation and exposure. This may lead to covering one's face with clothing or to avoiding eye contact altogether. What strikes me in Altman's analysis of privacy in different cultural contexts is its participatory nature; privacy is seen as a practice, requiring hard work, rather than as a given value or interest. Let alone a right. Though I am all for having a right to privacy, rather than 'merely'

its substance, this requires a proper understanding of what privacy is
about. An important asset of Altman's conception of privacy is its
relation to self-identity. Again, instead of taking identity as a given,
Altman emphasizes the constructive and ephemeral character of identity
as something that cannot be taken for granted. Privacy, as an enabler of
boundary negotiations, allows a person to build and rebuild her identity
beyond the continuous pressures of social stereotyping, public opinion
and dominant frames of reference. It thereby not only provides for a
safe cocoon to hide in, but also for a timespace in which unconventional
and novel practices and ideas can be fostered and cultivated. This –
subversive – aspect of privacy makes it a crucial asset for a viable
democracy, and the condition of possibility for a robust and agonistic
civil society. In the context of our emerging onli*fe* world, the joint
forces of hyperconnectivity and computational pre-emption urgently
require an innovative exploration of our need for privacy, to reinvent its
constraints in a radically different environment.

5.2.2   Privacy, Identity, Freedom and the Public Good

Inspired by Altman, I side with Agre and Rotenberg's innovative concept
of the right to privacy, defined as:[102]

> the freedom from unreasonable constraints on the construction of one's own
> identity.

This working definition does six things. First, it renders explicit the
relationship between privacy and identity.[103] Second, identity refers to
personal identity or selfhood. It does not refer to a collection of attributes
that defines a person, or to an identifier that allows someone to uniquely
identify a person, though both types of identity can be relevant for one's
personal identity. Third, it does not suggest that personal identity is
given, but implies a process of identity building that is as fundamental as
its dynamic result. Fourth, it sees identity and thereby privacy as
relational concepts, highlighting their emergence from the interactions
between different actors. Fifth, it thinks of privacy as the fruit of the
freedom from unreasonable constraints and the *freedom to* construct one's
identity, thus epitomizing privacy at the nexus of negative and positive
freedom.[104] Finally, sixth, it does *not* associate freedom or privacy with
the absence of constraints per se, but of *unreasonable* constraints. This
raises the difficult question of which constraints are unreasonable in a
particular context. In a world constituted by the ambiguities of natural
language, such difficult questions are inevitable. They protect against any

one party monopolizing the decision on what is unreasonable. In a constitutional democracy, such questions invite the political community that wishes to protect privacy to develop standards and guidelines to determine what is reasonable. Moreover, history has taught us that the protection this entails will only stand if the application of such open norms to individual citizens is left to the courts instead of either the legislator or the executive. An unambiguous answer to the question of what is unreasonable would result in rigid rules that lend themselves to mechanical application – reminding us of good old artificial intelligence. Luckily even machines do better, these days.

Understanding privacy as related to identity of course evokes a series of questions around the notion of personal identity that connect with my discussions of agency in the previous chapter. Intrigued by the issue of identity, I have made an analysis of the concept in terms of its dual meaning as, on the one hand, *idem*, sameness and identicalness, and, on the other hand, *ipse*, our sense of self or selfhood. Inspired by Ricoeur's analysis of *idem* and *ipse* in his seminal *Oneself as Another*,[105] I understand personal identity as a concept that respects the singularity as well as the contingency of the human person. In a rigorous and imaginative discourse Ricoeur demonstrates how *idem*-identity can refer to similarity, as with two different entities being similar in some or many relevant aspects, or identicalness, as with one and the same entity being the same in all respects over the course of time. The idea of something being identical with itself can be seen as a matter of logic or as an empirical fact, but it should be clear that as soon as we acknowledge the temporal aspect there is no way in which anything will be identical with itself in all respects. Unless energy is added, time seems to wear things out, bringing things down to an unruly and messy chaos. We could quote the second law of thermodynamics to understand this – but merely leaving a garden unattended demonstrates the point. A thing being identical with itself therefore implies continuity, which requires some kind of effort. In the meantime, we must acknowledge that the idea of the similarity of different objects, just like the self-identity of an identical thing, can only be established by taking an observer's or third person perspective. It relies on creating enough distance to be able to compare things, either with themselves or with other things. As to the human person we can safely say that self-identity is in constant flux and must be understood as an ingenious and dynamic combination of continuity and discontinuity. This is, however, not only a matter of similarity between different objects being viewed from an observer's or third person perspective. As discussed in the previous chapter, this objectification comes into its own when a person takes a third person perspective *towards herself*, thus constituting her own identity in the process. By either accepting or rejecting the third person perspectives that she takes other(s) to have formed of her, a person engages in a process of continuous – mostly intuitive – self-construction or identity building. This is the result of what I discussed in the previous chapter as the response to the primary address by one's first significant others, that initiates our emerging sense of self, or the 'me' that comes from taking the point of view of a 'generalized other'. Ricoeur saliently epitomized this as 'oneself *as* another'.

By relating privacy to the process of identity building, the dynamics as well as the fragility of identity become visible, highlighting that personal identity cannot be taken for granted as something that precedes our interactions with others. The relational character of identity explains why positive freedom (to build our identity) requires negative freedom (from unreasonable constraints); to make a difference between oneself and the world we need a time-out to recover from being addressed as a certain type of person by all the different others that engage us. Privacy enables us to recuperate earlier identifications, to realign ourselves, reconfiguring the roles that are attributed to us as mother, employer, lover, baseball player, violinist, dog owner, car driver, coffee addict or gourmand. Like sleep, that mysterious retreat from conscious perception, privacy increases or mends our resilience. It thus strengthens our resistance against being identified as whoever we don't want to be, which refers to its subversive aspect. As a retreat from social pressures, privacy ipso facto nourishes the germ of taking an unorthodox perspective, going against the grain of mainstream definitions of the contexts one stumbles upon. If this is what fosters difference and the strength to take a stand, this is also what generates an agonistic discourse – the kind that generates a robust outcome because it voices the incompatibilities that are at stake. It is interesting to note that both within democratic theory and within science, technology and society (STS) studies, the notion of agonistic discourse has been coined as preconditional for robust outcomes.[106] This leads me to an important point about the public nature of privacy.

The term privacy – often defined as the protection of private life – suggests that privacy is a private interest that is only at stake in the context of one's private life. This account is wrong on two points. First, though privacy can indeed be a private interest, many authors agree that it is also a public good; for instance, because it is considered conditional for free speech, or because its protection requires public intervention. Second, privacy scholars have shown that we care about our privacy in many public contexts. For instance, when driving on a public road or walking around in a public space, the anonymity of the crowd is what helps to gain a sense of privacy. One of the problems of defining privacy as the protection of private life is that it is unclear how we should understand private life. Is this restricted to one's innermost thoughts, not shared with anybody? This would equate privacy with a kind of isolation or seclusion. In view of an onli*fe* world that aims to pre-empt one's intent, this type of privacy will become increasingly precious. The idea that thoughts are necessarily private may soon be wishful thinking. However, more is at stake. Most would agree that we need to extend the realm of private life by adding one's intimate life, shared with close friends and relatives, admitting that what you share with your lover or child is not meant to become public unless you volunteer the information. Additionally, much of our social life, taken up in various identifiable contexts, such as sport clubs, the office, restaurants or concert halls also counts as part of private life, to the extent that boundaries are assumed within which most of this interaction takes place. In US constitutional law the right to privacy has been made dependent on a reasonable expectation of privacy, which is found to be absent if one discloses information about oneself to others who can share this information with third parties. Such sharing qualifies as 'making it public'.[107] This so-called third party doctrine leaves little room for truly private – in the sense of hidden – knowledge about the self. Privacy is then wrongly reduced to confidentiality or even secrecy. Though privacy as identity building can imply both confidentiality and secrecy, they form just one aspect of the boundary work that must be done in the social sphere, creating and maintaining the boundaries of the self in the midst of one's exploding social graphs. Here, what Nissenbaum calls 'contextual integrity' may be a more apt translation of privacy concerns in an information society.[108] Instead of focusing on an all or nothing policy with regard to which data is protected, she argues for criteria of *appropriateness* with regard to information flows within and between different contexts and criteria for the *distribution* of information within and across contextual borders. In line with this I contend that the appropriateness of specific information flows does not necessarily depend on individual preferences but rather on what fortifies identity construction and generates a resilient civil society, as well as on the fairness of the ensuing distribution of information (taking into account unequal power relations).

The notion of contextual integrity also links with Goffman's reference to audience segregation.[109] The roles one plays are directed to different audiences, and to preserve the integrity of our personhood we need to change masks to tune our performance to the specific context. The Latin word for mask is *persona* and refers to the identity we project to our audience. A person incorporates many *personae*, depending on the different institutions she navigates within the *Welt* she inhabits. Goffman spoke of 'impression management', long before users of social networking sites developed a new type of 'reputation management'. Keeping information within the contours of a specific audience thus also relates to privacy. However, in the landscape of pre-emptive computing described in Chapter 3, the notions of context and audience are blurring as much as the distinction between online and offline. Behavioural advertising is discussed in terms of 'creating and managing audiences'. So, yes there is audience segregation, but the control of audience segmentation is part of the business models for pre-emptive computing. Though we must admit that such market segmentation was initiated during the last century, it is important to detect the difference made by the resources of Big Data Space. While managing your privacy settings and thus your audiences and personae, the service provider is probably looking over your shoulder, feeding your behavioural data into the extended mind of her artificial agents. The concomitant blurring and manipulation of boundaries may require a more substantial rethinking of privacy as an enabler for effective boundary work.

Maybe the confusion over what constitutes the private sphere is caused by the opposition of private and public, and stems from the ambiguity of the term public. First, 'public' seems to refer to what is out in the open, disclosed and exposed to the gaze of an undefined set of others; 'publicness' or publicity defines this sense of 'public'. In qualifying 'publicness' as exposure to an undefined set of others we can distinguish 'publicness' from exposure to a defined set, for instance to a person's partner, family, specific friends or colleagues. Even if these others could share what they have seen, heard or read with third parties, the exposure should not count as public, insofar as there was no reasonable expectation that the exposure would end up with unknown others. So, 'publicness' comes close to transparency, but whereas something can be transparent to only one person or to a defined group of people, 'publicness' implies that anybody could at some point see what is 'public' in this sense. Habermas' 'Öffentlichkeit' comes to mind, emphasizing openness, depicting the public sphere as the domain where issues are discussed openly by the political constituency or civil society.[110] Habermas refines the discussion on the public sphere by distinguishing between the public sphere that consists of deliberating individual citizens (highlighting the role of the press in providing the platform for such deliberation) and the public sphere that is part of the state, notably public deliberation and decision-making in parliament. This public deliberation should ultimately ground public decision-making in the notion of the public interest. In making these distinctions Habermas disentangles 'publicness' from the realm of the state, arguing that precisely the 'private' public sphere is crucial for the functioning of the state's public sphere.

Next to the meaning of 'publicness', the term public denotes two other things. The second meaning refers to the realm of the state as the holder of public (state) authority. It should be clear that what is public in this sense is not necessary public in the sense of 'publicness'. Many operations of the state are confidential. For instance, most people would not appreciate the publication of the decisions of public authorities relating to their tax returns. Also, though foreign intelligence is typically tasked to a public authority, its operations are not usually published for all to know. The third meaning of public refers to the idea of a public good, a value or interest that cannot be reduced to individual taste or aggregated preferences,[111] and is meant to benefit the public in the sense of the joint citizenry. In fact, public goods such as privacy, justice and welfare may be conditional for developing and acting on private tastes and preferences.

If the term public is used without attention to its different meanings, public and private can easily be seen as dichotomies, pitting the interests of the state (public authority) or the collective (public goods) against the interests of individual citizens (for example private consumers and their private interests). Similarly, such dichotomies may lead to equating the interest of the state (public authority) with that of civil society (the public). Though, in a constitutional democracy, the core task of the state is to serve the public interest, this cannot be taken for granted. On the contrary, the idea of the Rule of Law is that citizens are given a position to contest the state's claims that it is acting in the general interest. A pivotal example of the undesirable mixing of different meanings of public can be found in the idea that privacy is either a public good that should be enforced by the state or a private interest that may be left to individual choice. This leads to situating the privacy of individuals in opposition to the security of the collective, which in turn leads to trading individual interests such as privacy against the general interest of security. These are false dichotomies, because both privacy and security are private interests as well as public goods.

A further refinement can be made by taking on Arendt's specification of the private, the social and the public, recalling that in her view it is the public sphere that may protect citizens from the tyranny of the social. In *The Human Condition*,[112] Arendt depicts the private as the sphere of bondage, she highlights the repetitive character of labour (cleaning house, tending the land, feeding ourselves) and the constraints of living under the imperatives of necessity. For Arendt, the private sphere, equated with that of the household, is not a sphere of freedom. She defines the social as the sphere of work, the context of creating artefacts defined by their functionality and of developing skills to achieve particular goals. Moreover, Arendt associates the social with social pressure, with the constraints of conformism, and the tyranny of public opinion. We might say – in more contemporary jargon – that she highlights the lure of herding behaviours and the manipulability of social influence.[113] Indeed, she defines the rise of conformism in terms of 'behavior [having] … replaced action as the foremost mode of human relationship' and explicitly relates the emergence of modern privacy as a defence against the social rather than the political sphere.[114]

Understanding the public sphere as the prototypical domain of freedom is no longer part of our common sense. We tend to conflate the notion of the public with either the realm of state authority or with the social (as in public opinion or publicness), and we often confuse politics with the mundane interplay of private interests at the level of the state. For Arendt, however, the public is the sphere of the freedom to act, whereby acting is not doing or making, but speaking. It is all about giving voice to one's dreams and desires about how to construct a shared world, about participating in the creation and maintenance of a sphere that enables a person to move beyond the satisfaction of one's needs (the necessary), beyond the dictates of public opinion (the plausible) and into the realm of natality (the possible). In protecting individuals from being framed and defined by the social, Arendt's public sphere in fact constitutes *the freedom from* unreasonable constraints, in order for individual humans to take *the freedom to* speak out for themselves and for what lies yonder. For Arendt, the public sphere is the stage on which we are challenged to reinvent ourselves, our minds and our societies. Perhaps, in order to reinvent privacy in the onli*f*e world, we must simultaneously discover, develop, conquer and defend a new public space, a networked spatiality that allows us to contest the plausibilities generated in Big Data Space.

This relates to a critical distinction to be made in the context of an onli*f*e world, distinguishing privacy between peers (social privacy) and privacy between an individual person and private or public organizations (institutional privacy). If we take the relational nature of privacy as boundary construction seriously, we must learn to speak in terms of privacy as something that plays out between an individual person and specific others, taking into account that we might want to share the same information with friends but not with colleagues, or with an acquaintance but not with an insurance company. Social privacy refers to how far a person is capable of segregating audiences consisting of peers, for instance friends on a social network site. Research confirms that privacy strategies at that level are becoming increasingly sophisticated.[115] Institutional privacy refers to the capability to manage and control, for instance, behavioural data that leak to institutional players, such as social network providers, advertising networks and data brokers. The same research demonstrates that hardly any privacy strategy is employed to guard one's privacy against institutional snooping. Widespread practices of AB testing confirm a lack of awareness and an absence of practical means to intervene in such privacy invasions.[116] AB testing follows a research design that tracks the impact of minor and major changes on the users of a service. For example, one half of the visitors to a website are directed to the current site (version A), the other half to a slightly changed site (version B). Based on various tracking technologies, the clickstream behaviours of the users are measured and compared. This enables an assessment of versions A and B, for instance in terms of purchasing behaviours. Whatever version is more profitable is chosen, and the same procedure can be automated for subsequent changes. AB testing can be performed automatically and with great speed, involving massive amounts of users. In the end it enables large-scale personalized targeting practices and pre-emptive computing. The lack of strategies to defend one's institutional privacy against this kind of invisible testing, which facilitates a systematic and permanent study of our so-called 'herding behaviours', threatens the shared public space. A vital public sphere depends on a private sphere that is free from unreasonable constraints on the building of one's identity.

Summarizing, within constitutional democracy, privacy is a public good in as far as it protects practices of identity building that are preconditional for a vigilant civil society. It is also – perhaps paradoxically – a public good in that it highlights the primacy of the individual above the collective, notwithstanding the fact that the individual self only emerges after being addressed by others and will always find itself thrown into an existing web of normativities (constraints) that form the dynamic backbone of any collective. Precisely to enable an individual to exercise her privacy on the basis of her personal preferences (privacy as a private interest), societal constraints must be put in place that allow for such an exercise (thereby qualifying privacy as a public good). The threats that pre-emptive STIs pose for privacy also threaten the public sphere; profiling enables the foreseeing of political preferences, and in a hyperconnected onlife world that thrives on access to Big Data Space these preferences can be managed on the basis of personalized news feeds and targeted campaigning. This leads me to further emerging threats, caused by the invisible visibilities of refined profiling, that is the threats against individual autonomy and the right to equal respect.

Though closely related to privacy and identity, these threats warrant a separate discussion.

5.3   STEREOTYPING AND AUTONOMY: RESISTING REAL-TIME DIGITAL SORTING

5.3.1   Social Sorting in the *Welt*

Though they differ from and cannot be reduced to privacy concerns, the issues to be discussed under the heading of social sorting will often overlap with privacy. Having explained privacy in terms of freedom from unreasonable constraints to build one's identity, it must be clear that social sorting is connected to privacy. To the extent that our identity is relational and co-constituted by how we profile others to be profiling us, social sorting has a bearing on the freedom discussed in the previous section.

Social sorting is an ancient custom. It allows us to categorize others as friends or enemies, natives or strangers, wine lovers or beer drinkers, parents or colleagues, children or adults, and so on. Social sorting is based on profiling, which is a form of pattern recognition. As discussed in Chapters 2 and 3, pattern recognition is the most crucial characteristic of living organisms, connecting perception with action, enabling an agent to foresee how its behaviours will affect its environment and how other agents will frame their signals. Once we move from an *Umwelt* to a *Welt*, it becomes trickier to describe pattern recognition as it becomes contingent upon the ambiguities of human language. Moreover, once the script and the printing press enter the stage, interpretation becomes critical, creating even more room for productive misunderstandings and reiterant shifts in meaning. In an oral society, a misunderstanding can be corrected while speaking, because communication is necessarily face-to-face. In that case misunderstandings can still be generated by messengers that travel from one person to another to convey a specific message. This would imply, however, that the message itself has been changed (for instance the wording, the syntax, or the intonation). Once we have script and print, the message is inscribed and its inscription remains the same, generating a plurality of alternative interpretations of the same inscription by different readers over time. The meaning of the text can no longer be controlled by the author; this is how text 'emancipates' itself from its author and acquires autonomous meaning. Autonomy, however, does not entail that text determines its own meaning. On the contrary, the relational nature of text triggers a web of meaning that is forever open to yet another interpretation. The meaning of any text is necessarily determined both in relation to other texts and to the world it references. The volatility of this web of meaning requires continuous attention to the internal and external sustainability of potential interpretations, that is, to the internal coherence of inter-textual dependencies and to the fit with the world they reference. The complexity of text and con-text is generated by the fact that the *Welt* that develops on the cusp of inter-textual and outer-textual reference is always already mediated by language. The outer-textual reference is thus constituted by inter-textual references. When I try to explain 'water' I will use other words (inter-textual references) and – if water is near – point to the thing I 'mean' by water. But most of the time the outer-textual reference is not around for pointing at and requires prior knowledge and further implication in more textual reference (for instance, a term like 'education' cannot easily be explained by pointing at something).[117] The reading mind is trained to achieve such inter-textual coherence and fit with the outer-textual world, combining conscious reflection with a reiterant intuitive reflexivity. Literate people inevitably perform their social sorting on the cusp of conscious and unconscious pattern recognition, accustomed to frame and reframe their profiles or stereotypes when confronted with written texts that challenge or confirm prevalent labelling practices. Literacy thus helps to infuse ambiguity and some instability in our social sorting practices. Text, and the need for reiterant interpretation, force the extended reading mind to reassess its profiling habits, hence inducing recursive reflection on the way we frame each other (and ourselves).

5.3.2 Digital Sorting in the Onlife World

The onlife world is built on newly extended minds that thrive on new profiling practices. The core difference here is that profiling is partly outsourced to data-driven agents, turning social sorting into digital sorting. As noted in Chapters 2 and 3 it is not easy to put one's finger on these new, autonomic profiling practices. Profiles can be reasonably stable, identifiable stereotypes, as in ordinary human profiling. For instance: 'black people and Muslims match with criminal intent or with low income'; 'CEOs of large companies are necessarily corrupt'; 'children of divorced parents need specific attention to get better grades in high school'; or, 'customers that buy diapers usually buy fewer alcoholic beverages' In the onlife world, however, profiles will often be more dynamic and complex, though simultaneously their occurrence is mostly hidden. The supermarket Target managed to figure out whether a customer is pregnant on the basis of her purchasing behaviours with regard to 25 products. The Guest Marketing Analytics department crawled through the volunteered and behavioural data of their customers, and was able to attribute a 'pregnancy score' for each shopper – based on the results of data mining operations. This enabled the supermarket to target pregnant women with ad booklets containing coupons for baby products, tempting them to choose Target as the preferred shop for their upcoming buying needs. However, once women got the idea that Target had such detailed knowledge of intimate parts of their life without their having volunteered the information, some customers got annoyed. According to Charles Duhigg in *The New York Times*, an anonymous Target executive explained:[118]

> 'With the pregnancy products, though, we learned that some women react badly,' the executive said. 'Then we started mixing in all these ads for things we knew pregnant women would never buy, so the baby ads looked random. We'd put an ad for a lawn mower next to diapers. We'd put a coupon for wineglasses next to infant clothes. That way, it looked like all the products were chosen by chance. And we found out that as long as a pregnant woman thinks she hasn't been spied on, she'll use the coupons. She just assumes that everyone else on her block got the same mailer for diapers and cribs. As long as we don't spook her, it works'.

This compares to a famous example given by Tal Zarsky in his paper on the effects of profiling on human autonomy. In 2003 he discussed – by way of hypothetical example – an online grocer that figures out that one of his customers is on the verge of quitting smoking. The grocer presents the customer with cigarette ads and with a complementary cigarette packet in the next grocery shipment. Zarsky addressed this particular type of profiling as a form of manipulation that confronts us with the so-called autonomy trap. He defines autonomy as a 'second order capacity of persons to reflect critically upon their first-order preferences, desires, wishes, and so forth and the capacity to accept or to attempt to change these in light of higher-order preferences and values'.[119]

Online and offline grocers, credit rating agencies, insurance companies, recruiting consultants, App developers, tax authorities and campaign advisors currently profile customers, web surfers, users of social networking sites, voters and tax payers by means of predictive analytics. They can then target an individual to pre-empt her intent, for instance, her intent to quit smoking or her intent to investigate where to shop for baby clothing, nappies, and so on. Clearly, it is still up to the targeted individual to make up her own mind. Nobody is forcing her hand. Nevertheless, her capability to reflect on the choices she faces is somehow influenced.

The asymmetry of information regarding these choices raises questions about the meaning of human autonomy in the era of proactive computing, notably because of the lack of awareness that a person is being spied on by software that may 'know' things about her that she may not even know herself. Predictive analytics may come up with statistical knowledge on significant health risks or employment prospects that are unknown to the individual whose data points match these profiles. The problem is also that the complexities as well as the dynamics of the profiles generated by statistical inferences make it hard to explain on what basis a person is being targeted, included, excluded, rewarded or punished. It seems that our cognitive make-up requires stable and relatively simple stereotypes as heuristics. Though some refer to this as our bounded rationality, suggesting that this diminishes our rationality, others highlight that the boundaries of rational choice are pivotal for our intelligence, helping us to be selective and enabling us to act under conditions of uncertainty.[120] The problem is that data-driven agents increasingly determine the course of information flows to influence our behaviours, based on highly complex computational profiles. It is difficult, if not impossible, to anticipate these profiles, making it increasingly hazardous to navigate the onli*fe* world in a manner that respects human autonomy.

5.3.3 Understanding Autonomy in the Onli*fe* World

In his definition of autonomy Zarsky refers to first and second order beliefs and desires. The seminal text on this distinction is Harry Frankfurt's 'Freedom of the Will and the Concept of a Person' of 1971. The title of this essay is interesting; it refers to the link between personhood and freedom and brings in the arduous issue of free will. The idea is that a person differs from other agents in 'the structure of her will'. Whereas animals obviously have desires, a person is an agent capable of having a desire about her own desires, an intention about her own intentions:[121]

> they [persons] are capable of wanting to be different, in their preferences and purposes, from what they are. … No animal other than man … appears to have the capacity for reflective self-evaluation that is manifest in the formation of second-order desires.

A person may have a strong desire for cookies at 3 pm.[122] Simultaneously that person may consider herself overweight, hoping to lose weight by getting rid of her 3 pm cookie-eating habit. She can sit down and develop strategies to kill the habit. For instance, she can engage with prayer or meditation, she can take care that there are no cookies in the house, or she can reward herself for avoiding the 3 pm challenge. In devising such strategies she can take into account the latest insights from neuroscience or behavioural economics. The bottom line is that she is in a position to reflect on her preferences and that she can redirect her habits. This goes for eating habits: do I want to become a vegetarian? It goes for investing in education: do I want to work and make money as soon as possible or shall I spend the coming years in school? It goes for shopping: do I want a green car that is more expensive or a cool car that boosts my prestige? And for onl*ife* privacy settings: do I want my data to be used for the construction of profiles of 'normal' citizens? Autonomy does not mean that I reset my preferences without being influenced by others. Second order desires are developed in confrontation with others, notably with the reflections that others have shared in written text. To act autonomously would mean that if I want, I can reflect on my own default settings or on those of my environment and reframe them to be in accordance with my second order desires. Autonomy is about the question of whether I want to be the kind of person who cannot stop eating cookies at 3 o'clock in the afternoon, or the kind of person who is forced to surrender her behavioural data to participate in the onl*ife* world. This means that others can violate my autonomy either by forcing me to adhere to my first order preferences, or by forcing me to adhere to the second order preferences of others. However, the most serious violation is when others diminish my capability to reflect on my habits or inclinations, for instance by taking my first order preferences for granted and catering to them before I become aware of them. Clearly, the kind of profiling that is performed by data-driven agents to pre-empt the intent of a particular category of persons flies in the face of this understanding of autonomy. The point is not whether someone forces me to buy nappies in Target, or a particular book at Amazon.com. The point is that the shaping of my intent is undercut such that I never get down to assessing my first order desires, let alone develop an intent about such desires.

From this perspective, we can understand the difference between social sorting and digital sorting in terms of a new category of profiles. The profiles that emerge from KDD and machine learning are usually based on aggregated data of very many people, and though they are applied to categories of individuals there is no guarantee that they apply at the individual level. From the perspective of marketing this need not be a problem. A marketer is not interested in me as a person, but in me as a specific type of person that may be lured into particular kinds of behaviours. In fact, commercial profiling is meant to make people transparent. Not in the sense of looking into their intimate self, but rather in the sense of *looking through* them to similar people. In the context of Big Data many authors speak of our 'data doubles', suggesting that our data trails become our double agents, available for further inferences. However, these data doubles are not necessarily used as individual profiles. More often, they are instrumental in matching us with inferences based on the aggregated data of many others. Once a match is found a person is grouped with her similes, those who are similar in a particular respect. This turns us into 'dividuals'; we are continuously and invisibly divided into an unlimited number of matching data points, measured against our proliferating similes that function as digital proxies. These similes determine what is being offered to us, what price we must pay, which jobs we may get, to what extent we will be monitored by law enforcement or foreign intelligence. We cannot see these calculated matching profiles, which are hidden somewhere in Big Data Space, but the machinery of the *onlife* world detects them and somehow acts on them. Living in an *onlife* world is living with invisible similes, employed as proxies for ourselves by the data-driven environment.

Social sorting in the *Welt* that is co-constituted by written text and human interaction is both ambiguous and contestable. It forms a part of our double contingency, as when I profile how others profile me. It enables people to join forces and start a revolution, based on a shared sense of being treated wrongfully. As long as we can foresee how we are being profiled, we can challenge the profile as incorrect or unfair. We can require of those who profile us to give good reasons for the labels they stick on us, especially if the label has a significant effect on our life. In an *onlife* world this is less obvious. With digital sorting, we find ourselves on the wrong end of a single contingency, extensively determined by the categorizations of hidden algorithms, shielded by the lucrative combination of trade secrets, intellectual property rights and national security arguments. On top of that, these categorizations are not only used to predict our future behaviours – which might leave us time to prove them wrong – but increasingly manage to predict the present, infusing our environment with multiple versions of 'autocomplete'. This is the bottom line of digital sorting in the *onlife* world; real-time adaptive environments that stick around (us) and transform as we navigate – making it ever harder to foresee how we might have acted if the surroundings did not cater to what they inferred about us.

5.3.4 Prohibited Discrimination

Finally, I will now pay attention to one particular type of social sorting that is prohibited by law, because it violates the fundamental right to non-discrimination. As a legal right, non-discrimination is a neatly defined notion that refers to specific forbidden grounds for discrimination and specific contexts in which such discrimination is forbidden. A variety of legal instruments at the national, international and supranational level articulate non-discrimination as a fundamental or human right, highlighting religion, race, health, age or sexual orientation as prohibited grounds of discrimination. Contexts like employment and occupation, health insurance, housing, social security and education may be regulated in more specific terms, depending on the jurisdiction.

The right to non-discrimination is related to the principle of equality, depicting the fundamental right to equal treatment. It should be clear from the outset, that a right to equal treatment does not mean people should always be treated as if they were equal. Rather, on the contrary, factual inequalities often warrant unequal treatment to compensate for unfair disadvantage. This, however, does not mean that people should be treated such that they all become equal. Without going into the nuances of factual and normative equality I would argue that the notion of equal respect that grounds both democracy and the Rule of Law also grounds the right to non-discrimination. It relates to democracy as it fosters the preconditions for individuals to partake in collective self-government and it relates to the Rule of Law as it provides for an enforceable right against unjustified exclusion. It combines concern for procedural equality, by providing means to develop capabilities that create a level playing field amongst fellow citizens, with concern for substantive equality, by discerning intolerable inequalities in the outcome of procedural equality.

As a fundamental right, non-discrimination is primarily a right of citizens against their governments. Nevertheless, governments are bound to ensure that the substance of this right is not violated by other powerful players. This means that employers, healthcare providers, utility providers, insurance companies, and so on are restricted in their freedom to contract or in the exercise of their property rights if this amounts to prohibited discrimination. It might be interesting to investigate how the right to non-discrimination fits with the fundamental right to conduct a business, as codified in the charter of the European Union. What if a company wants to serve or even create a market for gay couples, figuring out their specific preferences based on their behaviours on social networking sites? What if the company excludes – what it infers to be – straight couples from special offers, to elicit brand loyalty and exclusiveness for their targeted population?

It is important to stress that discrimination as such is not prohibited. As discussed, discrimination in the sense of making a distinction that makes a difference is typical of all living entities and indeed of all natural and artificial agents. An artificial legal subject, such as a commercial enterprise, will have to discriminate to survive in a competitive environment. Discernment may be a better term for this, as it is less likely to be understood in a pejorative manner. Notably, the idea of price-discrimination is a critical aspect of a market economy that requires companies to tune their price to the 'laws' of supply and demand, rather than merely checking the price against the cost. Price-discrimination is not prohibited as such and may even be termed beneficial for less advantaged consumers. For instance, paying a higher price for a business-class ticket may, in some cases, help to subsidize part of the costs of an economy ticket, thus creating a win-win situation that lowers the price of economy class tickets. Similarly, demanding a higher price for popular books may, under specific conditions, generate the funds to publish books rarely bought but considered worthwhile. This does not mean that price-discrimination is naturally beneficial; it may be the result of market failure, allowing companies to charge prices that consumers would never pay if they had knowledge of the actual costs or of the prices charged to others. In combination with personalized profiling and pre-emptive computing, price-discrimination may boil down to manipulation, enabled by the high transaction costs for individual customers, who have no idea of either the cost of a specific service or the prices charged to other consumers. This basically refers to the autonomy trap, discussed previously in section 5.3.2. In our current economic system, however, price-discrimination is not unlawful, unless it falls within the scope of discrimination based on a forbidden ground and/or in a context for which specific prohibitions have been enacted.

The legal prohibition of discrimination on specific grounds is not absolute. Rather, if differential treatment is based on a prohibited ground the question is whether this can be justified. Providing women with pregnancy leave, while denying men such a thing is obviously justified. However, the question is whether providing women with maternity leave while denying this to the men is also justifiable. If fathers are willing to take care of their infants, why should they be denied the privilege? The justification also relates to whether an intervention or decision that differentiates between people based on, for example, their gender is proportional to the goal to be achieved. A car insurance company may discriminate on the basis of gender, because its statistics show that women pose less risk than men. By using gender as a means to calculate a lesser premium for women they engage in direct discrimination. The goal of profitability that invites insurance companies to match risk to the insurance premium may not, however, justify systematic discrimination. The reason may be that such systematic discrimination is deemed not proportional to the goal of maximizing profit. The idea could be that spreading the risk can be achieved by charging women a higher premium than the statistics account for, while reducing the premium for men, thus attributing the same premium to both. In other words, proportionality also requires that if the goal can be reached by other – less-discriminatory – means, the making of a distinction cannot be justified.

A second complication in the law on non-discrimination is generated by the notion of indirect discrimination. This refers to making a difference based on neutral grounds, such as driving behaviour, which, however, results in discriminating between men and women because men drive more dangerously. Even if the insurance company does not use gender as a factor to calculate the premium, using the factor of driving behaviours will have the same effect and result in *de facto* discrimination on the basis of gender. Within the jurisdiction of the European Union such indirect discrimination is also prohibited. To prove indirect discrimination one may resort to statistics, showing that irrespective of the reason given for certain treatment the result significantly disadvantages people of a certain gender, race, political belief or other prohibited ground. As in the case of direct discrimination, indirect discrimination must be justifiable, or else it constitutes a violation.

In an onli*fe* world that enables surreptitious pre-emptive targeting, the threat of prohibited discrimination differs in two respects from that in a world untouched by Big Data Analytics. First, it may not be easy to figure out that one is the subject of discrimination on the basis of a forbidden ground, because the decisions taken by smart technologies are largely invisible. This concerns the difficulty of proving the existence of discrimination. The algorithmic adaptations of our smart environment are often intuitive and seemingly natural, meaning that users will not recognize their treatment as something that results from semi-automated decision-making. Just as we don't speak about our internal environment in terms of decision-making ('our heart deciding to increase its heart-beat'), we may not perceive the extent to which access to goods and services, their prices or surveillance of our person are a consequence of complex decision algorithms or artificial neural networks. The intelligence of the environment may thus hide the mere existence of prohibited discrimination, even if it is *directly* targeted to ethnicity, political opinion or gender. A further threat, however, derives from the way that pre-emptive targeting enables sophisticated *indirect* discrimination that is based on statistical inferences about risks or profitability. Taking into account that neural nets are basically black boxes, producing dynamic adaptive decisions based on complex calculations and reiterant feedback, it will be a huge challenge to identify their potential for invisible indirect discrimination. This relates to the transparency problem generated by smart technologies and pre-emptive environments. If the inhabitants of the onli*fe* world have no clue as to how they are sorted and targeted, it becomes very difficult – if not impossible – to exercise the right to non-discrimination. The lack of transparency of semi-autonomous decision systems is perhaps the most crucial threat posed by the invisible computational layers that constitute the onli*fe* world; it exacerbates any other threat by hiding it from our scrutiny.

5.4 THE PRESUMPTION OF INNOCENCE AND DUE PROCESS

5.4.1 The Presumption of Innocence

In the context of criminal law enforcement, public security and intelligence, specific categories of people may be targeted as potential suspects, or as more likely to develop unlawful behaviour. We can call this pre-emptive criminal profiling, as it is hoped that such targeting will reduce crime by staying one step ahead of its enactment. As long as a person is not charged with a criminal offence this does not violate the presumption of innocence in the strictly legal sense. From a broader perspective, however, we must take into account the consequences of 'merely' monitoring people on the basis of statistics that indicate a disposition to behave unlawfully or undesirably. Such pre-emptive monitoring seems to go against the grain of how most people intuitively understand the presumption of innocence.

Before discussing how pre-emptive criminal profiling affects the presumption of innocence, I will pay attention to the question of whether criminal profiling based on Big Data Analytics can be expected to contribute to crime reduction. In his *Against Prediction* Harcourt has convincingly argued why predictive profiling may be ineffective in the long run, notably with regard to policing and sentencing. Instead of 'merely' providing moral arguments 'against prediction', Harcourt has developed a sophisticated internal critique that challenges some of the vested assumptions of the cost benefit models that underlie pre-emptive criminal profiling.[123] These models assume that scarce resources of policing and fraud detection should be used to monitor those most likely to offend, leaving supposedly obedient citizens alone. They thereby assume, first, that monitoring potential offenders will prevent them from committing crimes, and, second, that those unlikely to offend will remain obedient citizens even when far less resources are dedicated to checking their behaviours. Much has been written on these assumptions in relation to racial profiling in the US, arguing that disproportional monitoring of black people will lead to skewed crime statistics and will in fact keep an entire group of people hostage to the bias that comes from directing disproportional resources to checking their behaviours. Though it seems easier to provide an external critique that confronts the unfairness of targeting people on the basis of them sharing characteristics with others who violated the law, behaving dangerously, or causing nuisance, it is important to test the argument that such profiling is at all effective in the long run. This is crucial, because measures that aim to reduce crime, while infringing privacy and non-discrimination rights, cannot be justified if they are not effective in achieving their aim. Harcourt's point is that by focusing attention on the category of citizens that is more likely than others to violate the law, one assumes that this will in fact prevent them from offending. At the same time, it is assumed that ignoring those less likely to offend will not influence their behaviours. To the extent that these assumptions don't hold, the cost-benefit analysis of pre-emptive criminal profiling lacks good reasons to focus all attention on suspect categories. Harcourt argues that by acting on the inferences of crime statistics behaviours will change, but not necessarily for the better, whereas the bias that is inherent in monitoring only specific categories of people blinds justice authorities to these changes.

One could argue that real-time ubiquitous monitoring – of all citizens – would solve this problem, allowing for a more dynamic and less biased version of criminal profiling. Surveillance is thus democratized and may seem to apply equal respect for each person to the extent that nobody is exempted from scrutiny. Though there may be some truth in this, in the case of pre-emptive criminal profiling we are still left with three problems: first, the profiling may be based on incorrect data, due to bad quality sensor-technologies, incompleteness or noise; second, the so-called no-free-lunch theorem demonstrates that there is not one correct or 'objective' way of mining data, which means that bias is unavoidable; and third, even if correct and effective, profiling may be unfair because it 'judges' people on the basis of an extrapolation of their past behaviours matched with patterns generated by other people's behaviours. In reference to the preceding section, we could say that judging people by their similes, addressing their inferred doubles as proxies for the person of flesh and blood, is incompatible with fundamental tenets of the criminal law in constitutional democracies. On top of that, ubiquitous monitoring of all citizens raises insurmountable privacy concerns, as it eradicates the substance of privacy; it would make citizens not merely transparent in the sense of looking straight through them to their similes and doubles, but render them transparent by putting the spotlight on all their machine-readable behaviours. One could rephrase this by acknowledging that it shows equal *dis*respect for all citizens.

Legally speaking, the presumption of innocence can be understood as a norm that addresses government officials after a person has been charged with a criminal offence. Until a court has spoken, a person is presumed to be innocent, meaning that the burden of proof is on the public prosecutor and that measures taken against the defendant cannot be seen as punitive interventions. Interestingly, the presumption thus depends on the charge, that is, on a suspicion. Only when the state has acted on its belief that a person may be guilty, can the state be held to account for treating that person as not guilty. Though this may sound contradictory, it is not. The monopoly of violence that grounds the *ius puniendi* requires countervailing powers to prevent abuse. The suspect that is the object of a criminal investigation must be provided with the status of a subject that is capable of contesting the charge, requiring the public prosecutor to prove beyond reasonable doubt that the suspect has committed a crime. Pre-emptive computing that enables police and justice authorities to act upon inferred proxies of potential criminals will not lead to a criminal charge, unless a specific charge can be made against a specific person. This implies that the presumption of innocence in the narrow sense is not at stake. People may be observed and monitored on the basis of data-driven criminal profiling, but they cannot be charged – let alone punished – until evidence is found to frame a specific person.

In a broader sense, however, one can argue that targeted monitoring of categories of people based on computational inferences ignores the foundations of the presumption of innocence. It seems to turn the presumption upside down by acting upon something like a potential for criminal conduct, somehow turning all citizens into potential suspects. Or, even more incriminating, turning specific subgroups into potential suspects, based on sophisticated risk analyses. Both types of pre-emptive criminal profiling are highly problematic. The first, because to select those inclined to criminal behaviours requires data on all citizens; the second, because it falls prey to Harcourt's critique of unjustified and ineffective surveillance of those supposedly prone to criminal conduct. In both cases, the problem seems to reside at least in part in the fact that people are not aware of how they are being profiled; they cannot contest the inferences drawn. They cannot disown their similes as proxies.

5.4.2 Due Process or the Right to Know and Contest Adverse Decisions

Little attention is given to the right to due process, though it relates in a direct way to privacy, non-discrimination and the presumption of innocence.

As a legal right, due process concerns the Fourteenth Amendment of the US Constitution, which stipulates, amongst other things, that no person shall be deprived 'of life, liberty, or property, without due process of law'. Due process in that sense can be equated with procedural fairness, based on substantive notions of equal respect and individual liberty. Art. 6 of the European Convention of Human Rights (ECHR) defines a similar right in more concrete terms, under the heading of a 'fair trial', requiring an impartial judge, a public hearing and verdict, immediacy of the trial before the judge, the presumption of innocence in the case of a criminal trial and equality of arms between the parties.

In a famous article on 'Two Models of the Criminal Process', Packer developed the idea that the administration of criminal justice is driven by two types of values, namely those of 'due process' and those of 'crime control'.[124] Whereas the first emphasizes the value of individual rights and liberties, the second focuses on effective regulation and control of criminal conduct. He speaks of a fundamental normative antinomy at the heart of the criminal law, thereby accepting a double instrumentality of the criminal law: on the one hand it functions as a means to repress criminal behaviour, and on the other hand it must take into account that trade-offs between reliability of evidence and speed of conviction cannot be made on the basis of a mere calculation of costs and benefits. One could rephrase by saying that whereas a pure crime control model might be informed by a utilitarian ethics, favouring the maximum utility for the greatest number (and thus sacrificing the utility of an individual for the greater good), the due process model is inspired by a deontological ethics, respecting individual autonomy in the face of majoritarian trade-offs and efficient and effective crime control. Packer saliently compares the crime control model to an assembly line that aims for a smooth progression of the different stages of the criminal process, whereas he likens the due process model to an obstacle course that inserts principled impediments in each and every stage of the same process. For our purposes due process must be taken in its broad sense of fair procedure, with an emphasis on what has been called the 'equality of arms' in the context of the fair trial of Art. 6 ECHR. Equality of arms means that if a person wishes to contest an accusation, charge or claim she must be in a position to argue her case on the basis of equal access to relevant knowledge in comparison to the prosecutor or claimant. This is also coined as the maxim of internal publicity of the fair trial. As a legal right one could argue that due process requirements only apply in the relationship between a government and its citizens, but in a more general sense due process is relevant for all interactions between powerful organizations on the one hand and individual citizens on the other. Even from the perspective of law and economics, due process would be advantageous in so far as it creates a level playing field. Traditionally adding obstacles to a course of events is viewed as adding transaction costs (think of Packer's metaphor of the obstruction course), but in fact exercising one's due process rights may distribute transaction costs instead of leaving them all on the side of the weaker party. It should thereby not impede pareto-optimal solutions but enable pareto-optimal solutions that are also fair.

The narrow – legal – meaning of due process is tied to the context of criminal investigation and criminal procedure. In the broader sense due process refers to the capability to contest adverse decisions. Such a capability matches, first, the right to know about the existence of such decisions and the reasons that inform them and, second, the right to contest them if one deems them to be inappropriate or unfair. This moves us from law to ethics, though the right to due process in this broad sense is connected to a number of legal rights that can been seen as an expression of due process. For instance, 'fair play' in administrative law, transparency rights such as freedom of information in constitutional law, and various information duties in the context of tort law and the law of contract, all seem to embody the fundamental notion of equality of arms and to contribute to the system of checks and balances of the Rule of Law. Due process may indeed be the normative core of law in a constitutional democracy, the ethical grounding of such a law, distinguishing law from mere administration or even regulation. As an unwritten principle that is never exhausted by its codification in legislation or its assertion in case law, due process may in fact provide the critical potential to reinvent ourselves in the shift from *Welt* to the onlife world.

How does the principle of due process fare with pre-emptive computing systems? Pre-emptive analytics accumulates knowledge on the side of whoever owns the databases and the software. This knowledge is not easily available for those it describes and predicts, which is partly due to the fact that mining this data will produce non-obvious knowledge; for instance, non-trivial inferences about earning capacity, health, credit risk and employability. When people are not aware of this knowledge they have no way of defending themselves against actions taken on the assumption of its validity and relevance. A person cannot contest incorrect or unfair decisions that impact her life if she has no clue that and how decisions have been reached. The increasing knowledge asymmetry that is thus produced, coupled with the invisibility inherent in current 'visions' of smart environments will thus violate due process even – and especially – if people are unaware of being targeted. Ubiquitous computing has been described as thriving on hidden complexity. This is not necessarily in opposition to due process. One can imagine an environment that is saturated with intuitive interfaces enabling smooth interaction with the underlying decision systems, whereas whoever wants access to the computational intestines of the ambience is provided with similarly intuitive tools to investigate how one is being targeted. But at this moment such tools must still be invented, while the business models of the onli*f*e world thrive on the trading of personal data and profiles in the context of a proprietary model for cloud provision, databases and the analytics that nourish the monetization of data. This last implies that there is no business model for effective transparency tools, though there certainly is a business model for tools that merely simulate transparency. Real transparency would easily threaten the monetization of data, disabling the profitability of pre-emption itself.

Privacy and non-discrimination are often violated precisely because of the absence of due process in the broad sense. In the context of pre-emptive profiling, due process would mean that there is a way of effectively and reliably intuiting how one is targeted and how this relates to one's behaviours. This would allow a person to change her behaviours to change how she is profiled, but due process implies that she could also choose to contest her similes as proxies. Thus, due process is a precondition for a person to effectively prevent privacy violations as well as manipulative social sorting and unjustified discrimination.

5.5   CONCLUSIONS: THE RIGHT TO CO-DETERMINE HOW WE SHALL BE 'READ'

Privacy is about a social setting that permits a person to prevent, ward off or contest unreasonable constraints on the construction of her identity. This presumes that a person can anticipate and co-determine how the environment 'reads' her. The advantage of speaking in terms of 'being read' instead of merely defining privacy in terms of 'control over personal data' is that what matters is *what others may infer from these data*. The same phrase captures what is at stake with non-discrimination, the presumption of innocence and due process; it highlights the categorization that is inherent in proactive and pre-emptive computing, and marks the importance of having access to the similes and doubles that may be employed.

In a salient account of what she calls the 'inference problem in pervasive computing' Dwyer has suggested that what people care about is not so much the sharing of individual data per se, but the invisible consequences of disclosure. She convincingly argues that privacy should not be seen as an attribute of a data element, nor be reduced to control over personal identifiable information. Against such reductive conceptualizations of privacy, Dwyer contends that privacy is:[125]

a culturally and socially constructed property of relationships and groups.

This links her position to Altman's relational conception of privacy, as discussed previously.[126] Privacy can then be seen as a strategy to construct, define and sustain boundaries between self and others, building on tacit knowledge that is both intuitive and dynamic. Most of this boundary work is not deliberate, as it requires real-time assessment of the extent to which others can be trusted with what kind of disclosures. Our bounded rationality precludes extensive calculations of risks and opportunities. This is not necessarily a drawback as it may save us from complicated deliberations.[127] Cognitive science now confirms that there is no time to deliberate over the numerous choices made in the flux of everyday life, and managing one's public persona as well as one's private self is a matter of hunches and guesses rather than the application of preconceived rules. The practice of privacy is, in other words, largely autonomic, though this does not at all rule out reflection or autonomy. Such reflections are often the starting points for the formation of new habits, nourishing novel automations. Thus, becoming consciously aware of our habits and their implications is part of a learning process that can result in rewiring our behaviours.

However, to the extent that smart environments shield the relevant inferences from their inhabitants, reflection becomes unattainable and developing new privacy practices becomes impossible. If we cannot grasp or intuit the inferences that allow the environment to read us we cannot sustain our boundaries (having no clue where they have already been erased), we cannot prevent unjustified or undesirable discrimination (having no clue to what extent we are in fact categorized and treated differently), and we cannot exercise due process rights (having no access to the inferences that are protected as trade secrets or by means of intellectual property).

6. The other side of privacy: agency and privacy in Japan

6.1 WHY JAPAN?

The Japanese term for privacy, *puraibashi*, is of foreign origin. It has been imported from the English language and many authors suggest that the Japanese legislation on privacy and data protection has been enacted merely to comply with the demands of Western trade partners.[128] This seems a bit over the top, considering that in Japanese case law a right to privacy has been recognized since 1964, and legislation regarding the processing of personal data by the administration has been in force since 1988, followed by a more comprehensive Act on the Protection of Personal Information in 2003.[129] In some ways Japan seems ahead of the USA, as Japan has opted for general instead of sectorial regulation. Though we must admit that much is left to self-regulation and it is unclear to what extent the legislation is implemented,[130] this has been a recurrent complaint about all regulation of informational privacy, also in Europe and the USA.

This chapter is not focused on the current legal framework, which seems relatively up to date. Instead I want to explore privacy practices that have been part and parcel of Japanese culture, even before the notion of privacy entered the Japanese vocabulary. I contend that absence of a concept does not imply that the relevant practices were absent; as long as we are willing to concede that these differ substantially from our own. In Japan, to recognize and qualify particular interaction patterns as a manifestation of privacy requires sensitivity to privacy as a relational concept, rather than an attribute of individual persons. The question is not whether a person 'has' privacy, but whether the environment 'affords' a person a degree of privacy. The 'environment' refers, first, to the material surroundings of an individual person, such as walls made of stone or paper or the presence of specific monitoring technologies, and, second, to the interpersonal and institutional environment that determines disclosure of our various identifications. Note that both the material and the institutional environment are artificial, but real. Building on the previous chapter I take privacy to refer to a variety of practices that allow agents to co-constitute and negotiate the borders between self and environment. In the Japanese context, an example of such a practice may be:[131]

> In fact, bowing at a distance of one meter is still a common form of greeting in Japan and creates a sense of familiarity for people by letting others know that one will not violate their privacy. This formal maintenance of distance is an important element in the communicative style of the Japanese.

To uncover which Japanese practices can be seen as privacy practices we need to engage a concept of privacy that abdicates from a common denominator in the practices to which it refers, instead requiring a family resemblance;[132] no genus-species relation but a more complex entanglement between different ways of self-constitution, distantiation and retreat. From that perspective, privacy can be seen as a habit, even a life-preserving habit, safeguarding an individual agent from invasion, attack or manipulation. Altman proposed that in this broad sense: 'the concept of privacy is central to understanding environment and behavior relationships; it provides a key link among the concepts of crowding, territorial behavior, and personal space'.[133]

Human privacy differs from that of other agents in that humans engage in reflection. The Western notion of *a right to* privacy builds on this reflection. It introduces a legal framework that allows individual citizens to practice their privacy in the face of a modern state that tends to encroach on their personal life in a myriad of ways.[134] This involves a more explicit conceptualization of privacy.

This chapter will explore practices developed in Japan that can be qualified as privacy practices, whether or not they have been conceptualized as such, and it will speculate how these practices enable people to deal with smart technologies. The reasons for investigating Japanese culture are threefold. First, the particular types of boundary work that are engrained in Japanese society provide an alternative way of understanding privacy in a pre-emptive environment. This highlights the other side of privacy, namely as a gift or a duty rather than a right; the attention goes to grace or obligation rather than entitlement. Second, the distinct relationships between people and things within the Japanese tradition may be instructive for the challenges of grappling with animated *things*. The latter is highly relevant for the capability to view things as agents, without necessarily attributing human agency to them. This engages yet another side of privacy; namely privacy granted by things instead of people. Third, we need to assess how the Japanese tradition relates to the right to privacy. What is the added value of an individual right as compared to a deeply ingrained duty to respect another's privacy? This leads up to the third part of the book, where the focus shifts to the relationship between law and technology.

6.2 THE JAPANESE TRADITION

To detect what can be understood as privacy practices we need to understand the interaction patterns that constitute Japanese culture, tradition or *Welt*, terms that I will use interchangeably at this point.[135] Japanese culture seems unhampered by the ideas of unity, universality and binary logic that inform Western traditions. Actually, speaking of *the* Japanese tradition would be a precarious undertaking that only makes sense if we accept its eclectic as well as complex nature. Japanese culture has fed on foreign influences ever since the Chinese script was imported in the beginning of the 5th century AD, opening Japan to the repositories of a millennium of Confucian and Buddhist thought. The indigenous oral tradition of what has later been called 'Shinto' is usually labelled as animistic;[136] meaning that important 'things' (the sun, mount Fuji), concepts (birth, growth, fertility) and beings (animals, ancestors) are seen as manifestations of *kami* or spirits. These *kami* should, however, not to be equated with gods in the Western understanding of that word.[137] The introduction of Confucianism and Buddhism did not replace Shinto but infused it with novel meanings, complemented it with different rituals and produced a culture that enabled people to hold on to a diversity of partly overlapping and even contradictory practices.[138]

In *The Japanese Mind* Davies and Ikeno discuss the concept of *iitoko-dori*,[139] which refers to the Japanese way of adopting foreign elements, highlighting the selective and transformative character of this adoption. They stress the coexistence of different beliefs and the lack of conflict over religious convictions. Seemingly incompatible beliefs are not only tolerated between their respective adherents, but routinely negotiated within a single individual. Macfarlane suggests that due to a number of circumstances the Japanese have managed to transform the core of both Buddhism and Confucianism while integrating them into everyday life.[140] Though Confucianism had its influence on social stratification, stressing harmony and compliance with traditional expectations, it seems that both Shinto and Buddhism had a more comprehensive influence on everyday life. This is visible in the rituals that celebrate, and show deference to, the Shintu *kami* and their Buddhist counterparts, *hotoke* (ancestors, dead people, enlightened ones).[141] Interestingly, ethnographic research suggests that these rituals are not based on *beliefs about* either Shinto or Buddhism, but rather produce an *embodied moral order* grounded in a variety of reiterative ritual actions.[142] One can argue that all beliefs are ultimately grounded in some form of interaction, but the Japanese intercourse with *kami* and *hotoke* seems non-intellectual and even non-spiritual in comparison with the written religious traditions that transformed both the West and most of Asia. Macfarlane compares *kami* to radio waves or electricity. He goes on: 'The difficulty of comprehending this in a monotheistic Christian context is very great since our distinctions between natural and supernatural, spirit and matter, human and divine do not apply.'[143]

This confirms what have been termed the five 'axiological orientations that are deemed to persist throughout the history of Japanese thought'.[144] First, authors underline an emphasis on 'immanence over transcendence in defining spirituality'. The spirits are somehow part of the same reality as humans, instead of being worshipped as on the other side of an ontological divide. Second, contextual pragmatism overrules and precludes the establishment of universal principles; there is an acuity and discernment in perceiving and enacting reality that flies in the face of attempts to use general propositions. Third, reason is combined with affect to provide knowledge or insight, instead of trying to separate feeling from argument. This is connected with Buddhist practices to gain knowledge of the self by preventing the suppression of emotion. Fourth, theory is formulated in conjunction with the practice to learn the theory. This ties theoretical knowledge into contexts, situations and interactions, providing a more precise attention to the singularity of its applications. Fifth, textual authority is important but there is no single authoritative text such as the Torah, the Qur'an, the Bhagavad Gita or the Analects. This rules out monolithic attempts to restrict the interpretation of one authoritative source of knowledge, insisting on the need to fit textual cogency with the complexity of daily interaction. If we can put aside the idea that kami are spirits in our sense of that term, we may come to understand how Japanese society enters the era of AI and what kind of onl*if*e world it has under construction.

6.3 JAPANESE-STYLE AI: SOFT AND SOLID

6.3.1 Ubicomp: Softwired Environments

In the past, Westerners may have contented themselves with the thought that Japan's success was based on technology transfer and imitation; although one had to admit that they often did a better job in the end. In the meantime, after excelling in quality control, the Japanese have managed to venture ahead in microelectronics,[145] robotics and ubicomp. Indeed Japanese culture, with its emphasis on situated pragmatics, its distance from textual authority and its focus on immanence, favours a more realistic approach to AI than the acontextual 'brain-in-the-vat' type of AI that reigned in the West. As indicated in previous chapters, the heyday of old-school AI with its Cartesian dreams of disembodied intelligence and top-down engineering is long gone; software has made a turn to machine learning while robotics has ventured into embodied intelligence and behavioural robotics.[146]

This has resulted in an open mind to Japanese-style AI, operating on the nexus of atoms and bits, as with ubicomp and robotics.[147] In their chapter on ubiquitous computing and interfacing technology Pfeifer and Bongard recount how in 1984 the Japanese computer scientist Ken Sakamura of the University of Tokyo started thinking about the future of computing beyond the laptop computer, developing a vision that he called 'computing everywhere'.[148] They discuss 'The Real-time Operating system Nucleus' (TRON) Intelligent House' that he built in a district of Tokyo at the end of the 1980s – a smart home incorporating invisible technologies to enable proactive and autonomic computing. Though Weiser is forever credited as the 'father' of ubiquitous computing,[149] it seems that Sakamura was already on track with his own project of calm, invisible, hidden, pervasive, everyday, sentient, amorphous computing. It is not impossible that this actually prepared the ground for what Philips and the European Commission later coined as 'Ambient Intelligence'. 'Computing everywhere' is equivalent with ubiquitous computing or ubicomp, framing the computational infrastructure for pre-emptive ICIs. Pfeifer and Bongard understand it as 'scaffolding': designing an environment for an agent, instead of the other way round. They describe it as a smart way of 'off-loading' tasks to the environment. As discussed in Chapters 2 and 3, such 'off-loading' is not new. Clark and Latour have pointed out that the usage of tools basically integrates them into our extended mind or delegates cognitive tasks to *things* that subsequently restrict or enlarge our 'action potential'.[150] However, as Pfeifer and Bongard explain, there is a key difference between the 'old ways' of involving tools and the emergence of ubicomp. The latter thrives on connectivity: 'you cannot network pans and hammers, but you can network communication devices'.[151] Adding communication devices to pans and hammers thus enables the networking of previously stand-alone devices. Another salient difference between hammers and doorknobs on the one hand and ubicomp on the other is that the latter not only augments our 'sensing' capabilities, but can also act on what it perceives.

A smart environment will thus develop its own type of sensor and perhaps even motor capabilities, turning a network of *embedded systems* into a larger autonomous system,[152] and – depending on the circumstances – into a series of *embedded agents*. In Chapters 2 and 3 I have discussed the agency characteristics of our *onlife* world as the most salient novelty as compared to what we now call our offline existence. Moving from bits to atoms adds movement and manipulation to this, coming closer to what was termed 'complete agents' in Chapter 2 above.

This brings us close to what makes ubicomp so very interesting and different. Not merely in comparison to unconnected tools, but also from the perspective of the software revolution. The general purpose computer has enabled the translation of the analogue world into a digital code that can be processed with great ease, thanks to the invention of the tubes, transistors and integrated circuits that embed the bits and bytes generated by computer programs. This has afforded an entirely novel type of ICI, with real-time remote communication, decision and control mechanisms, based on unprecedented predictive analyses and the simulation of highly complex processes. It has indeed generated highly abstract theories of information that tend to Platonic understandings of information as the holy grail for understanding reality, deeply committed to mathematical renderings of the real. Often, data are equated with information and whatever pattern is detected in the data is assumed to be relevant for real life. The so-called information revolution, however, has flooded us with data instead of information, triggering awareness that data is not necessarily information. Similarly, at some point even the most enthusiastic Big Data aficionado will have to admit that inferences drawn from all this data must be tested against the resistance of real-life circumstances. The implementation of ubicomp is part of a return from bits to atoms. It wires software into the hardware of our physical environment, as it turns individual things into parts of a distributed hardware system. It does not really make one's fridge smart, but connects the fridge with a distributed multi-agent system that turns it into a component of a smart home, a smart energy network, a remote healthcare system, or a smart grocery delivery system – though these may overlap or even compete for the fridge's attention. By softwiring our things into adaptive systems the difference between bits and atoms becomes even more artificial. The software (bits) that was always already embedded in chips and circuits (atoms) meets the 'stuff' (atoms) of our environment that is reconfigured as part of a larger system, based on any kind of software (bits). Full circle.

It may be that Japanese involvement in ubicomp is somehow connected with a sensitivity to animated things that is out of bounds for the Western mind. Though *kami* cannot be equated with artificial agents, they induce expectations with regard to the 'thingness' of our surroundings, infesting things, concepts and beings with intentions that can be foreseen and influenced, though not controlled. This is a disposition we need in the onli*fe* world. It is even more obvious in the case of robotics.

6.3.2   New Robotics: Solid Encounters with Compliant Others

As a matter of fact, the difference between ubicomp and robotics is less absolute than it was before the ubiquity of interconnectedness. Especially if we take the advent of cloud robotics into account, where a robot connects with the cloud to access Big Data or to receive an update of its operating system, the difference becomes more subtle. One could even say that advanced stages of ubicomp turn most devices into robots that connect with one or more smart systems. Robots have been defined as:[153]

> a machine designed to execute one or more tasks repeatedly, with speed and precision. There are as many different types of robots as there are tasks for them to perform.

Robots operate in the physical world, though some would include webbots (software agents) under the general heading of robots. The definition above seems to include all automated machines, even when operated by a human being. In that sense a car – an auto-mobile – is a fine example of a first generation robot, while some would add that robots must be electro-mechanical devices to qualify as such. Others may want to restrict the term to those machines that are controlled by a central processing unit capable of representing the environment and producing adequate behaviour based on that. Even more advanced, one can require that for a device to be named a robot it must be capable of learning behaviour based on its navigation in the physical world. And, finally, public perception tends to associate robots with physical machines that look like humans or animals, giving the impression of autonomous action.

   I would side with roboticists like Pfeifer and Bongard, who find that contemporary robotics is no longer an attempt to program human behaviour into a machine, but an endeavour to build 'complete agents' that require what they call 'design for emergence'. In Chapter 2 this was discussed as the most ambitious form of artificial agency. It fits with the approach of robot developers like Rodney Brooks, who initiated 'behavioural robotics', and built one of the most successful consumer robots ever: the autonomic vacuum cleaner Roomba. Based on the same approach, Brooks' MIT start-up 'Rethinking Robots' has built Baxter, an example of collaborative robotics aiming to make robots that can safely interact with human colleagues on the work floor. Behavioural robotics is focused on fabricating machines that are *mobile* in an intuitive manner, capable of *manipulating* objects without crushing or dropping them, while interacting with a world that is fundamentally *messy*, instead of merely operating in the constraint environment of a laboratory or factory. The idea is that real-time navigation outside the laboratory requires *morphological computation* instead of the numerical representation that underlies control by a central processing unit. Numerical computation in a central control unit takes too much time to guide real-time mobility in the physical world, since it is based on representing the world by means of computational models followed by calculations of the consequences of alternative behaviours. Too much calculation on data sets, too many complicated mediations. Living beings are embodied in a way that enables smooth movements, well fitted to their particular niche. The 'design' of their material embodiment – the shape, elasticity, texture and friction of the material they are made of – takes into account the physical constraints of their environment, including gravity, wind, light, and so on. This makes possible direct interactions between body and world, without a need for complex calculations. For example, recent experiments with soft robotics show how designing robots with compliant, flexible materials emancipates robots from the limited degrees of freedom (DOF) that have so far determined their capabilities for mobility and manipulation. The limited DOFs of conventional robotics explain why they are generally stiff and slow. Morphological computation thus integrates two advantages over numerical computation:[154]

> [I]t is well known that some problems are numerically more difficult than others and that this difficulty may have nothing to do with the intrinsic properties of the problem.
>
> [c]onventional computing requires the encoding of the whole of the relevant physics. A morphological control process, by contrast, can exploit the fact that the physical system used to perform the computation already incorporates the physics.

By designing for morphological computation we can, first, prevent investing time and money in computational problems that are not related to the problem we want to solve, but only with its numerical translation, and second, delegate problem-solving to the shape and texture of the embedded system, plus third, I would add, morphological computation can prevent harm to human beings that encounter robots, by using compliant instead of rigid materials.

Baxter combines numerical with morphological computation that can be used in a workplace setting where humans interact with robots; it extends the mainstream implementations of industrial robotics, which depend on a predictable nonhuman environment. Next to industrial robotics we now have the promise of service robots (for instance in healthcare) and companion robots. Service robots require safe interaction with humans, for instance when lifting or feeding an elderly person, or when a robot is employed in the context of surgery. In these cases soft robotics enables the leapfrogging into mass employment of mobile robots capable of adapting tactile interaction to the vulnerability of the human body. The most far-reaching challenge is in 'social robotics', which requires both sensitivity to the risk of physical harm and fluency in human machine interaction (HMI).

Japan has been ahead in the development and usage of robots in everyday life.[155] One of Japan's most famous robots, the *manga* and *anime* character Tetsuwan Atomu (Astroboy) is depicted as an amiable and benign companion for its human friends. Apart from industrial robots, Japanese manufacturers have developed a number of famous humanoids (Asimo) and robot companions (Aibo, Paro). Some authors date the Japanese interest in robots to the mechanical dolls (*karakuri ningyo*), crafted during the Edo Period, while I have already pointed to ancient Shinto and Buddhist practices in relation to animated things, that may have enabled a more smooth integration of robots into everyday life. These practices do not necessarily assume beliefs in specific religious dogmas. They do, however, provide for concrete bodily operations that enable interactions with things, animals, ideas and ancestors usually reserved for humans in the West. In Japan, industrial robots have been taken up in ritual consecration, given names or flowers, even qualifying – according to some – for attaining Buddhahood.[156] Japanese enthusiasm and affection for robots contrasts with the Western reception of robots, where they are generally understood within a rationalist utilitarian framework. For the West, smart technologies are tools, means to ends that are determined by humans. In a Memorandum for the National Science Foundation, Shinohara observed about the Japanese:[157]

> Rather, they deal with these robots as pets and friends. Thus, whereas robots are seen as [a] 'labor source' in the western world, in Japan they are being treated like living things with which humans work or live together.

As indicated in the previous chapter, the Western tradition of moral philosophy dictates that only human beings qualify as addressees and 'addressants' of the Kantian categorical imperative: only humans should never be treated as merely a means to an end.[158] The flipside of the Kantian moral standard is that we can treat nonhumans as merely a means to an end. Thus, the categorical imperative supports utilitarianism in dealings with nonhumans. This may not be evident in a culture that feeds on *kami* worship, and on Buddhist negation of the self, that is seen as an illusion standing in the way of enlightenment. It may be interesting to recall the five axiological orientations mentioned above to describe Japanese culture. The lesser emphasis on authoritative text and transcendence, coupled with contextual pragmatism and integration of reason and affect, as well as the idea of theory as a practice all soften the demarcation lines between nature and culture, human and nonhuman, spiritual and everyday life. Technology is not just mediation, but more easily encountered as an 'other' that invites something like respect and discernment. This could have as a consequence that the construction of smart technologies is seen as a challenge that evokes awe and alertness rather than fear or exultation.[159] At the same time, Japanese consumers may connect more easily with the thrill of new types of companionship, based on playful experimentation.

This is easier in the case of solid encounters, with identifiable – robotic – agents, than with distributed softwired ubicomp environments. The same goes for the surge in wearable smart devices that are used as gateways and interfaces to the onli*fe* world: from smart phones to smart watches, glasses and clothing that enable augmented reality, access to SNSs and self-quantification with regard to biometric behavioural data for health and sports monitoring. These devices, other than human implants, can be encountered, reset, thrown away, unplugged, tweaked. They are visible and external, they mediate our relationships with the onli*fe* world, but we can also stop and check the mediator. However, we should not be misled. Both robots and wearables are most often connected with service providers and third parties in the cloud; they will be updated automatically and despite their embeddedness they necessarily hide the complexity of their extended mind. By default, they will mostly be connected with the digital unconscious of Big Data Space.

The question is how this relates to the notion of privacy and what can be learnt from the Japanese intercourse with others: family, work, friends, ancestors, animals or things.

6.4 PRIVACY AS BORDER CONTROL IN JAPANESE CULTURE

6.4.1 The 'Inbetween' (*Aida*)

One way of looking at Japanese culture is by stressing the primacy of what has been called the 'inbetween' (*aida*) of human beings (*ningen*), which is seen as constitutive of both individuals and their society (*ningen*).[160] The word for both human beings and society consists of two Chinese characters: *nin* for human and *gen* for between.[161] This 'in-between' is a space, often depicted as an emptiness that nourishes both the selves and the society they originate in and depend on. Although it might be tempting to qualify the relational conception of the self that is inherent in this perspective as collectivist, this is not necessarily implied. As discussed in the previous chapters, Western philosophy and cognitive science have developed similar notions of relational selves, without denying the importance of individual minds.[162] On the other hand, we need not be blind to the fact that in the course of Japanese history this 'inbetween' has often been monopolized by entities such as the state, which had an interest in generating compliance from its subjects. To the extent that such monopolization succeeds,[163] the individual may indeed have less room to (re)negotiate her borders and may thus 'have' less of what we qualify as privacy. But this by no means follows from the priority of the 'inbetween' and would actually violate the emptiness it protects. In Western democratic theory similar notions of an empty 'inbetween' have been developed, for instance by Claude Lefort, who notes the importance of recognizing the place of sovereign power as an 'empty place' that – within a modern democracy – can no longer be fully occupied or monopolized by one person or one party.[164]

Apart from monopolization by the state, the members of the particular group a person belongs to may also impose themselves by crowding the empty space of the 'inbetween'. This goes for a person's next of kin, colleagues or others. Arendt's apprehension of 'the social' and Mill's warnings against the tyranny of public opinion caution against the impact of social pressure. Especially those who are higher ranked may take advantage of their position, disturbing the fragility of the 'inbetween'. In both cases we must, however, remember that these are violations of a space that makes and breaks both the individual and her *Welt*. Below, the significance of belonging to specific groups and of discerning rank will be further discussed under the heading of *basho*.

The concept of the 'inbetween' offers a fresh perspective on the pitfalls of pre-emptive infrastructures. By acting on inferred future or even on inferred current behaviours, such infrastructures may destroy the emptiness of the space that holds us apart while constituting us, creating the critical aperture for reinvention of the self. Pre-emptive computing stocks and occupies the 'inbetween' with projections and inferences to which we have little access, while they reconfigure the onli*fe* world we navigate. Though the 'inbetween' is always a stage for projections and inferences, the danger sits in the overfill and the overdetermination of computational decision-systems that pre-empt our intent. Like the tyranny of either a state or social pressure, these infrastructures are prone to colonize the 'inbetween'. We urgently need to invent new ways to prevent any such colonization, as we did with regard to the state as well as social control.

6.4.2 Politeness as 'Face' or 'Place' (*Basho*)

Let's hold on to the fundamental empty space of 'inbetweenness' while investigating another approach to Japanese border control, namely that of politeness. Mainstream theory on comparative politeness practices has been based on Goffman's notion of 'face'.[165] This is especially relevant here, because the concept of privacy as boundary negotiation is sometimes based on Goffman's notions of 'face' and 'role'.[166] Within 'politeness theory' 'face' has been defined as both positive 'face', that is, the wish to be desirable by at least some others and as negative 'face', that is, the wish not to have one's actions constrained by others. Positive 'face' thus has some Hegelian overtones, highlighting our need for recognition or *Anerkennung*, while negative 'face' assumes a cross-cultural wish for personal autonomy and control over one's own actions. Politeness is then seen as behaviour that aims to redress a potential threat to either positive or negative 'face' *of the other*. It is a matter of saving the face of one's fellows. As such, it provides a highly ritualized way of accommodating the need for recognition as well the need to act freely. It seems a 'manner' of not imposing oneself on others while also showing respect. To the extent that privacy is a relational conception, politeness can be seen as the duty to protect the privacy of others, or the duty not to violate their borders, taking into account that since politeness is an institutionalized pattern of behaviour it has some 'objectivity' and does not merely depend on good intentions. In a culture that emphasizes the 'inbetween' (*aida*) of human relationships as constitutive for individual action as well as society, politeness may protect this 'inbetween' rather than merely the individual's need for recognition and autonomy. In other words, the protection may concern the group to which the one addressed belongs, since the 'inbetweenness' on which this person feeds occurs within that group.

A more specifically Japanese analysis of politeness can be found by investigating the concept of *basho* (place) as pivotal for understanding politeness practices in Japan. Investigations into *basho* suggest that the concept of 'face', as a cross-cultural instrument of comparison, does not explain Japanese politeness practices. Haugh, for instance, has suggested that Japanese politeness can better be understood in terms of a sense of 'place', because the notions of personal autonomy and individual control are not necessarily part of Japanese culture.[167] Haugh distinguishes between two types of *basho*, namely location (*tokoro*, *uchi*) and position (*ichi*, *tachiba*). Location (*tokoro* or *uchi*) refers to the fact that interacting individuals are – or are not – part of the same group (work, family, nation), whereas position (*ichi* or *tachiba*) refers to the hierarchical relations between partners (boss-employee, father-son, emperor-subject). One's sense of place, then, depends on whoever one is communicating with or about, in which context, in whose presence: first, does it concern a person from the same or another social group; and, second, does it concern a person of lower, equal or higher rank? Such ranking is in fact inherent in Japanese language: '[a]ll Japanese verb endings must denote relative rank. Even if two people are exactly equal in age, social status and gender, they are forced to speak as if the other is their inferior or superior'.[168] Instead of being focused exclusively on the individual needs of one's partner in communication, the Japanese concept of politeness stresses the relational aspects of another's identity: inclusion in a particular group and ranking within or between groups.[169] The sensitivity to one's in-group should not be equated with collectivism in any straightforward sense of the word. What is required in politeness is an acute responsiveness to a highly situational context; since people are part of a number of groups and fulfil a number of roles within these groups, both the location (inclusion) and the position (ranking) vary per situation. It depends on who is talking to whom, in what context and also, crucially, on who else are present. For instance, whereas speaking truth to power may be entirely unacceptable within the domain of the office, it may be desirable and accepted after work during drinks with one's colleagues and boss, though not when members of another group (company) are present.[170] The emphasis on a variety of communities rather than a separate individual has been coined as 'groupism' with regard to Japan. If we manage to avoid mistaken beliefs in rigid collectivism, the idea of something like 'groupism' may help to understand how privacy relates to individuals that depend on dynamic attachments to a variety of groups. Alas, the idea of Japanese 'groupism' or *shudan-shugi* has been used to explain the success of the Japanese economy in the 1980s, based on a misconceived romantic and holistic rendition of Japanese culture.[171]

To make sense of the way the Japanese anticipate the required level of deference – while steering clear of romantic renderings – contextual pragmatism offers some interesting clues: both 'groupism' and ranking require an unceasing, situational and acute discernment (*wakimae*) that feeds on a combination of tacit background knowledge and wakeful attention. Just like in the case of *Shinto* and Buddhist ritual practices, Japanese politeness may not depend on extensive *beliefs* regarding stratification. Instead such stratification is *produced and maintained* in a permanent dynamic reiteration of interaction patterns. The fact that beliefs about these interactions are neither primary nor explicit, however, does not imply that they are neutral or innocent or do not involve power relationships. The philosophy of 'as-if' that is inherent in the complexity of role play that pervades Japanese society may end up reinforcing existing stratification. As one author noted, this would amount to a philosophy of 'as-is',[172] violating the subtle difference between a performance and a straightjacket. By taking a pragmatic view, Western observers of Japanese politeness rituals should at least avoid projecting their own need for reasons and beliefs, when trying to explain them.

The hyperconnectivity of the onli*fe* world affords dynamic relationships with people within and without the groupings that incorporate us; it enables us to initiate and develop new, transformative online communities that extend into the 'offline' world, thus grounding the experience of an onli*fe* integration. New manners of discernment must be discovered, invented and learned as people increasingly opt in and out of hybrid groupings that mix face-to-face with electronic communication. Though deference may sound like an out-dated concept of the feudal era, a keen awareness of power and authority is required to navigate the chemistry of hyperconnectivity and pre-emptive computing. Losing discernment as to power and status does not imply that relationships of power and authority are no longer at play. On the contrary, these relationships now emerge from the hidden complexity of the computational infrastructures that surround us. They are mostly invisible and harder to scrutinize. Perhaps we can learn from the awareness of implicit belongings and the tacit sensitivity to power and rank that is pivotal in Japanese society, as it may also teach us how to protect ourselves against the unspoken colonization of the 'inbetween'.

6.4.3   Situated Discernment (*Wakimae*) and the Culture of 'As-If'

In the context of the Japanese concept of online privacy the notion of situated discernment is pivotal:[173]

> There is no neutral ground, one must always consciously construct a self appropriate to the situation.

This, for instance, explains why a business card is so important for a Japanese person. It reveals whether the other is part of one's group and how she should be ranked: 'it gives the clues as to what "self" is called for'.[174] This clearly indicates that Japanese thinking does not assume one integrated and coherent self that remains the same self in any context. Navigating Japanese settings requires a repertoire of different selves, always tuned to the situation at hand. This nicely fits with Agre and Rotenberg's definition of privacy as the freedom from unreasonable constraints on the construction of one's own identity. Though this definition can be interpreted as a portrayal of negative 'face', freedom from external constraints, assuming a sovereign self in full control of its own identity, the definition seems more in line with a relational and interdependent notion of the self. In that case privacy protection goes well with the protection of a constitutive 'inbetween' that requires effective constraints for identity to emerge, but also warrants the rejection of unreasonable constraints that overrule the construction of the self. Both concepts of self ('inbetweenness' and 'identity construction') share an emphasis on the reconstructive and dynamic nature of the self, which is neither seen as a given substance nor as a set of properties or attributes that uniquely describes a person.

Some authors have differentiated between descriptive privacy, that is the extent to which an environment happens to afford privacy, and normative privacy, that is the extent to which the social framework instantiates privacy as a social norm.[175] Noting that in Japan people often live close to each other, with thin walls that allow their fellows to overhear intimate exchanges (thus apparently affording little privacy), a strong form of normative privacy is called for. It requires that people refrain from imposing on each other by acting 'as-if' they have not overheard, seen or understood whatever is considered inappropriate. The *Welt* instituted within the Japanese context thus entails a duty to respect the privacy of others by either simulating ignorance or interiorizing a kind of normative veil that hides information that should not be disclosed.[176] For example:[177]

The as-if tradition requires that information overheard but not explicitly given, is treated as if one did not have it. This allowed, for example, spouses to have arguments without the rest of the household treating them as though their marriage was in trouble, unless one or both partners approached a third party for help or advice in the matter.

Obviously, for people to feel safe with having their information disclosed to others who are obligated to act 'as-if' they have no access to the information, there must be an elementary level of trust between them. This trust depends on the extent to which the relevant others are part of one's own group. This raises important issues when privacy comes to depend on the willingness of those outside one's own group to refrain from sharing the information.

Adams, Murata and Orito provide an interesting framework to understand how this dependence works out, while also explaining how people protect their informational privacy against people they had better not trust.[178] To begin with, the authors introduce the *uchi/soto* model of Japanese relationships that refers to inclusion (*uchi*) and exclusion (*soto*) in the context of one's social group (family, colleagues). Next, they explain the *honne/tatemae* model of speech that refers to truthful (*honne*) and deceitful (*tatemae*) talk. To protect oneself against undesirable sharing of information, a person can engage in deceitful talk. Outside a trusted relationship such deceit is not necessarily considered shameful. Finally, they discuss the *ura/omote* model of the self that refers to, respectively, one's core identity (*ure*) and one's projected image (*omote*).[179] This seems to connect with Goffman's distinction between frontstage and backstage behaviour.[180] Adams, Murata and Orito summarize their threefold model by saying that:[181]

> Omote is the identity or personality presented by tatemae speech to soto individuals, while ura is the identity or personality presented by honne speech to uchi individuals.

The authors add that:[182]

> acceptance of the necessity of, a lack of total openness in communciation is reflected in the social meaning of the Japanese word *uso* (lie) which lacks the significant negative connotation of the word in English ...

Their model of *uchi/soto* is both nuanced and dynamic, it differentiates *watashi* (self), *miuchi* (family), *uchi* (inside), liminal, *soto* (outside) and *tanin* (everything else, even beyond the outside). With people categorized as *miuchi* and *uchi* there is a basic trust, which allows people to safely communicate their feelings,[183] whereas in dealing with people considered *soto*, a person will be careful to share only the appropriate information, using honorific forms. Davies and Ikono observe how people preserve their privacy within the closeness of *uchi* relationships by 'simply staying together' without explicitly sharing their thoughts: 'They should not know what the others are thinking even though they know what the others are doing.'[184] *Soto* refers to others that are not part of one of the groups one identifies with; these others may for instance be part of competing groups. *Tanin*, however, refers to strangers that do not concern one, since there is no connection at all.

In the context of hyperconnectivity, the difference between *soto* and *tanin* seems crucial. Because people categorized as *tanin* are seen as entirely irrelevant, there is no fear of sharing information with them. Adams, Murata and Orito noted that many young Japanese shared personal information on the Internet, assuming that they were dealing with either *uchi* (friends) or *tanin* (others). Therefore they abstained from *tatemae* speech (part of the 'as-if' culture) and thus forgot to protect themselves against possible abuse. Similar confusion was apparent with young Japanese exposing their private thoughts in webdiaries.[185] Normally, *tatemae* would function as a kind of privacy protection, not based on the respectful 'as-if' behaviours of one's *uchi*, but based on one's own 'facade', on one's own 'as-if' behaviours in relation to one's *soto*. But in so far as users of online social networks believe they are dealing with disinterested strangers, they fail to protect themselves. This is not specific to Japanese users. All over the world people have been learning how to segregate their audiences. As briefly discussed under the heading of privacy in section 5.2.2, research shows that young Facebook users have developed intricate and dynamic privacy strategies, by changing their privacy settings in relation to the targeted audience of their postings.[186] Facebook has indeed become a reputation management system, used to project the intended *omote* or frontstage persona. However, this regards only one's peers, friends of friends, parents or potential employers. Awareness of whatever the social network provider 'does' with the postings, or with one's clickstream behaviour on the network, is absent. Not only Japanese users, but most of us do not care, considering these providers to be *tanin*. This results in a lack of protection, as was extensively discussed in the preceding chapter. Recognizing the cogency of the difference between *soto* and *tanin* may add to the salience of the difference between what has been termed 'social' and 'institutional' privacy. 'Social' privacy plays out between peers or others that one is somehow familiar with, whereas 'institutional privacy' concerns the relation with organizations that we have little personal contact with, such as social network providers, telecom providers, data brokers, government agencies, and advertising networks. One of the most arduous challenges of the *onlife* world thus resides in coping with the invisible collection, sale and processing of personal data by one's *tanin*, notably by the software of largely invisible corporations and governmental departments.

6.4.4 The Indulgence of Restraint and Acuity: *Amae* and *Enryo-sasshi*

The last form of border control I want to discuss is concerned with the concepts of *amae* and *enryo-sasshi*, as originally coined by Doi, a Japanese psycho-analyst who wrote extensively about *uchi/soto*, *honne/tatemae* and *ura/omote*.[187] Here I will focus on *amae* as a conceptual tool to understand the regulation of communication within the intimate sphere (*uchi*), allowing for a measure of frankness that is not encouraged between more distant relationships (*soto*). The concept of *amae* builds on:[188]

> the cravings of a newborn child for close contact with its mother, and in the broader sense, the desire to deny the fact of separation that is an inevitable part of human existence and to obliterate the pain that this separation involves.

The term refers to a relationship of dependence and is usually translated as 'presumed indulgence', indicating that a measure of frankness is 'safe' within one's own group. This would, for instance, imply the trust that those who overhear quarrels in a home due to the thinness of the walls will not abuse this knowledge and actually show restraint (*enryo*). This may even entail a denial of the fact that conversations have been overheard.

The idea is that *amae* has two dimensions, one being 'a lubricant of self-assertion' and the other being 'a facilitator of *enryo-sasshi*'.[189] *Enryo* stands for constraint or indirect communication and *sasshi* can be understood as a particular type of mind-reading: picking up what is intended even though it has not been directly expressed. As such, both *enryo* and *sasshi* connect to politeness and privacy as they protect the other's intimate feelings and expressions by means of a simultaneous recognition (*sasshi*) and non-disclosure (*enryo*).

Obviously, indirect communication, which can only be successful if coupled with acute discernment, is not unique to Japan. To the extent that this type of communication is used to promote the myth of a Japanese enigma, we must be careful not to engage in naïve essentialism. However, the practice of a complex pattern of openness within the safety of *uchi* contacts, alternating with restraint as well as *tatemae* speech in relation to members of other groups, has been refined to a level that is not common in many other cultures. In that sense there is a uniqueness to Japanese privacy practices, which do not depend on written laws but emerge from an oral culture, emphasizing attention to the here-and-now (mindfulness), situational pragmatics, and a sensitivity to reason as well as affect (discernment, acuity or *wakimae*). Mutual trust is not merely a matter of reading another's concerns, but also of reading them correctly and of making 'fine discriminations in recognizing limits in "caring for", and to make just the right response to those concerns'.[190]

Again, we may learn from the subtle manners of Japanese protection against invasion of the self. The challenge would be to investigate whether the computing systems that ground the on*life* world are capable of discernment and restraint: can they act 'as if' they have not read us? Can they actively forget what they should not have heard? Is this a technical question on how to reconfigure the affordance of the ICI, or do we need legal injunctions to carry the day?

6.5   PRIVACY: AFFORDANCE, DUTY OR INDIVIDUAL RIGHT

6.5.1   Robotic and Ubicomp Others

Smart technologies, at least those displaying agent-characteristics, necessarily develop their own border control. To the extent that they are designed for emergence, they will learn to sustain themselves, challenging the salience of Asimov's Laws of Robotics. His Three Laws of Robotics were:[191]

> A robot may not injure a human being or, through inaction, allow a human being to come to harm.

> A robot must obey any orders given to it by human beings, except where such orders would conflict with the First Law.

> A robot must protect its own existence as long as such protection does not conflict with the First or Second Law.

Though the first law seems laudable, its meaning is unclear if a robot is no longer entirely programmed. Does it, in that case, have a choice to ignore the 'law', just like its human counterparts? What if a self-driving car has to choose between driving forward and potentially driving into a bus with school children and avoiding the collision by driving its owner into the wall? The second law seems to assume that humans are in full control, which is no longer the case if smart technologies are designed to come up with unforeseeable solutions. Does this mean that robots are to be treated as Hegel's dog (disciplined into compliance),[192] or should we accept the possibility that they will develop an 'own' moral sense and demand emancipation from serfdom? Similar questions are raised by the third law, as it presumes the salience of the first and second.

The previous chapters have made clear that the implications of agent characteristics make a difference for privacy. Smart technologies are capable of anticipating us and of acting upon that, to test the accuracy of their anticipation. This is a novel situation, since we are not used to being anticipated by artefacts. In terms of an extended mind, it seems that we may become the cognitive resource of robotic systems and other types of ubicomp. This obviously makes a difference in terms of privacy, because the extent to which these technologies can cross our borders is extended exponentially. On top of that, we have not yet developed the interfaces and interactions that allow us to anticipate how we are being anticipated. We are in the dark, which may in fact eradicate our privacy, even if we don't know it.

The response given above is typical for my Western mind-set or *Welt*. The idea of animated artefacts that 'know' about me (by learning from their interactions with me, combined with tapping into the digital unconscious) is novel and raises fears about manipulation. I may feel apprehensive about taking an 'intentional stance' towards nonhumans, reserving both autonomy and intrinsic value for rational subjects. Japanese consumers may have less problems here, because they are less dogmatic about separating nature and culture and they are already 'in the habit' of respecting nonhumans as beings that matter beyond their utility.

In having an open mind they can more easily make room for a novel 'inbetween', now between themselves and their robot companions, ready to feed on the interaction they generate. They may develop intuitions for the extent to which smart devices or infrastructures must be considered as *uchi*, *soto* or *tanin*, instigating a sense of place (*basho*) and a measure of discernment (*wakimae*). In so far as they qualify these devices or the infrastructure as part of *soto*, they may practise *tatamae* speech and emulate the as-if culture to protect their own intimate sphere. And similarly, they might design *enryo* (restraint) into their technological companions, in order for them not to impose themselves.

6.5.2   Forcing Robots and Ubicomp to NOT 'Read' Us

I am aware of being speculative here. I have not done any empirical research into Japanese intercourse with either ubicomp or robotics. This is not a tractate on the sociology of Japanese attitudes towards artificial intelligence, which would actually raise the question of who is doing the observation and how she is qualifying what she observes in terms that may be familiar to sociology but irrelevant in the *Welt* she is describing. My interest resides in tracing alternative understandings of the relationship between humans and things in a *Welt* that is radically different from our own, while still being familiar. My knowledge of this alternative understanding is based on relevant literature, but most of all, it is part of a thought-experiment. What if we were open to *things* as beings that have some kind of power over us and deserve some kind of respect? And what if we had no individual right to privacy, but developed patterns of interaction that protected the 'inbetween' as well as our individual selves and the *Welt* we would share? What if, in this particular *Welt*, we develop a singular acuity in reading each other's gestures and utterances and display a distinctive restraint when encountering another? The acuity is critical because we protect ourselves against invasion by means of *tatamae* speech and acting 'as if', which requires a discernment beyond the explicit and the obvious in those subjected to such speech and performance. What does it mean that we expect both discernment and restraint in our significant others? This expectation is not based on legal entitlement but on a deeply ingrained persuasive normativity, which cannot be enforced in a court of law.

When ubicomp and robots invade the social space by calculating moods, emotions, preferences, inclinations and capabilities, one can see them as *tanin*, *soto* or *uchi*. Ubicomp environments are difficult to address as such or even to identify as an agent. Perhaps the embedded systems that tap into the cloud to form a smart environment will be somewhat identifiable as the entities that pre-empt us and help us to navigate the onli*fe* world. A fridge, a PDA, the remote control for the heating system and the software that summarizes a report for its reader could at some point be addressed as others that must be convinced, ordered, reset or tweaked. This is even more likely in the case of companion or care robots. We tend to attribute intention to such entities, get attached to them, give them a name and welcome them into the family *(uchi)*. If most people name their Roomba,[193] we can be pretty sure about this for the robot that carries us to bed. Taking the intentional stance is not a bad thing, as it implies awareness that the 'other' is involved in anticipating our behaviours. This awareness is urgently required to start coping with emergent artificial agency all over the onli*fe* world. However, I see two caveats. First, awareness that things display something like intentional behaviour does not imply understanding of what goes on behind the screen, in the backend system, so the say. The intent on the side of the embedded systems is mindless and once it builds on Big Data it will not be so easy to figure out. Second, this awareness may lead to a kind of trust that fits with *uchi*, whereas the service providers that can access one's dealings with the ubicomp systems or the robots should be understood as *soto*. As recounted, seeing the mindless agents as *tanin* would also be a mistake. Despite being strangers, the service providers and third parties involved are not disinterested – business models are built on one's data and profiles.

Would it be possible to design these devices as mindless agents so as to incorporate both acuity (*sasshi*) and restraint (*enryo*)? To have them guess their onli*fe* human companions while restricting their access to what they have inferred? Could they be engineered in a manner that forces them NOT to read their user, consumer, patient, client, or however the human is qualified, unless and to the extent permitted in the relevant context? Can these embedded systems be forced to forget or anonymize inferences that can be used to manipulate their human counterparts? I believe these are interesting challenges, that can only be articulated if we take into account, first that these companions, systems or environments develop agency, whereas, second, they are – for now – mindless. With mind I refer to the capability to attribute meaning based on human language and self-consciousness. Perhaps we must add the capability of suffering, even if it sounds queer to qualify this as a capability. Without the experience of suffering, empathy remains a simulation. Though pain does not imply self-consciousness it is probably a part of consciousness, which depends on a central nervous system. Animals with such a system exhibit behaviour that signals their capacity to experience pain. As such, pain would then also be a necessary condition for self-consciousness, noting that it is the self-consciousness that transforms and extends pain into suffering, adding reflection. Ubicomp environments and robots may come to simulate emotional states, or even pain, but without conscious-ness – let alone self-consciousness – the acuity and the restraint we can program into their system remain 'as if'. In so far as this works to protect us, that is fine. But we should not confuse 'as if' with 'as is'.

6.5.3 The Need for an Individual Right

If another person shows restraint, while displaying acuity, she respects my privacy. I will enjoy the substance of privacy: 'the freedom from unreasonable constraints on the building of my identity'. This can be seen as a gift, in so far as she had the power to invade my space and cross my boundaries. She may not have provided this gift as a matter of doing whatever she liked best, since she may have felt obliged to me, to her self and society. Respecting my privacy may have been a moral duty that she takes seriously. If I had a legal right to privacy, which I could have enforced if needed, there would be no gift. The moral duty to respect the 'inbetween' would have disappeared from view, taken over by the legal obligation to refrain from violating my right. Within a trusting relationship we may depend on the moral duty and the gift of privacy, though power imbalances might displace such trust. Beyond the trust network, however, it becomes more risky to depend on a gift; we may require more resilience to negotiate non-interference. To enjoy the substance of privacy in that wider context, I must be willing to use violence to defend it. Or, in another setting, I may have to pay for my privacy.

It is interesting to speak of ethics, codes of conduct or self-regulation. Moral philosophy may come up with a number of good reasons to require that people behave ethically correctly, respect the autonomy of their fellows and refrain from violating shared values or rationally inferred moral rules. In the context of power relationships a gift of privacy is laudable, and we may applaud those who manage to negotiate their privacy against whoever intends to disrespect it. In the context of a hierarchical institution, such as the state, it could be even more difficult to obtain the substance of privacy if its obstruction pleases the sovereign. Enlightened despotism has been described as the state where one is dependent on 'le bon plaisir du prince'; though the prince can be good, he is free to be bad. And, to be honest, his idea of what is good may not be your idea of the same. A company may claim that its motto is 'Don't do evil', but who gets to decide what is evil here? The CEO, the employers, or the customer – or whoever suffers the consequences of its operations?

This is where the law comes in and the notion of an individual legal right that can be enforced if necessary. I sometimes find that we take this notion for granted to an extent that makes us exceedingly vulnerable. Actually having individual rights is not self-evident, and it will require robust institutions and hard work for such rights to be sustainable in the onli*fe* world. If we do not insist on preserving and protecting the law as an architecture of coercive authority, its current system of checks and balances will not survive the rise of pre-emptive computing. Those who abhor any type of authority forget that human rights, such as privacy, depend on the authority of the modern state for their enforcement. This has been called the paradox of the Rule of Law: we can call upon the state to protect us against the state, and to require that same state to protect us against powerful players that violate our privacy. The division of internal sovereignty has made this possible. We should not do away with it until we have found and tested other mechanisms to protect individual human beings from dictatorial or totalitarian regimes, whether instituted by people or their mindless smart machines.

The notion and practice of individual rights are historical artefacts. Not a universal property of human society, or an achievement that will stay with us no matter what. The idea of an individual rights-holder, as opposed to a clan, person or institution bound by a social, religious or moral duty, is relatively new.[194] It shifts the attention from the addressee of a duty to the holder of rights. It has a history, the beginning of which was written down by Hugo Grotius, the Dutch lawyer who authored two famous tractates, on the laws of war and on the law of the sea. Grotius' perspective was that of natural law, that is, a law that naturally follows from human reason. Writing in the beginning of the 17th century, his choice for human reason was an innovation. By attaching natural law to human reason instead of divine reason or revelation, he laid the groundwork for the architecture of the Peace of Westphalia (1648) that instituted the system of internal and external sovereignty as two sides of the same coin. It was the era of the religious wars in Europe, in dire need of a secular system of states bound by international law to respect each other's external sovereignty (recognizing states as equivalent legal subjects) and internal sovereignty (prohibiting interference in internal affairs, such as religion). Grotius went on to discriminate between perfect and imperfect rights, depending on whether a right can be enforced or merely determines the legitimacy of a claim. We should remember, however, that thinking in terms of individual right-holders was novel and – once part of the *Welt* of the modern era – it created a new social order. The idea of the social contract as a pact between free individuals that decide to institute a government over themselves, is contingent on the idea of natural rights that can be exchanged for personal safety and public welfare. The move from natural law, based on human reason, to positive law, based on the authority of the state, is grounded in the social contract, whether theorized as a historical fact or hypothetical postulate.

Individual rights emerged as ideas in the writing of Grotius, Locke and other Enlightenment thinkers. They were used in the French Revolution to leverage a new social contract in the form of a written constitution that tied the sovereign to the law. Of course, in so far as the sovereign was the nation, the law could not provide protection against a legislator that was allowed to interpret his own law. Similarly, in so far as the state could exercise its own subjective right in the realm of administration, individual rights were limited to those emanating from private law. The next innovative move, which made individual rights effective against the state, was the institution of independent courts capable of overruling both the legislator and the administration. Without such independence individual rights remain contingent upon 'le bon plaisir du prince', or, in the case of democracy, on majoritarian benevolence.

I once asked my audience whether they would prefer the substance of privacy to a right to privacy. I was happy to see nearly all hands up in favour of the right to privacy. This is not obvious. A person could object that having a right without the substance is of no help; it reminds one of Anatole France's famous dictum: 'In its majestic equality, the law forbids rich and poor alike to sleep under bridges, beg in the streets and steal loaves of bread.'[195] If you have no privacy in the first place, what is the use of requiring the government to respect it? This introduces the horizontal effect of human rights, which imposes a duty on governments to enforce respect for a particular right on other societal players. It is critical to admit that such protection depends on the state's capability to unilateral enforcement of individual rights, which grounds the protection of privacy in the monopoly on violence of the modern state.

In the last part of this book I will investigate the role of the law in the onli*fe* world, by inquiring into the peculiar relationship between law and technology. I will argue that only if we come to terms with the specific technological embodiment of modern law, can we begin to reinvent its alliance with the Rule of Law and guarantee an effective technology neutral law.

6.6 CONCLUSIONS: LESSONS FROM ANIMISM AND PRIVACY AS A GIFT

In a curious text under the title of 'Reclaiming Animism', Isabelle Stengers writes about how scientists 'presume to be the ones who have accepted the hard truth that we are alone in a mute, blind, yet knowable world – one that is our task to appropriate'. Her text ends with:[196]

> Reclaiming animism does not mean, then, that we have ever been animist. Nobody has ever been animist because one is never animist in general, only in terms of assemblages that generate metamorphic transformation in our capacity to affect and be affected and also to feel, think, and imagine. Animism may, however, be a name for reclaiming these assemblages, since it lures us into feeling that their efficacy is not ours to claim. Against the insistent poisoned passion of dismembering and demystifying, it affirms that which they all require in order not to enslave us: that we are not alone in the world.

In the course of the text, Stengers has explained that an 'assemblage' is the English translation chosen by many for the Deleuzo-Guattarian notion of 'agencement', which she explains as a 'coming together of heterogeneous components' that animates our existence. 'Agency belongs to the assemblage', it springs from the hybrid that animates us as the beings that we become. We do not precede this animation, but originate in its productive moment. This could be another way of saying that technologies invent us while we invent them. What captures my attention in this engagement with animism is the uncompromising pragmatic approach. Stengers refuses to speak in terms of a belief system, instead focusing on the effective assembly of human and other components that inspire specific modes of existence. She requires from the scientists and those under the spell of Science to accept projects and beings that raise other questions and provide other answers than those of experimental or theoretical science. Her point about animism is that 'we' should not disclaim its eventual success by means of, for instance, a scientific explanation based on the neurological effects of a placebo. I would add that the question of cause and effect is open, even in the case of the placebo. Instead of denouncing placebo effects as a matter of tricking the brain into healing on false grounds, we might want to celebrate the coalescence of, for instance, the manipulation of particular objects, the focused attention of prayer or meditation, the drinking or eating of specific substances, dance or song, resulting in good health, consolation, physical strength, mental endurance or delight. I say 'might' celebrate, because animism can mean many things in different contexts. Whether a specific 'agencement' that we label as animism, actually results in good things depends on the context, on the humans and nonhumans that participate, and, on who gets to judge.

The Japanese demonstrate that animism can continue to sprout in a high-tech environment, perhaps signifying that being animated by things helps the process of creating technological systems. On the other hand, those involved in the 'agencement' of ubicomp and robotics may have a particularly mathematical mindset, abhorring the 'superstition' of their fellow Japanese. Let's not romanticize. Nevertheless, there is an interesting coincidence, which may not be so coincidental after all, in the creation of mindless agency in a context that is highly conducive to hybrid and nonhuman animation. Perhaps, the better translation of 'agencement' is precisely that: animation, initiating *animus* or agency on all sides. What we can learn is to be pragmatic. We should not to fall into the trap of either attributing all kinds of beliefs to those who worship their *kami*, or of believing that to become successful ubicomp or robot designers we must develop a belief in the spirits of things. That is neither the point of Shintu practices nor of Stengers' 'reclaiming animism'. We must – indeed – learn to encounter things that have mindless intentions, that could manipulate us, and that 'run on' a distributed polymorphous digital unconscious that is not even transparent to those who 'run' them. We must learn how to persuade, assuage and contest these hybrids, to acquire the skills for playing with them in a meaningful way while instituting and protecting our own boundaries.

This brings me to privacy practices and the role of the law. Sometimes I feel that we move to what is called subjective legal rights too soon, without any sense of what we are protecting. Rather, we are just shouting about our right to this or that. By checking into the various ways that Japanese border control is effected, we may become aware of the tenacity of privacy issues and the fragility of human identity as multiple and in constant flux. It reminds us that depending on the gift of privacy is wonderful as well as horrible. I hope that this has brought home the need to reclaim the notion of individual rights, not merely as an intellectual trope, but as a robust, sustainable manner of protecting the self against invasion. Even if that invasion comes from machines tapping in a digital unconscious.

PART III

The end(s) of law

7.   The ends of law: address and redress

7.1 WHY LAW?

The third part of this book inquires into the implications of smart
technologies and data-driven agency for the law. There are two good
reasons for this. First, an investigation of the threats detected in the on*life*
world clarifies that a number of fundamental rights are at stake. As
argued in the chapter on agency and privacy in Japan, it is crucial that
these issues are not only discussed in terms of ethics and duties, but also
in terms of enforceable individual rights. In Chapter 9 I will address this
point by means of an inquiry into the fundamental right to data
protection, as stipulated in the Charter of Fundamental Rights of the
European Union (CFREU). This allows me to demonstrate how this
particular right overlaps with some of the other rights that are at stake,
while enabling an approach that is specifically relevant to the implications of data-driven intelligence. The second reason concerns the
question of how pre-emptive infrastructures affect the mode of existence
of modern law and what conception of law we need to cope with the
challenges it faces. By mode of existence I mean nothing more than the
way that law exists, since it obviously does not exist in the same way as
a table (which is a matter of matter and function and form and meaning),
or in the same way as a religion or the economy (which generates
functions and forms and meaning while developing complex relationships
with tables and candles and manufacturing and prayers). My take is that
the mode of existence of modern law is deeply dependent upon the
printing press and the way it has shaped our world. Especially the binary
character of legal rules, the complexity of the legal system and the
finality of legal decisions are affordances of – amongst things – the ICI
of the printing press. In this chapter and the next I will discuss how
modern law exists and how it attributes legal effect, and in the last
chapter I will see how this fares with the new ICI of data-driven
intelligence.

To make the case, however, I need to explain how lawyers and
philosophers of law understand their own trade in light of the role that
law plays in human society. What kind of protection could the law offer

in relation to the threats discussed in Chapter 5, and does modern law indeed offer more than the gift of privacy, as suggested in the last part of Chapter 6? What are, in other words, the ends of the law, and how can we sustain these ends in an on*life* world?

7.2 CONCEPT AND CONCEPTIONS OF LAW

7.2.1 Law as an Essentially Contested Concept

The German legal historian Uwe Wesel made a salient point when he wrote: 'What in fact is law? Answering this question is as simple as nailing a pudding to the wall'.[197] Is this because law itself is a vague and polymorphous thing, or because it is many things that partly overlap and partly contradict each other? Or, is it because it is one thing to some people and another thing to other people, for instance, depending on whether they are in a position of power, or have gained a monopoly on defining law, or simply depending on how the law treats them? Is the flexible but sticky texture of the pudding perhaps an advantage for what the law is supposed to achieve, and might it be that its 'unnailability' is an asset in view of competing eadibles?

I dare say that most philosophers of law (philosophers studying the law) and even many legal theorists (lawyers taking a theoretical perspective on their own discipline) would agree that law is an essentially contested concept, bound to generate dissent over its meaning and the role it plays in the configuration of human society. Gallie, who coined the term 'essentially contested concepts', has argued that such concepts are conditioned by the following seven characteristics:[198] the concept denotes something valuable [1]; it covers intricate complexities [2]; that make it inherently ambiguous [3]; and necessarily vague [4]. Being a matter of value, of complexity, ambiguity and vagueness, those who use the concept are forced to acknowledge the fact that others hold opposing or different views, requiring them to contest other conceptions, while defending their own [5]. And, although people may hold competing opinions on the meaning of the concept, they share an idea of what counts as an example of the concept in the past [6], and, finally, the persistent competition about the meaning of the concept helps to sustain and develop what has been achieved by that example in the best possible manner [7].

Even those who see law as a mere instrument tend to value its contribution to societal order and dispute resolution [1], and admit there are strong disagreements about the content of the concept [5]. It seems clear that law depends on human language and shares its inherent ambiguity [3] and open texture, which Gallie qualified as vagueness [4]. This is even more obvious for modern law, since this is a complex, multi-layered historical artefact [2]. When speaking of law most scholars will think of modern Western legal systems, which provide clear examples of what counts as law [7], while the pervasive discussion on the meaning of the concept of law enables a continuous learning process based on competing argumentations for one conception or another [6]. So, we can be sure that the concept of law is an essentially contested concept, keeping lawyers, politicians, citizens and market players alert to changing circumstances that require novel understandings of what law is, and how it exists. Whereas some scientists believe that disagreement about the object of study is a sign of immaturity, Gallie portrays the notion of an essentially contested concept as a positive contribution to our understanding of whatever the concept refers to. This is related to the value-aspect of such concepts, which invites their users to take a normative position and to reflect on its implications. The contested nature of these concepts also relates to their open texture that enables application in novel circumstances, reconfiguring their meaning. Essentially contested concepts help us to log into changing environments.

In the case of law, competing conceptions vie for the attention of those who use the law to order society, to distribute wealth or to decide on disputes. Within the context of political philosophy, for instance, John Rawls developed a theory of justice that advocates a particular conception of justice, namely 'justice as fairness',[199] taking a stance on the meaning and the relative importance of equality as compared to liberty. The bottom line of his theory is that those who manage to enlarge the cake that we share are entitled to a larger piece, provided that the least advantaged are not losing out compared to their previous share. This should incentivize people to innovate, while in the end everybody is better off. An application of his theory could be that if companies build their business models on the behavioural data of their customers, they should share the profit they make and be transparent about the monetary value of the data they sell. At this moment nobody knows how one's data contributes to the added value that is created, while it is also unclear what added value is actually created, because the amount of players in the data economy are multiple and many operations remain hidden behind the curtain of trade secrets and intellectual property rights. If we restrict ourselves to Apps, we have App developers, App providers, platforms that support the App, SNSs that enable users to log-in via their service, advertisers, advertising networks that mediate between the App provider and the advertiser, the provider of the data analytics that feeds the business model, and so on. Often, the same company has several roles, or the same role is distributed over different players. Quite apart from the question of whether the data are anonymized and whether the processing of the data violates a fundamental right, 'justice as fairness' would require us to consider these questions.

Within the context of philosophy of law, Ronald Dworkin developed a theory he called 'law as integrity'.[200] Dworkin found that lawyers facing so-called hard cases, where the interpretation of a legal rule is not obvious, are often confronted with essentially contested concepts such as causation, fairness, equality and reasonableness. He contended that to resolve the case a lawyer should ask herself which conception of such a concept best fits the implied philosophy of the legal domain it belongs to. If a person asks the court to order a large search engine provider to remove an old news article from its search results, because it is not relevant and distorts his reputation, the court will have to consider the whole of the relevant legal framework. This is a complex undertaking, because it involves several fundamental rights: the rights to privacy, data protection and freedom of expression, which includes the right to freedom of information. At the same time the right to conduct a business and the right to intellectual property may be involved. The balancing act this requires must – according to Dworkin – be performed in light of the underlying principles of the legal framework. We should not be surprised that such principles are themselves contested, but this cannot mean that anything goes. The court will have to decide in a way that respects the integrity of the legal system as a whole, keenly aware that any decision it takes will affect future decisions on related cases. Law is not a bran tub of rules but an architecture with interdependent layering, which requires acuity and vigilance to remain sustainable.

Rawls and Dworkin both argue that there is a best conception of justice or law; they take a normative stance on how to interpret the foundational concepts of the law. Others claim to merely describe law, warning against confusing law with morality. In this part of the book, I will develop a normative position on what conception of law best fits the historical artefact of the Rule of Law. I believe that any description of a value-laden concept such as law inevitably has normative implications. This does not mean that one's conception of law is a matter of taste or mere subjectivity. Rather, it means that we should acknowledge and stand for the normative angle we choose, and be willing to explain it.

In view of the changing ICI described in the first part of this book, we need to explore what substantial reconfigurations of law are at stake. In this chapter I display some of the mainstream conceptions of law, followed by an inquiry into the ends of law. In the next chapter I will frame three types of conceptions of both law and technology, arguing where my preferred choice fits in and explaining the intricate entangle-ments of modern law and the printing press. This enables me to provide a taste of the challenges facing law in the onl*ife* world.

7.2.2 Formal Legal Positivism

Common sense understandings of law and legal norms can be situated somewhere between the positivist accounts of three scholars of legal theory: 'the command theory of law' attributed to John Austin, 'the pure theory of law' of Kelsen, and 'the concept of law' of Hart.[201] Legal positivism heralds the importance of positive law. The term positive does not refer to a positive evaluation of the law. On the contrary, positive law can be defined as the valid law that exists at a certain time within a certain jurisdiction, irrespective of whether it is deemed good or bad law. Positive law is defined by what counts as law, not by what counts as good law. Its positivity refers, first, to the fact that it has been *posited* as such by whatever legal body has the competence to enact or decide the law. Second, the term refers to its *positive existence*, discriminating it from past law, future law or desirable law. The positivity of law is obviously tied up with the state, which provides modern law with its teeth. Positive law is enforceable and its validity and content are in the first place a matter of political decision-making. Most conceptions of modern law mark the importance of positive law, but legal positivism turns it into the hallmark of the law.

Austin, writing in the first half of the 19th century, basically claimed that laws are the commands of a sovereign, emphasizing the relationship between law and the sovereign state. In opposition with the natural law theories of the 17th and 18th centuries that made law dependent on the tenets of natural reason, he viewed law as man-made, artificial, and depending entirely on the power of the sovereign to impose general rules on his subjects. By restricting the concept of law to that of positive law, he made a strict distinction between what the law 'ought to be' and what it 'is'. This has been called the separation thesis. The command theory of law makes the law dependent on a sovereign, capable of unilaterally imposing its will. Though this may sound harsh, authoritarian and undemocratic to us, it does solve some of the problems posed by natural law in so far as this claims to be the ultimate standard on the validity of the law. Natural law theories that understand law as directly aligned with morality imply that there can be no difference between what 'is' law and what 'ought to be' law: unjust law is not law. Posited law can thus be tested against natural reason to determine its validity. Austin's point was that law is not necessarily the result of applying justice or reason, and if a law is found to disagree with morality people are nevertheless bound by its tenets. This should provide for legal certainty and trust that help people to anticipate what is expected from them, and gives them the bottom line of what they can expect from others, notably from their government. All this is closely connected with national jurisdiction that determines the territorial scope of a particular system of positive law. One of the major challenges in the onli*fe* world is the crumbling of jurisdiction. The Internet is transnational and raises continuous issues about, first, what law applies, second, how to deal with overlapping jurisdictions with contradictory law, and third, whether a government can enforce its law to protect its citizens outside of its own territory. The idea of mutually exclusive jurisdictions that lies at the heart of modern law is persistently challenged. States have found a number of ways to resolve these problems, for instance, by concluding treaties or by requiring companies to abstain from targeting their citizens. However, powerful states increasingly engage in extraterritorial enforcement of their own laws, for instance by means of cyberattacks. This blurs the borders between war (between states) and criminal law enforcement (within the state), reducing the authority of the sovereign state, because this authority is based on a strict separation of internal and external sovereignty. Though some may applaud a reduction in state authority, we should remember that, for instance, human rights protection ultimately depends on the power of the state to enforce such rights.

Kelsen made a similarly strict separation between law and morality. Writing in the first half of the 20th century, he described the 'is' of the law as a set of rules that form a pyramid of hierarchically ordered normative rules, which in the end all derive from one 'Basic Norm' (*Grundnorm*). This 'Basic Norm' guarantees the unity of the legal system and the validity of all the legal rules, which should be seen as derived from it. As in Austin's command theory, law always depends on the authority of the state, but according to Kelsen this authority also depends on the law. The state is a legal construction; they are mutually constitutive. Kelsen's conception of law is focused on the coherence of the legal system as a whole, on its architectural quality and on the need to attend to correct deductions, while avoiding contamination with elements from morality or politics. To allow a moral evaluation of the law, Kelsen found, one must first describe its normative content, taking into account the deductive logic that determines the connections between different legal norms. This description is part of legal science. Though a moral evaluation is always possible, in his view, it is neither part of the law nor of legal science; the title of his masterwork was *The Pure Theory of Law*.

Kelsen's legal system is a pyramid; it has a hierarchical structure that assumes a strictly systematic architecture.

Many authors have indicated that the idea of a legal system is no longer relevant – if it ever was – because we have been moving towards a network society and this cannot be reined in by the logic of another era. These authors claim that modern law must move from a pyramidal to a network configuration, or invent a mix of both, depending on the legal domain.[202] However, it is important to acknowledge that the systematic character of the law protects us from unreliable, arbitrary legal decisions. It requires that the legislator, the administration and the courts consider how their decisions affect other parts of the system and how they influence similar decisions in the future. The systematic character of the law induces reflection, deliberation and argumentation. It forces courts, governments and legislators to take into account what expectations are raised on account of any decision they take. This is a matter of trustworthiness. If a copyright holder requests a court to force an Internet Service Provider to filter Internet traffic in order to block a website that facilitates the unlawful sharing of copyrighted content, a court has to take into account a number of different legal regimes: those of copyright, those of enforcement, those of privacy and data protection, and those of ecommerce and competition law. Without a legal system this would be a matter of weighing different interests, based on political preferences or economic power. The systematic character of the law forces the court, however, to compatibilize these different regimes as far as possible, seeking a decision that aligns with the legitimate expectations of all the players. In that sense the complexity of legal systems protects against mere power play, which could turn the moral standards of a powerful party into those of the polity.

Hart, writing in the second half of the 20th century, took a similar position on the separation of law and morality as both Austin and Kelsen, although the nature of 'his' law was defined in terms of social interaction instead of orders backed by threats or 'purely' normative statements. While Kelsen's 'Basic Norm' can be understood as a hypothetical rule that ensures the unity of the system and the validity of its elements, Hart's 'Ultimate Rule of Recognition' is firmly rooted in social acceptance or what he calls the internal aspect of legal rules. Hart went on to discriminate between primary and secondary legal rules. Primary rules define which conduct is prescribed, prohibited or allowed, while secondary rules define the competence to recognize, change or adjudicate the primary rules. This distinction has developed into a canonical approach within law and legal theory. For instance, whether collecting location data is prohibited depends on a primary rule, while who decides the content of this primary rule depends on a secondary rule.

In short, Austin linked law to the power of the sovereign to impose general rules on his subjects, Kelsen elaborated the systematic character of the body of legal rules and their clear distinction from moral rules and political competence, and Hart understood law as a complex system of social norms, coining the difference between primary and secondary rules. Roughly speaking, legal positivism seems to emphasize that law is a system of general rules, which depends on the authority of the state and must be strictly separated from morality and politics.

7.2.3 Hermeneutic and Pragmatic Conceptions

Hermeneutic conceptions of law   Many scholars of law and legal theory have objected to these tenets of legal positivism, which has led to further refinements and alternative positions.[203] Most famous is Dworkin's objection that it makes no sense to define law as a system of rules. He argues that for the interpretation of legal rules we need guidance by principles that give direction to the application of legal norms. These principles have a certain weight, depending on the context. They speak the language of balance rather than application, and do not share the binary application of rules.[204] For instance, if we must decide whether the collection of personal data is a violation of the right to privacy, we cannot proceed straightforwardly. Within Europe, the collection of a name or a social security number is not necessarily an infringement of the right to privacy. This depends on whether such collection infringes private or family life, the home, or one's correspondence. To determine that, we have to assess the case law of the European Court of Human Rights (ECtHR), and here we will encounter unwritten principles of law that give direction to those applying it. An important principle in this respect is that of proportionality. It is not written explicitly into Art. 8 ECtHR, but it can be inferred from the case law. If we move from the right to privacy to the fundamental right to data protection, which are not the same, different rules apply. The collection of names surely does fall within the scope of 'processing personal data', thus entering the realm of the right to data protection, which is explicitly protected in the Charter of Fundamental Rights of the European Union (CFREU). However, if there is a legal ground for such collection and a clear and legitimate purpose for which it is being processed, there is no violation of data protection law.[205] Again, we are confronted with case law and other sources of the law, to figure out how such cases are decided in specific contexts. The challenge is to flesh out the principles that guide such decisions. Dworkin emphasized the need for coherence in the interpretation of legal rules, but argued that this coherence amounts to more than just logical consistency, requiring what he calls the integrity of law. With the notion of integrity he introduced moral standards into the law, though not those of an individual judge or activist legislator. He explained that the moral standards that are unavoidably implied in any act of interpretation must be inductively generated from previous legal decisions (enacted law, court judgements), to sustain the moral integrity of the law. He used the metaphor of a chain novel to highlight the temporal aspect of law-making. Understanding – and thereby making – law is a continuing story that is rooted in the background philosophy it draws on and constitutes. Dworkin held that the implied philosophy of law in a liberal democracy finds its basic expression in a right to equal respect and concern for each individual. This is the origin of both democracy and the substantive conception of the Rule of Law; it grounds the idea of one (wo)man one vote, while also protecting individuals against the tyranny of a majority.

Dworkin's approach to law is hermeneutical. Hermeneutics is about interpretation in the sense of establishing the meaning of a term or an action. Interpretation, however, is not necessarily about meaning; even mindless agents are continuously engaged in interpretation, since they thrive on the feedback loop between action and perception. The attribution of meaning depends on human language. Hermeneutics, as the science of meaning attribution, assumes self-consciousness and reflection on potential meaning. It is firmly rooted in the productive ambiguity of human language. A hermeneutical approach to law entails that any legal decision implies interpretation and requires creativity, precision and argumentation. The complex architecture of modern law entails that legal decisions are always situated in a network of similar and different decisions that must be taken into account; if a particular decision was not aligned with the network of past and future decisions on similar cases, this would violate the legitimate expectations of those under its jurisdiction, who would be subject to arbitrary rule.

The emphasis on interpretation in contemporary legal discourse is not surprising. Modern law centres on text and printed matter. The script and the printing press form the preconditions for the modern legal systems that depend on them, as will be further elaborated in the next chapter. For now, it is important to acknowledge that hermeneutic conceptions of law do not deny the positivity of modern law, or the far reaching implications this has for the bite of the law. Rather, hermeneutics highlights the intricate and multiple relationships between law and morality that render the separation thesis somewhat shallow, while underlining the fact that the emphasis on positive law does not solve the problem of interpretation.

This relativizes the positivist concern about validity; knowing that a law is valid does not provide us with a correct interpretation. Moreover, in law, interpretation is performative. *Law does things with words.*[206] When a judge speaks, legal effect is attributed, which changes or confirms rights and obligations. This brings us to the pragmatic conceptions of law.

Pragmatic conceptions of law When discussing legal positivism I loosely defined positive law as the valid law that exists at a certain time within a certain jurisdiction. In legal theory, legal positivism is divided into two streams: formal and realist. Both have a strong concern for positive law, but very different conceptions of what makes law positive. Whereas the positivity in formal legal positivism rests on formal criteria for the validity of the law, legal realism takes a sociological or pragmatist approach. Holmes, for instance, claimed that:[207]

> The prophecies of what the courts will do in fact, and nothing more pretentious, are what I mean by the law.

Holmes was less concerned with formal validity than with the actual operations of legal decision-making and with their effect. Note that he does not speak of what the courts do or did, but of our anticipation of how they will decide. This anticipation is crucial and aligns Holmes' legal realism with the hermeneutic emphasis on interpretation. To foresee how the courts will decide a case one has to interpret past decisions in the light of the case at hand, and vice versa. That is what lawyers do; this is their everyday business. Interpretation in law is always anticipation. Basically Holmes argued that the law is, in fact, what we expect it to be, because it is this expectation that regulates our actions.[208] Such expectations are grounded in past decisions, but if these were entirely deterministic of future decisions we would not need the law – we could settle for logic and simply calculate the outcome of future decisions. No need for interpretation. Holmes claimed, however, that 'the life of law has not been logic. It has been experience.' This correlates with a specific conception of intelligence. As we have seen in Chapters 2 and 3, rule-based artificial intelligence, which tried to solve problems by means of deductive logic, has been superseded by machine learning (ML), based on experience. Anticipation requires experience; mere logic only works in a strictly controlled environment. Those versed in pragmatist philosophy will not be surprised by the emphasis on anticipation. The famous pragmatist maxim goes:[209]

Consider what effects, which might conceivably have practical bearings, we conceive the object of our conception to have. Then, our conception of those effects is the whole of our conception of the object.

If we translate this into statistical forecasts we arrive at judgements resulting from ML. However, neither logic nor statistics can attribute meaning. ML-based court decisions would remove the fundamental ambiguity of human language from the centre stage of the law. As noted above, this ambiguity is connected with the value-laden aspect of the concept of law. It is not a drawback of natural language, but what saves us from acting like mindless agents. My take is that an approach based on statistics would reduce judicial or legislative decisions to administration, and thus collapse the Rule of Law. This is not to say that a number of administrative decisions could not be taken by smart computing systems. It is to confirm that such decisions should be brought under the Rule of Law, notably by making them contestable in a court of law.

7.3 THE ENDS OF LAW

7.3.1 The Performance of Law: Functions and Ends

Speaking of the ends of law is not the same as speaking of its functions. The concept of a function is a sociological notion that refers to the operations of the law within a societal structure, allowing an observer to check how the law actually works, irrespective of how people intend it to work or believe it to work. This requires an external perspective on the law. Though it is an important test to verify or falsify claims made from the internal perspective, I will discuss the ends of law from a legal perspective to clarify how the law is meant to operate. This should at some point help to answer the question on whether the law is functioning well or not, because if there is no yardstick by which to judge this, such a question cannot be answered.

The ends of law are the goals, objectives or purposes of the law. When speaking of the law, I am not talking about a particular statute or judicial verdict, but about the law as an institutional normative order, a practice or a specific 'regime of veridiction' (I will explain this later on). At this point, we are not interested in specific ends like achieving environmental safety, the protection of intellectual property rights or punishing a burglar for theft, which may be the end of a particular statute or verdict. Instead, we need to explore the ends of the law as a normative order that guides professional lawyers, individual citizens, corporations, government agencies, and those who study the law. How do they decide what is the legal problem, after hearing the facts of a case? What determines the choice of legal norms they apply to a legal problem? Who decides what counts as a legal solution and how is legal interpretation different from any other interpretation? The answers to these questions must be derived from the law itself, to count as correct answers from a legal point of view. Of course we can ask an economist what she thinks about the difference between justice and lawfulness, but although she may come up with an interesting opinion we cannot be sure that this opinion tells us something about the law, or about the kind of decisions lawyers make. This means that we must take an internal point of view to explain the operations of the law and the ends it serves. However, law is a societal practice; it is not – in the end – merely the business of legal practitioners. The ends of law must been seen from the perspective of the legal order as what holds together, in a very specific way, the people, things and institutions that form the polity. The ends of law – though deeply entwined with their internal validation – are thus co-determined by the needs of the society it serves and co-constitutes. They must be mined from the operations of the law, but with a keen eye for how this positions individuals and their various groupings, as well as the relationships of power and authority that are instituted, tested, restricted and legitimized by the law. The internal perspective must therefore be seen in close relation with a mitigated external perspective that can only be invoked by taking the role of other 'regimes of veridiction', such as politics or economics.

The operations of the law can be described in the simplest manner by noting that the law articulates legal conditions for legal effect. Legal effect is a legal term that denotes the legal consequences of a certain event, action or state of affairs. A legally relevant event is one that has legal effect though no one had the intention of creating legal effect, whereas a legal action implies such intent. An example of the first is causing a traffic accident, where the legal effect may be an obligation to pay compensation to the victim or even the liability to be punished for criminal conduct, all depending on the precise circumstances and the relevant jurisdiction. An example of a legal action is the conclusion of a contract that creates legal obligations, for example to deliver a service or good and to pay the price. An example of a state of affairs with legal effect is 'being a specific type of corporation', which has the legal effect of qualifying as a legal person. Legal personhood is the capacity to act in law, to have and generate legal rights and obligations. Dogs and cat, hammers and houses are not legal subjects. But corporations may be, and all human beings are – even if their capacity to exercise these rights may be restricted, for instance, because of youth or mental illness. Being a legal subject is not a natural right but something conditioned by positive law; animals used to be liable under the criminal law and artificial agents might one day become liable under private law.[210]

Connecting legal conditions with legal effect bypasses descriptive analyses of how the law functions, or whether it is always enforceable in practice. Whereas descriptions are interesting and important, the knit between condition and effect in law is performative. Law actually *does* things, it is not a social science that describes things, nor a set of policy recommendations that hopes to get things done, nor a computer program that operates effects based on digital calculations. When a civil servant declares a couple man and wife, she is not describing something; her declaration actually *performs* the act of marrying two people. Neither the couple, nor the witnesses *perform* the marriage in the legal sense. The legal effect of being married is instituted by the stipulations of the law. Marriage is – what some call – an institutional fact. The law stipulates *what counts as* a marriage, that is, the legal institution that generates a specific set of rights and obligations to the partners as well as third parties. Usually the marriage has to be registered in the civil registry to take effect, because of the effects on third parties, such as children and other kin (legal status, inheritance) and creditors (who may have redress against the assets of both partners). These legal effects underline the importance of a clear moment in time when the marriage is concluded and a clear form of evidence that this moment has indeed passed. The performative aspect of legal effect differentiates it from other occurrences. It highlights that legal effects are *institutional facts* of a very specific type, dependent on a very specific *regime of veridiction*.

The concept of institutional facts was coined by another Austin, in a famous work (1962) titled *How To Do Things with Words?*[211] He highlighted the fact that some utterances do not (only) describe a reality, but actually bring it into being. 'I declare you man and wife', is an example of this. Such institutional facts depend on institutions, such as marriage, the church, universities, money or contract. Austin's institutions are what Latour would call 'regimes of veridiction'; they clarify the truth conditions for the facts that we determine as such. Or, as Austin and Latour would say: they constitute the conditions of felicity for the actual institution (Austin) or fabrication (Latour) of a fact. For instance, if I put my thumb up, a natural scientist could describe all the myriad interactions that take place within the body, including the physics, the chemistry and the biology, based on her knowledge of bodily movement in the context of her science. This will not, however, convey the meaning of the gesture within a specific group. For a correct description of such meaning we must rely on another set of truth conditions that help us understand what people mean when they 'do' the thumbs-up. In a society where the thumbs-up institutes the conclusion of a contract, we may need a legal expert to clarify the relevant 'regime of veridiction'. Latour has placed truth regimes in the context of the constitution of what he calls different modes of existence, a term inspired by Souriau:[212]

> This banal and quasi-ecological expression refers to a specific speech act – each with its peculiar felicity and infelicity conditions – to which is added the claim that a highly specific type of world is being inhabited. Souriau's argument is not to say that there are several ways to talk about one world but several ways for the worlds (in the plural) to be addressed.

This is an interesting proposal. It relates to the notion of a life world or *Welt*, as introduced in Chapter 3, but basically admits that we do not inhabit one monolithic *Welt*, but necessarily navigate different *Welts* that determine different dimensions of our reality. This reality is plural and depends on hard work, namely on addressing the modes of existence to sustain their existence. It probably implies that Latour is not interested in concepts and conceptualizations as ways of *seeing* the world, but in the way such concepts *shape* the environment in which we live. It can be related to the notions of 'agencement', affordance and enaction. The first highlights the way that different entities *animate each other* when forming a hybrid, while the second underlines the fact that a mode of existence *affords specific roles, actors and actions while constraining others*, and the third notes the reiterant feedback loop between action and perception as *performing our world*. This seems an excellent proposition to understand and investigate how the law operates, what conditions of felicity it institutes and what work is required to maintain and preserve its mode of existence. I believe that Latour, however, would not understand the law as an 'agencement'. Instead he would expect different entities to come together, confronting and inspiring the law as test cases for its 'regime of veridiction'; such new 'agencements' can be found in the onli*fe* world, forcing the law to face the transformation of its environment. In the next chapter I will argue that different conceptions of law implicate different modes of existence that vie for dominance. Here, I will build on a particular understanding of law as a value-laden concept and practice, to ground and suspend the ends of the law that are at stake in an onli*fe* world. In the next section I will explain why the ends of law must not only be grounded but, most importantly, be suspended in the thin air of the *Welt(s)* we inhabit.

7.3.2 Law as a Value-laden Concept

Law may be a pudding, but it is not any kind of pudding. Its texture, elasticity, form and identity matter. One way to find out how they matter, is to figure out what values law incarnates. In doing so, we should avoid both idealistic renderings that conflate law with justice and instrumentalist perspectives that deny the value-aspect of law. In the next chapter we will return to these reductions, because they play an important role in attempts to sterilize the law as an independent construct, or to instrumentalize the law for political or economic purposes. Here, I will elaborate on the work of a lawyer and philosopher of the first half of the 20th century, who turned the productive tensions between the different aims of the law into its agonistic core.

Gustav Radbruch was Minister of Justice in the Weimar Republic that witnessed the emergence of the Nazi regime.[213] Though he understood the crucial role of decision-making in law, and the dangers of identifying law with justice, he steered clear of the glorification of the positive aspect of the law that informed the philosophy of the famous German constitutional lawyer, Carl Schmitt. In fact, in his *Political Theology*, Schmitt went even further, by emphasizing the non-legal political grounding of the law, stating that 'sovereign is who decides on the exception':[214]

> If there is some person or institution, in a given polity, capable of bringing about a total suspension of the law and then to use extra-legal force to normalize the situation, then that person or institution is the sovereign in that polity. ... Any legal order is based on a sovereign decision and not on a legal norm.

While Schmitt aligned himself with the Nazi regime, his insights into the nature of law's mode of existence should not be discarded. On the contrary, they must be taken into account to avoid the trap in which those who struggle with the relationship between law, power and the modern state so easily get caught. After the war, Radbruch wrote a famous pamphlet, called 'Five Minutes of Legal Philosophy',[215] in which he restated his earlier views on the law, in direct relation to the way German lawyers had dealt with Nazi law. The bottom line of his view was – then as before – that unjust laws may still be laws, unless they can no longer be understood as *aiming for* justice. This assumes that a court should not refuse to apply unjust laws, unless it finds that a law is not directed to achieve justice. This means that if a law can no longer be understood as aiming for justice, the court must indeed refuse to apply it. Radbruch's view was that such a law cannot be qualified as law anymore; we could paraphrase that it does not fit the 'regime of veridiction' of the law and cannot be addressed as a mode of existence of the law.

In suggesting that a law can be unjust while being directed to justice, Radbruch achieves two things: first, he discriminates between the concept of law and the aim of law; and second, he shows the tension that suspends and sustains the law as a form of mediation. His distinction between a value-laden concept and the aim(s) it presumes is rooted in his attention to language and concepts as cultural artefacts. Values and aims do not refer to some abstract universal maxim, but are generated by and productive of their cultural habitat. Culture roughly equates with what has been discussed as a *Welt* in the first part of this book: a web of meaning that institutes our environment, ourselves and our minds. Law, for Radbruch, is a cultural artefact, not a universal entity. This is why it would be a mistake to qualify Radbruch as an adherent to natural law; the ends of law are cultural artefacts, not moral universals. So, according to Radbruch, the concept of law describes the law, while the idea of law describes its aims or ends. What makes this interesting is the argument that one cannot describe the law without paying keen attention to its aims.

If all this were to result in a unilateral unambiguous call for justice or utility or certainty, his concept of law would be unconvincing. What has triggered so many lawyers and philosophers to study his work is: first, Radbruch's emphasis on the *antinomian* character of what he terms the three aims of the law; and second, his accentuation of the fact that law is defined by these *aims*, not by the requirement to have achieved them. Radbruch names justice, legal certainty and purpose as the ends of law. None of these dominates the others entirely, though legal certainty has a slight prominence. For Radbruch, legal certainty is directly connected with the positivity of the law:[216]

> The order of living together cannot be left to the particular conceptions of law of individual citizens, as different people may well have contradictory ideas, requiring a unitary regulation from a supra-individual position. ... If nobody can establish what is just, somebody must decide what should be lawful, and positive law should fulfil the assignment, to end the contradictory conceptions of law by means of an authoritative verdict. The positivity of the law must depend on a will that can impose itself against any contradictory conception of law.

The prominence of legal certainly can also be explained by the predictability that is implied in justice as equality; treating equal cases equally to the extent of their equality clarifies how the law will operate on a case-by-case basis. Legal certainty requires foreseeability and trustworthiness, thus partly overlapping with justice as equality. Also, in so far as law is used to achieve certain purposes, it will benefit from foreseeability and trustworthiness. However, Radbruch makes clear that a law that is only focused on legal certainty could not qualify as law. Neither can we expect the law to achieve legal certainty to the full, precisely because it must attend to justice and to purpose. If the attribution of legal effect could be automated, for instance by using a computer program capable of calculating all the relevant circumstances, legal certainty might be achieved. But this can only be done by eliminating the ambiguity that inheres in human language; it would reduce interpretation to mindless application. From Radbruch's point of view this would fly in the face of the cultural, value-laden mode of existence of the law. It would refute the performative nature of the law as an artificial construction that depends on the reiterant attribution of meaning and decision-making by mindful agents. One is reminded of Derrida's 'Force of Law',[217] which celebrates the untenable tension between law and justice, making sure that any law that is claimed to have achieved justice is by that very fact dangerous and should not qualify as law.

Justice, legal certainty and purpose are antinomian. This implies that though the law always strives to achieve these ends, their application in specific situations will often be incompatible. It may be tempting to resolve the ensuing tension by reducing the goals to one overarching goal or by reducing them to each other. In fact, Radbruch speaks of the generic goal of justice in the broad sense, but this must be understood as the agonistic space where the antinomian aims vie for dominance. Indeed, I believe that Radbruch's insistence on the unruly agonism of the ends of the law is not unlike Latour's principle of irreduction. Though the reader may understand irreduction as the recognition of the irreducibility of a thing or a value, this easily reduces to a kind of essentialism. As if justice, purpose and legal certainty could exist and play out independently, on their own, without being tested against each other. Latour's irreduction would, on the contrary, mean that they cannot translate into or reduce themselves to each other, but – on the contrary – only come into their own in their mutual confrontation. Yes, they must be respected on their own terms, but these terms become clear only when challenged by the other aims. This type of irreduction confirms that lawyers will have to cope with difficult choices that must be accepted as an invitation to consider all that is relevant, to suspend judgement until all parties are heard and relevant arguments deliberated. While still ending with judgement.

7.3.3 Justice and Equality

Within the general concept of justice, that gives direction to the law, Radbruch distinguishes between justice in the narrow sense, legal certainty and purpose. Justice in the narrow sense is defined as equality, which I dare call the hallmark of modern law (definitely not the hallmark of previous types of law). Equality, however, can mean many things to many people:[218]

> Justice requires us only to treat equal cases as equal and unequal cases as unequal, however, it does not provide us with the perspective from which they can be seen as either equal or unequal; it furthermore only provides us with the relationship, but not with the content of the treatment. Both questions can only be answered on the basis of the purpose of the law.

Aristotle has made a wonderfully lucid analysis of the ethics of equality that Radbruch elaborates for the law. First, Aristotle distinguishes between distributive and corrective justice. Distributive justice is about sharing one piece of cake equally between a number of people; corrective justice is about equal compensation between two people. Distributive equality has a geometric structure; it departs, as it were, from a centre, to provide equal access, opportunities, goods or services to all. Who is all, however, depends. It can refer to all citizens, all residents, all humans, the humans in a certain territory, all employees, all patients, all those without income or all those under or above a certain age. In Aristotle's time it probably referred to all free men. Radbruch points out that the equality that is established here does not clarify the measure of what is being distributed. For instance, if we think of punishment, we may believe that all offenders must be punished equally for having committed an equally serious crime, but this does not tell us anything about the measure of punishment. This may depend on the offence, which brings us to corrective justice. The measure of the compensation should, in this case, be equal to whatever must be compensated: the more serious the crime, the higher the sentence. This is another type of equality, not geometrical but arithmetic. This has also been also called proportional justice, suggesting that the proportion that is compensated is equal to the proportion of what requires to be compensated. Corrective justice is not only relevant in the case of criminal law, but also in the case of contract and tort, in so far as they are grounded in proportional reciprocity. However, just like in the case of distributive justice, it is not always clear what compensation is proportional. Should a person who stole a piece of bread be punished with a fine of 10 euros, or with 1 day in prison?

Should they be convicted on the basis of the measure of their culpability, instead of the seriousness of the crime – or should both be taken into account? Is the price for a certain good really decided by the cost made to produce it, or does it depend on what other people are willing to pay, or on what other producers are charging? The latter seem based on distributive rather than corrective equality.

In the case of law, we can see that any type of corrective justice must always be balanced with distributive justice. Once the legislator and the courts decide on a punishment for a specific crime they must take this into account when deciding on similar crimes. If a company charges a certain price for a specific product, it may not charge a higher price to another person just because that person is a woman or black or homosexual. In that sense non-discrimination law is focused on distributive justice. However, if a company wants to charge different prices to different customers because they are willing to pay different prices, the law does not prohibit this. Here we see how the freedom to conduct a business and the freedom to contract provide private parties with a space for strategic interaction, enabling them to gain a profit from the creation of added value.[219] It should be clear that the freedom to contract includes the possibility to conclude contracts that obligate only one of the parties, without providing any type of corrective justice. For example, the contract of a gift, or the institution of a trust, exemplifies that mutual consent enables legal subjects to ignore corrective equality. In the case of tort law this is obviously different, here the law requires full compensation, based on the proportional reciprocity of the mutual causality, the culpability and the wrongfulness. Nevertheless, strict liability may disturb the measure of corrective equality, while still adhering to distributive justice: the strict liability will apply to all similar cases. The purpose of such a deviation from corrective justice may be to ease an impossible burden of proof for the weaker party, or simply deterrence of dangerous behaviour.

Though in the private sphere citizens and companies enjoy the freedom to act as they wish unless they violate specific prohibitions, the public sphere has a different regime. Whereas a private party cannot be forced legally to consider the public interest in all of its actions, the government should always act in a way that is at least compatible with the general interest. The notion of the general interest does not imply that there is one particular interest that everyone agrees on as being the one and only general interest. There is no such thing. It is rather a criterion for decision-making, notably when a number of general interests are incompatible in a specific situation, requiring the government to investigate and decide how they can best be served. This brings us into the realm of politics and purpose. It relates to equality and justice, because whatever the government does, it should take into account the distributive justice that gives everyone her due. It returns us to Dworkin's notion of 'equal respect and concern' as the basic premise of constitutional democracy.

Distributive and corrective justice do not dictate how individual decisions must be made. They do restrict, however, the decisions that can be taken, requiring that they show consideration for both types of justice where they apply. This has been called reconstructive justice, demanding that whatever a government does must be 'reconstructable' in terms of the general interest.[220] This puts a burden of productive hesitation, the suspension of judgement and a convincing motivation on the state. Cumbersome, yes. But living in a complex world requires acuity and conscientious attention to all the different interests that are at stake, while taking into account the effects of any decision on power (im)balances and, especially, on those least advantaged. Distributive justice does not imply communism, but it does necessitate fairness. I believe that Rawls' maximin principle is the best practical translation of such fairness: whoever creates added value can claim a larger piece of the cake, provided the least advantaged have some share in the growth of general welfare. This, however, cannot be the sole end of the law. Law is not equivalent with justice.

7.3.4   Legal Certainty and Positivity

Radbruch finds that equality requires proportionality of distribution or compensation, but does not provide the measure of whatever is distributed or compensated. This, he states, depends on the purpose. For instance, if we want to deter people from displaying certain behaviour, we can seek equality in punishment in relation to the seriousness of the crime and raise the bar to a level that overrules the benefits gained from committing the offence. If, on the other hand, we wish to address the intention of a person to undertake certain actions, we had better seek equality in punishment in relation to the wrongfulness or culpability, which involves other types of investigation that may be more intrusive than merely establishing the past existence of certain behaviour. In any case, we will probably always disagree on these purposes and to have an effective law that is capable of guiding our interaction, the decisions of the legislator and the courts must be binding even on those who do not agree with them:[221]

> The certainty of the law requires its positivity: if it cannot be determined what
> is just, it must be decided what is lawful, and this from a position that is
> capable of enforcing the decision.

This aspect of the law is typical for modern law. It aligns law with
sovereign authority and unilateral decision-making, notably with *res
iudicata est* and *litis finiri oportet*. These two adages are the crown
jewels of modern law. They look like maxims of Roman law, but they are
not. Actually, they are part of the medieval reception of Roman law,
connecting law with territorial jurisdiction and internal sovereignty.
Though many scholars categorize pre-war Radbruch as a legal positivist,
because of his emphasis on the crucial importance of positive law, this is
not a very productive understanding of his work. In his masterwork,
Legal Philosophy (1932), he writes that '[f]inally, too, it will appear that
even the validity of positive law that is unjust and wrong cannot be
maintained unqualifiedly hence the question of validity may be considered not only from the standpoint of legal certainty but also that of justice
and expediency'.[222] This clearly indicates the continuity with his postwar writings on the lack of validity of a law that does not even strive to
be just. His point is, however, that this is an exceptional situation,
whereas under normal conditions a court must apply the law, even if it
considers it unjust, precisely because we may not agree on what is just or
unjust and at some point it is more important that we know what to
expect than to continue the hesitation about what must be decided. *Res
judicata est* means that once the highest court has spoken the parties
must accept the final verdict and third parties can rely on the fact that this
is what positive law dictates. The parties cannot go back for another
appeal if they do not agree. Though we may think this is a natural
component of the law, this is not at all so. Societies without internal
sovereignty cannot enforce the verdicts of the court and their dispute
resolution is in principle voluntary. The position of the judge is that of an
arbiter and his authority is persuasive; power relationships between the
parties and the groupings they belong to are far more decisive for the
solution and,[223] mostly, neither the law nor the verdicts are written down.
This has implications for the equality of rule application and the
generality of the rules that apply. Neither is evident and anthropologists
like Geertz have warned against translating the complex web of legal
norms in oral societies into our own rule-based understanding of law.[224]
Litis finiri oportet means that the legal struggle must be ended; both the
parties and the third parties that may be involved benefit from knowing
where they stand, legally speaking. The performative nature of modern
law comes into its own in the unilateral and final decisions taken by the

legislator and the courts. Rules, once enacted, cannot be negotiated on the basis of the economic or military power of those under its jurisdiction – or so we hope. The end of law is to provide certainty about what counts as a legitimate expectation as to the legal effect of one's interactions. In small-scale societies this can be inferred from the patterns of face-to-face interactions, but in large-scale societies that have outsourced part of their cognitive resources to the script and printed text, a more abstract certainty must be provided. Besides that, legal certainty is capable of taming the potentially unfettered powers of internal sovereignty by bringing it under the Rule of Law, forcing it to abide by the rules it enacts. And, taking into account the issue of interpretation, legal certainty is always the result of a hesitation; it is the outcome of a deliberation on how to interpret the law in the face of different potentially valid applications. The complexity of the legal framework and the task of attending to its coherence whenever a legal decision is at stake, prevent automated application and link legal certainty firmly with the aim of making just decisions that serve a legitimate purpose.

7.3.5 Purposiveness and Instrumentality

As discussed, justice as equality involves both distributive and corrective equality. This raises two questions that cannot be answered by justice itself: 'whom to consider equal or different and how to treat them'.[225] These questions require a teleological inquiry, pointing to the *telos* or purpose of the legal norms that must be applied. Since modern law is tied up with the state, which it empowers and legitimizes, and on which it depends, we can reframe the question as follows. How do the legislator, the administration and the courts determine the purpose that informs the articulation, enactment, application and judicial interpretation of legal norms? Is it desirable and possible to answer this question by stipulating a particular purpose that all legal norms should aim to achieve, such as individual liberty, collective welfare or great works of art and science? When introducing the concept of the ends of law, I noted that this is not about the particular ends of particular laws. However, when discussing the purposiveness of law we seem to return to this point. Since the law aims to be instrumental for achieving policy objectives, because this instrumentality is one of the critical ends of the law, we need to pay keen attention to the types of purposes legal norms can serve. As to these types, Radbruch was a convinced relativist. He signified relativism as a crucial assumption of democracy, because '[d]emocracy refuses to identity itself with a definite political view', since 'no political view is demonstrable' and therefore 'each view is to be fought from the standpoint of an opposite view'.[226] The end of the law is not necessarily to achieve social welfare, redistribution of income, or public healthcare, or to guard individual liberty or public security, nor to reserve all its resources for higher education and the arts. These kind of decisions, on how to organize the life of the polity and how to attribute what legal effect to which events, actions or states of affair, are political decisions that belongs in the realm of democratic practice. However, the purposiveness of law implies that the law lends itself to being an instrument for achieving the particular objectives selected by the democratic legislator. Though it cannot decide on the relative importance given to welfare, liberty or equality, it must provide the specific legal framework to institute the relevant policy choices. The purposiveness of the law thus depicts its instrumentality. This by no means implies a one-way affair between law and politics, where politics dictates its terms to the law. This would be instrumentalism, to which we shall return in the next chapter. Instead, the instrumentality of the law derives from the legality principle that requires the state to base its operations on legal competence instead of bare sovereign power. While serving the purposes decided in the realm of democratic politics, the law imposes its own 'regime of veridiction'. Legality thus institutes the law as an instrument of democratic political power, while simultaneously attending to justice and legal certainty. It is not suggested that this can be done without making difficult choices.

Legality, finally, should not be confused with legalism, which makes legal certainty the final end of the law. The legality principle is closely connected with a substantive conception of the Rule of Law, which binds the government to its own enactments, while providing for a system of checks and balances and a set of effective human rights. It underscores that governments are obliged to restrict themselves to the specified, legitimate purposes for which they have an explicit competence, attributed by law. This limits their freedom and provides transparency as well as accountability. Though governments might find that in the short term the legality principle obstructs the expediency of their work, the limitation of governmental powers marks the difference between the rule of an enlightened despot and a constitutional democracy. It forces government to deliberate on the purposes it wants to achieve, knowing that once the competences are defined in terms of purpose, it has to stick to them. This has been called the purpose binding principle, which is a direct descendant of the legality principle. In both administrative law and criminal procedure the use of a competence for another purpose than the one provided for by law, has legal effect. It may be that such usage renders a disposition or an injunction of a public authority invalid, or leads to the disqualification of evidence in the context of a criminal trial. This legal effect makes the principle of purpose binding effective. The fact that the administration cannot decide for itself whether its decisions violate the principle of purpose binding prevents arbitrary rule; ultimately a court will test the legality of the decision.

The wisdom of the principle of purpose binding relates to Odysseus' encounter with the Sirens. As the story goes, the Sirens lured passing sailors with the enchantment of their seductive voices, causing their ships to crash on the rocky coast. Odysseus wished to hear their song without causing a shipwreck; he wanted to have his cake and eat it too. While he has himself tied to the mast of his ship, his men have their ears plugged with beeswax. They are ordered to keep him tied tight, and to refuse any orders he gives to the contrary, while being under the spell of the Sirens as they pass their island. And indeed, though he is lured and would have caused death and destruction if his men had not been so instructed, the ship sails on. This is called self-binding. But it is more than that. There is a division of tasks that prevents him from untying himself. He is forced by others to live by his own rules. This is what purpose binding does for a constitutional democracy.

In Chapter 9 data protection law will be addressed. In the European context some scholars claim that the principle of purpose binding that governs the processing of personal data is the core of data protection, rather than consent, contract or a legal stipulation. It is curious to see that already in 1980 the Guidelines of the Organisation for Economic Co-operation and Development (OECD) herald purpose binding as a core element of the fair information principles. These principles and the legislation that has been built on them apply to private companies as well as governmental agencies. It seems that a derivative of the legality principle that addresses the powers of the state has been transplanted to the private sector, requiring a similar limitation on the powers of private enterprise. It may be that this particular principle flies in the face of all the added value that is to be created from data analytics; it seems to pre-empt pre-emption by requiring prior, specific and explicit notice. Outside the EU, scepticism rules, especially with regard to the fact that under EU law a person cannot waive the right to implementation of the purpose binding principle. The principle may, however, be our only hope for keeping the onli*f*e world free from successful attempts to persistently pre-empt our intent. We will return to this point in Chapter 9, but we will first elaborate on the various relationships between law and technology.

7.4 CONCLUSIONS: ADDRESS AND REDRESS

Law is the business of lawyers, but in the end it addresses all those with legal subjectivity, that is, all those capable of having rights and obligations. In the end, it is their law. In the end, law does not describe or prescribe; it predicts what legal effect will be attached to what event, action or state of affairs. This effect is performed, not caused. Law is – perhaps – a stage where we are all actors, invited to perform our shared lives. But this performance is for real, thanks to its hard-core artificiality; it is not an imaginary narrative or something for spectators. It co-determines who gets what, under what conditions, whether the 'what' concerns money, goods or services, punishment, an entitlement, an obligation, or a status that enables specific actions otherwise denied. In abiding by the law or violating its stipulations people address the law; they try to twist its hand to their own advantage, or confirm its normativity by acting in ways compatible with its 'regime of veridiction'. The ends of the law are simple but complex; modern law aims for justice in the sense of distributive and corrective equality, legal certainty in the sense of a monopoly on enactment for the legislator and another monopoly on adjudication for the courts, and, finally, purposiveness in the sense that law is instrumental in serving the objectives set in the political arena.

Corrective justice redresses violations of the legal framework by attaching legal obligations to compensate damage, or a legal right to punish, notably for harm caused. Redress, however, also concerns the legality principle that is ingrained in constitutional democracies. I dare say that the legality principle typifies the agonistic struggles between justice, legal certainty and instrumentality, which must be sustained instead of overcome. Legality cannot be reduced to legal certainty (which would equate with legalism), nor to justice (which would equate with natural law) nor to expediency (which would equate with instrumentalism). It ties the state to its own legal rules, but also instantiates a system of checks and balances that safeguards against the Sirens of tyranny or those of market fundamentalism, and, finally, legality relates to fundamental rights that prevent it from turning into legalism.

Legality connects the instrumentality of the law with the political arena, where the purpose of government policy is determined. It implies that governmental action is restricted by the fact that it must serve a legitimate purpose that must be specific and explicit to count as such. This enables transparency and accountability of government intervention and explains the role of purpose binding in a constitutional democracy.

Legality addresses the government as an actor with specific loyalties to the public good, thus redressing a potential bias to serve its own semi-private interests. Such redress must be arranged by means of a system of checks and balances, notably setting up countervailing powers where powers accumulate. Purpose binding is implied with legality; it demands that governments are always clear about the purposes for which they intervene in the lives of their constituents, enabling others to test whether their behaviours and decisions are in line with those purposes.

It is interesting to see that purpose binding has developed into a core principle of data protection in the age of data-driven agency, although the lure of the Sirens (business models and homeland security) remains a perpetual challenge.

8. Intricate entanglements of law and technology

8.1 WHY LAW AND TECHNOLOGY?

After exploring the ends of law in the previous chapter, we shall now relate law to technology, while reflecting on the nexus of philosophy of law and philosophy of technology. The question is whether modern law can afford to remain unaffected by the changing ICI, and if not, whether and how it should be *transformed to sustain its identity*. To answer these questions we need to investigate to what extent modern law has distinct characteristics that were triggered by the ICI of the printing press, because if so, such characteristics cannot be taken for granted in an environment that thrives on data-driven agency.

To prepare the ground for an inquiry into the interrelation between law and technology we first explore different conceptions of both technology and law. This confronts the preliminary issue of technologically neutral law that concerns the mode of existence of modern law and asks the question whether law exists independently from its technological embodiment. In the next chapters, the question of how modern law could transform to sustain its identity will be addressed, by investigating the role of data protection law and the notion of legal protection by design.

8.2 THREE CONCEPTIONS OF LAW AND OF TECHNOLOGY

8.2.1 Different Conceptions, Alternative Modes of Existence

Law is an essentially contested concept that gives rise to competing conceptions. In this chapter we will group these conceptions under three headings that are equally pertinent for the concept of technology. Within the philosophy of technology we can discriminate between those who view technologies as mere tools to achieve a purpose, and those who believe that Technology has an autonomous, independent dynamic. Finally, there are those who see technologies as instruments that reinvent us, while we invent them.[227] In this book 'technologies' refers to instruments that have a material component, whereas 'techniques' is reserved for methods used to achieve a goal.[228] Techniques will often involve technologies, while technologies assume consolidated techniques to handle them. However, we could say that spoken language is a communication technique that does not involve a technology. When I write technology with a capital T, I refer to a conception that tends to technological determinism, and views Technology as a separate dimension of our artefactual environment. Speaking of technology or technologies without capital T refers to the set of actual technologies under discussion, assuming that whether technologies are deterministic of human behaviour is an empirical question and depends on the specifics of the material components and the architecture of the technology, on how it connects with other technologies, and on how it has been taken up in human society. Based on current scientific research and the core tenets of philosophical anthropology,[229] I understand human beings as fundamentally entangled with the technologies they use; being human implies making and using tools. This also means that human society is always also a technological society.

In philosophy of law, we can distinguish similar conceptions of law. There are those who view law as a mere instrument to achieve certain policy ends, whom I will call instrumentalists, and those who believe that law has an autonomous, independent existence. Finally, there are those who see the law as an instrument that embodies and constitutes the core values of a society, neither a mere instrument, nor an independent domain. Though I term the first conception instrumentalist, the third can be termed instrumental because it does not deny that law is an instrument. Rather, the third conception emphasizes that instruments co-constitute both their users and the goal they should help to achieve.[230] This fits with the conception of law that was developed in the previous chapter, where the purposiveness or instrumentality of the law is taken to be one of its crucial ends. A law that does not aim to be effective does not qualify as law.

When you think about it, these different conceptions of law and technology refer to how the law and how technology are deemed to exist, to their supposed mode of existence. In the previous chapter we have already touched on this by referring to Latour's work. Let's take this a step further. In his *An Inquiry into Modes of Existence*, Latour saliently cuts through the usual business of opposing epistemological and ontological issues, based on the philosophical distinction between how we know things and how things exist. Within that framework *conceptions are about knowing* and *modes of existence are about being*, leaving us with an insurmountable gap in between. Latour builds on Austin's speech act theory, and Ryle's category mistake, to explain how a 'regime of enunciation' connects with a 'regime of veridiction', that basically determines the conditions of felicity for the truth of an enunciation. In his view, science, religion, politics, law, economy each produce their own facts, based on their own truth conditions. He argues that instead of requiring such different disciplines or domains to mix their 'regimes of veridiction' into an interdisciplinary soup, they should instead learn to respect each other and join forces without betraying their own modes of existence. My investigation differs in that I am concerned with different ways of speaking about law (detecting alternate conceptions of their 'regime of enunciation'), which is connected with different views on the force of law and legal effect (which determine law's 'regime of veridiction'), ultimately resulting in different understandings of the mode of existence of the law.[231]

For instance, we can ask whether law is merely a technique for dispute resolution or for governing one's subjects. Does law exist as an idea of which the fundamental characteristics remain the same throughout (pre-) history? Is it tied up with morality or does it exist in a separate dimension? In the previous chapter we have already encountered these types of questions, and the position that was developed resonates throughout this chapter. Similar questions can be asked about technology: is it merely a physical tool whose existence, once created, can be described without reference to its maker or user? Or, does Technology exist as a mode of thinking of which actual technologies are mere examples? Does law exist as an institutional fact, built on the performative interplay of human society, whereas technology exists as a brute fact, built out of atoms and nowadays bits (which are, by the way, also made of atoms, inscribed on silicon)? Or, should we admit that modern law is both an institutional fact and a brute fact, since it has been embedded in the technology of the printing press? Law *is about* text, or should we admit – more precisely – that law *exists as* text? If the latter is true, should we expect that artificial intelligence – as a technology – transforms the mode of existence of the law? This question will be explored in the next section (8.3). Before that I will first discuss the relevant conceptions of law and technology in terms of their assumed modes of existence: as a neutral instrument, as an independent actor, or, as a mediator that exists on different levels and is capable of transforming its makers, its addressees, its users and the human-machine fabric that holds them together.

8.2.2 The Neutral Conception: Law or Technology as Mere Instrument

The mode of existence of technology as a mere instrument   The first conception of technology can be termed instrumentalist, because it considers technologies as a means to an end without paying attention to either the way they enable and shape the ends for which they are employed, or to the way they influence the person, business or other organization that uses them. The instrumentalist understanding of technology sees technologies in general, first as tools that can be clearly separated from the objectives they serve and, second, as objects that must obviously be seen as separate from the subject that operates them. A hammer should not be confused with the table it is supposed to help make, nor with the carpenter who does the hammering. Though the analytical clarity this provides is laudable, thinking in terms of separation mystifies the mutual shaping of means and end, subject and object. In that sense it does not clarify at all. The instrumentalist perspective inevitably connects with a utilitarian point of view of technology, highlighting that the moral evaluation of a specific technology can only be based on its effectiveness and efficiency in achieving the goal that was set by its user. The moral evaluation of the goal itself supposedly has nothing to do with that; it is set by the user and should be evaluated on its own, not in relation to whatever tools were used to reach it. The goal can thus be evaluated from a deontological perspective, by asking if it is the right goal, considering whether it accords with moral imperatives. An instrumentalist conception takes technologies to be neutral tools, which can be used for good or for bad, but have no normative implications of their own accord. In a famous maxim, Kranzberg has summarized the main objections against this position:[232]

> Technology is neither good nor bad, but never neutral.

Taken by itself (if at all possible), a specific technology is neither good nor bad. However, this does not imply that its affordances do not have a normative impact on its users, their environment, those affected by its use, and the kinds of objectives enabled by the technology. The term 'normative' is not used here as equivalent with moral. Normative refers to action patterns that are induced or enforced, and inhibited or ruled out by the use of a specific technology. A car enables one to drive. It does not force one to drive, but once in the car there are things one can do and other things one cannot do. The car is not merely an instrument for driving, because the act of driving is *constituted by* the car. You cannot drive a horse or a bicycle, though at a higher level of abstraction one could say that horses and bicycles, as well as cars enable one to travel. It would be silly, however, not to acknowledge that driving a car has a different impact than riding a horse or a bicycle on the person who travels, on her relations with family, friends, work and leisure, or on the health of those who drive a car or become the victim of a collision. Technology thus always has a normative impact, because it changes the affordances of the environment of the human person who uses it. Whether this change is for the good or for the bad is a matter of moral evaluation. Before we can perform such evaluation, however, we must first recognize the transformation of action patterns that is afforded. Viewing a technology as a neutral tool thus hides its normative implications and suggests that the moral evaluation of a technology only concerns its wrongful use; if it is used for a bad purpose or used badly for a good purpose we can condemn the action as abuse or misuse. An instrumentalist conception of technology thus focuses on harm and abuse, avoiding a discussion of the technology itself, turning a blind eye to its affordances and how they reconfigure the fabric of human society. For, instance, an online social network will be considered a tool that can be used for good or bad purposes, depending on the individual person or organization that engages with it. Suggesting that, irrespective of the bad intentions of whoever abuses the network, it may restructure the 'in-between' of groups and individuals, thus impacting privacy by its mere usage, makes no sense to those who wish to stick to clear separations between means and ends, and subjects and objects. I believe that understanding technologies as mere means amounts to taking a naïve and even dangerous position. Such an understanding blinds us to the potentially far-reaching consequences of engaging with new technologies. This is neither to say that these consequences are necessarily bad or good, nor that we can always foresee them.

The mode of existence of law as an instrument for social engineering   In philosophy of law we discriminate between ruling by law and the Rule of Law.[233] Ruling by law is basically a rule of man by means of law. This brings those subject to the law under the arbitrary will of whoever rules. The difference with the Rule of Law is the lack of a system of checks and balances that brings the legislator and the administration under the reign of the law. By separating the bodies that legislate and administrate from the body that ultimately decides on the scope and meaning of the legislation, that is, the court, the Rule of Law prevents the legislator and the administration from being judges in their own case. Ruling by law has certain advantages, compared to other means of ruling one's subjects, for instance by means of dispute settlement or by means of military, economic or religious power. Ruling by law allows the government to impose general rules on its subjects, hoping they will contribute to the behavioural changes that it deems desirable or necessary. The rule-based character of such government creates a framework of rule-based expectations that is instrumental in keeping the peace, to the extent that it provides legal certainty. Historically, absolutism in 17th- and 18th-century Europe was a prime example of the rule by law by the sovereign. At that time the courts served under the reign of the sovereign and the magistrates decided cases in the name of the king. If a judge decided against the king's wishes, he could be overruled by his sovereign.[234] In that sense, legal certainty was rather limited, because the law was easily bent to the private interests of the king.

Those who frame law as a neutral instrument for social engineering basically invite those who govern us to rule *by* law, instead of adhering to the Rule of Law. The latter would, surely, imply that law is not a neutral instrument, but an instrument that is co-constitutive of the 'regime of veridiction' of the Rule of Law and thus defined as expressing a set of norms and values that are part and parcel of the Rule of Law. The neutral conception sees law as a way to govern that can be replaced or freely mixed with other policy instruments; the only criteria for preferring one instrument to another are its effectiveness and efficiency in achieving policy goals set by the legislator or the executive. This heralds the instrumentality of the law as its only final end. Legitimacy may come in as a means to generate acceptance, hoping to bring down the cost of law enforcement, but otherwise legitimacy plays only at the level of politics, which determines the goals to be achieved.

Viewing law as merely an instrument fits the so-called regulatory paradigm. This paradigm reigns in policy circles, and also in policy science, which is a social science inclined to take an exclusively external perspective on the law. Somehow the paradigm has also infested law and legal theory,[235] inviting lawyers to think about law in terms of regulation, that is:[236]

> A process involving the sustained and focused attempt to alter the behaviour of others with the intention of producing a broadly identified outcome or outcomes.

Thus defined, law is a mere instrument to influence behaviour in view of policy goals. Citizens are not addressed as subjects of the law, but – in an attempt to get rid of the command and control model of authoritarian law – they are now framed as entities whose behaviour must change to achieve some greater good. The language has shifted from regulating the *actions* of legal subjects, to regulating the *behaviour* of groups or individuals.[237] The regulatory paradigm is not about providing normative orientation coupled with the means to contest governmental intervention in a court of law. It simply aims to influence people (in a sustained and focused manner). We can imagine the confusion that occurs when technology comes into the equation. Why not use technologies as neutral means to achieve policy goals, if they provide for more efficient and effective ways of guiding people? If the idea is to influence behaviour instead of addressing action, and if the means are interchangeable, why not opt for a means that is less visible, less contestable and thus more influential in getting people to behave in alignment with policy objectives? Techno-regulation is a prime example of what rule by law ends up with; replacing legal regulation with technical regulation may be more efficient and effective, and as long as the default settings are a part of the hidden complexity people simply lack the means to contest their manipulation. This is why Lessig's famous *Code and Other Laws of Cyberspace* is deeply disturbing.[238] Lessig discusses four ways of regulating our behaviour: law, market forces, social norms and computer code. This is clearly in alliance with the regulatory paradigm; the mix of regulatory instruments is then necessarily based on utilitarian considerations. Though Lessig has done wonderful work in showing the normative impact of computer code and architecture, his cure for the problems this causes is deeply entwined with the classical law and economics approach of the Chicago School.[239] The assumptions that underlie the game theoretical background of this school cannot frame law other than as a neutral instrument to be judged based on its efficiency and efficacy in reaching policy goals. It sees human beings as rational agents that try to maximize their utility. The same goes for approaches based on behavioural economics, which admit the bounded rationality of human agents and basically advise policy makers on how to cater to the irrational biases of their citizens.[240] Why not use nudging to influence your constituency, if it 'works' better than law? Why indeed?

8.2.3 The Autonomous Conception: Law or Technology as Independent

The mode of existence of technology as an autonomous and independent force   In the field of philosophy of technology we confront two types of technological determinism: utopian and dystopian. Both attribute a dynamic to technology that is independent of its human inventors, or at least determines its own impact on human society. Both also tend to speak of technology in general terms, as if there is no need to investigate the actual empirical affordances of a specific technology in a specific environment; Technology with a capital T runs the show, whatever its various incarnations instantiate. The optimistic strand of technological determinism can be detected in the opinion that any problems created by a specific technology will – in the end – be solved by new technologies. Or, taking it further, the belief that any problem can – theoretically, but often also practically – be solved once the right technology has been applied to it. To validate the latter belief, problems will be defined in a way that enables us to translate them into the frame of a particular technology. Big Data is a case in point. The near-religious belief of many adherents of Big Data Solutionism (BDS) shows a tendency to redefine the flux of life in terms of machine-readable data that can be operated upon to compute solutions to any computable problem one might want to imagine. From reducing the greenhouse effect, distribution of food resources, health problems to critical infrastructure, the task is to reorganize the world in a way that enables pervasive data flows, Big Data aggregation and the employment of ML and other techniques of AI. The assumptions that problems are translatable into computer code and that solutions will be computable once there is enough computing power and the right type of AI are unsubstantiated. The fact that the problem can be solved in Big Data Space does not imply that the problem will also be solved in the world that is supposedly represented in the data. Meanwhile, the widespread faith in BDS drives new business models as well as governmental investment in data-driven government. One could object that this type of belief is mainly found with non-experts, who are unaware of the actual obstacles to computability and tractability. It seems a naïve version of techno-optimism, rather than an argued philosophical determinism. However, its widespread adherence in policy circles and business makes it, perhaps, even more noteworthy than the more radical prophecies of grounded expertise. Examples of the latter concern beliefs in trans- and posthumanism,[241] based on advances in neuroscience and artificial intelligence, combined with synthetic biology, nano-technology and robotics. Kurzweil's famous singularity where the universe implodes into a single point of unsurpassable intelligence is also a case in point.[242] To the extent that such scenarios are presented as the inevitable result of technological evolution, they disclose themselves as examples of technological determinism. In the end such determinism cannot be proven; it is an article of faith, like any other attempt to create certainty in the face of the openness of the future. The lure of utopian determinism is that it presents the uptake of new technologies as inevitable and worthwhile, qualifying criticism and critique as inapt attempts to delay a better world.

Dystopian views of our technological environment have similarly been infested with the virus of technological determinism. The idea that our current age is one of computational thinking, driven by a technological eco-system that transforms our relationship to ourselves, can be found in the work of a series of mainly continental philosophers. In itself this point of view need not couple with determinism. Many authors in the fields of media studies and science, technology and society (STS) studies observe and describe the impact of specific technological affordances on the structure and institution of self, mind and society, without suggesting that the mutual transformations of technology and society are in any way determined. Influential philosophers such as Heidegger and Ellul,[243] however, have clothed their concern over the calculative mode of being that comes with automation in a dystopian determinism. They attribute a kind of autonomy to Technology that is hard to counter, because it is not based on empirical evidence, but on assumptions and definitions that allow them to explain societal developments in terms of their pre-conceived ideas of the technological world. The lure of this form of determinism is the attraction of knowing in advance that proposed solutions will not be of help and can only create the illusion of stopping the decline of civilization or human evolutions.

Whereas viewing technology as a mere means can be termed naïve and dangerous, seeing Technology as an autonomous force that cannot be stopped is similarly naïve and equally dangerous. When assessing how specific technologies influence and determine the constitution of our-selves, mind and societies, we need acuity and discernment, not the simplification that is inherent in instrumentalism and faith or fear. This is even more important when analysing and imagining the impact of ICIs. Keen attention to empirical detail is needed and a perspicacious sensitivity to the affordances of the AI that we are constructing, without taking for granted that the design of our ICIs entirely determines their consequences in the real onlife world.

The mode of existence of law as an independent autonomous discipline or practice The autonomous conception of law can be equated to some extent with legal positivism, which refers to a specific understanding of positive (valid, existing) law. Positivism is deeply concerned about the validity of law. It is important to understand why this is the case, and why legal positivism adheres to a strict demarcation of positive law from social or moral norms on the one hand and politics on the other. This is related to the binding character of modern law that enables and con-strains those under its jurisdiction, thus imposing a specific configuration of mutual expectations between citizens. Other than in the case of social or moral norms, these expectations relate to enforceable rights and obligations. The enforcement is ultimately based on the power and authority of the state that holds the monopoly of violence that in turn co-constitutes the internal sovereignty of the modern state.[244] Modern law can best be understood as the articulation of the conditions for legal effect. The notion of legal effect should, however, not be equated with a sociological notion such as influence or function. Whereas the neutral conception of law tends to view law from an external social science or economic perspective, the substantive conception takes an internal legal perspective, emphasizing that the mode of existence of the law is not 'social' or 'moral' or 'political'. Legal effect denotes the consequences that legal norms attach to specific actions or states; legal effect changes the legal status of a person or other entity and attributes the ensuing rights and obligations to legal subjects. If I fulfil specific conditions, stipulated by the law, I will become the owner of a house, I will be married, or I will be liable to pay compensation for having caused harm. The definition and interpretation of these specific conditions have significant effects. A broad definition of a criminal offence will imply that more conduct falls within its scope and entails that more people will suffer the consequence of punishability. A vague definition or an erratic interpretation of the conditions for concluding a valid contract would generate uncertainty, because people will not be sure of the legal effect. A measure of analytical rigour is therefore an act of benevolence in the context of the law; it safeguards the foreseeability of legal effect. This underlines the crucial importance of the determination of the validity of positive law, and the demarcation of what falls within its scope. Legal positivism tends to direct all its attention to the latter questions: those of validity and law's separation from what is not law. It is based on two 'separation theses'. First, law is separated from politics, and second, it is separated from morality. These separations are, however, complex. Though law is separated from politics, its enforceability depends on the powers of the state. These powers are, paradoxically, legitimated by the law. The law basically denies the state any powers that have not been attributed by (constitutional) law, and subsequently turns powers into competences when attributing them.[245] For instance, the power to punish is transformed into a competence to punish, once the state's power to punish is formally attributed by a law that also conditions the exercise of this power. A legal competence thus both constitutes and restricts the powers of the state. This shows that, though politics is what produces law, politics is also bound by law, at least in so far as we are speaking of a state that adheres to the Rule of Law. Some speak of a historic bargain between law and politics: as long as the legal profession leaves the enactment of law to politics, the latter will leave the interpretation of its law to the courts.[246] In the context of the autonomous conception of the law, however, the Rule of Law must be understood in a formal and procedural manner. As long as the legislator follows the legal rules on how to make law, and the administration acts in accordance with the law that has been enacted, it is deemed to comply with the Rule of Law. I will call this formal conception of the Rule of Law legalism, and will later distinguish it from a substantive conception, that vouches for legality instead of legalism. Under the autonomous conception of the law, the validity of the law cannot depend on its content, as this would conflate law with morality. The validity of the law – in this view – depends on the authority of the state and on its societal acceptance as a system of interrelated legal rules that requires obedience from those under its jurisdiction. Note that in common law jurisdictions legalism may be associated with strict rule-based interpretation of legal precedent, instead of putting the emphasis on enacted law as with civil law jurisdictions.

The consequence of this conception of law is that it need not concern itself with other domains in science, or with other practices than that of the legal profession. The autonomous mode of existence enables clear demarcations between law and sociology, between law and politics and between law and morality. It entails that transformations within other domains of science or society cannot affect the law, because it is supposed to develop independently. It also entails that technology cannot change the mode of existence of the law, or challenge its conceptual architecture. Finally, adherents of this conception will claim that there is no need for lawyers to engage in in-depth reflection on the onlife world, or to worry about the effects of ICIs on the substance of legal rights and obligations, other than in the course of solving cases that require legal solutions. They will assume that most, if not all legal problems posed by the onlife world can be decided within the framework of the existing legal framework. If not, the legislator should act by making new laws, and this is not a matter of law, but of politics.

8.2.4 The Pluralist Conception: Law or Technology as Relational

The mode of existence of technology as multistable   In the philosophy of technology several strands stand out for acknowledging a mode of existence that is both relative and relational, entailing a pluralist conception of technology. We have social shaping of technology (SST), social construction of technology (SCOT) and actor network theory (ANT). These understandings of the relationship between technology and society all confirm that the point is not so much whether a particular technology necessarily has certain effects; the point is how a specific design and how a specific uptake of a technology determines its affordances. When I use the term design, I refer to the development of hardware and software, their architecture, the interfaces, including requirements engineering, computer science, and electrical and software engineering. In some communities design is strictly separated from engineering, seeing the first as secondary to the second, as if only engineering determines functionality, whereas design is merely about developing user-friendly interfaces. Or, quite the opposite: as if engineering is merely about technical functionality, whereas the creative process of designing determines the user experience and thus the eventual uptake of a technology. To prevent endlessly detailed differentiation I will use the notions of design and engineering as interchangeable, though I am aware of pertinent debates on the difference. The same goes for the difference between software engineering and electrical engineering, and between computer science and software engineering. My take is that these differences matter, but not necessarily for the argument I am making here. What does matter is the difference between affordances in the sense of Gibson, as I have been using the term so far, and in the sense of Donald Norman, who popularized the term in design studies in his *The Psychology of Everyday Things*, later titled *The Design of Everyday Things*.[247] For Gibson an affordance does not depend on whether an agent actually perceives it, as long as the particular environment makes certain things possible or impossible for that particular type of agent (a bat, a dog, a human being, a cloud based robot, a self-driving car). Gibson spoke of affordances as 'actionable properties' that are inherently relational because they always depend on the characteristics of the agent. Norman was less interested in the question of 'actionable properties' than in the perceived affordances, while also distinguishing affordances from constraints. His focus was on how things can be designed in a way that enables people to intuitively understand how they should be used without needing guidance in text. However, what matters for an ICI is what it affords, not merely what people perceive as its affordances. This is important because many affordances of pre-emptive computing are hidden.

Engineering makes a difference because the design and the default settings of the hardware and the software determine its potential uptake (its affordances), while the actual uptake by humans and other machines determine its functionality. We should take the term functionality in the broad sense. A technology can be functional in the sense that it was intended, but most of the time there are many other ways that it is functional or dysfunctional. An SNS may be functional in enabling people to share information about themselves, in managing their reputation, in connecting them with old friends they would not have located otherwise and with new friends they would not have known to exist. It may also be functional in protecting their privacy, in enabling personalized advertising, in generating extensive profiles on political preference or sexual orientation, in enabling the SNS provider to calculate a number of personal traits based on 'liking behaviours' or in protecting people against surveillance by a government. All this will depend on the underlying infrastructure of the Internet and the web, on the default settings that cannot be changed, on the default settings that can be opted out of, or on granular choice as to who gets to see which postings and on which third parties can access one's SNS social graph and online behaviours. The social fabric into which the SNS arrived will have to reconfigure itself while accommodating the novel attachments, and this will depend on whether and how people engage with the technology, to what extent they force the provider to change its policies, what new applications are developed and admitted on top of the SNS and on whether alternatives become available that force the provider to compete on functionalities it previously neglected. Technologies are inherently multistable, as Ihde holds.[248] While nesting into, infringing upon or even disrupting the existing social fabric, they will develop and transform until a balance is reached that consolidates the mutual expectations around the technology, making it more difficult to return to its initial malleability. But this stabilization is not entirely determined; most technologies enable a multiplicity of stable entanglements. Indeed, current ICIs seem to favour a continuous flux, even after a technology has been taken up beyond the threshold that signals its stabilization. Some have called this the generative nature of the Internet,[249] which enables ever novel applications to be built on top of its hyperconnected infrastructure. Nevertheless, the idea of a threshold is crucial, since ICIs depend on it to be a success. Users flock to the SNS that has managed to seduce their friends or colleagues, because this is seen as the major function of the SNS: to be able to reach out to a maximum amount of potential friends, creating, segregating and reconfiguring the audiences that help to construct one's identity.

If the mode of existence of technologies is multistable we need a pluralistic conception of technology. How a specific technology exists will then depend on its actual affordances, which are always relative to its environment and to the perceptive and enactive capabilities of those who use it, or, rather, those who interact with it. To understand the future impact of a technology we must, therefore, not restrict ourselves to an investigation of the intended usage or its foreseeable functionalities. What is required is scrutiny as to potential usage and required functionalities. The latter cannot be restricted to utilitarian projections. They need to incorporate the norms and values we wish to sustain, and to enquire how their potential usage will transform or disrupt these norms and values. Technology assessment, then, requires up-stream involvement of those who will suffer and enjoy the consequences of its potential use. Not merely of its abuse. It should be clear that whereas abuse is a threat that must be countered, an ICI that threatens the normative fabric of our society by its use is a far greater concern. Not because the normative fabric is inherently good, but because we need to pay attention and ask ourselves the – ultimately political – question of what kind of society we wish to remain or become.

The mode of existence of the law as relational   A relational conception of law sees law neither as instrumentalist nor as autonomous. First, it denies that law is a mere instrument, because its instrumentality depends on the legal subject that enacts, administers or adjudicates the law, and on the ends it aims to achieve. Second, it denies that law is independent from its societal, scientific and professional environment, because its existence depends on the performative nature of the social fabric it constitutes and by which it is constituted. The latter indicates that in so far as this social fabric is articulated by means of particular ICIs, the mode of existence of the law co-depends on the ICIs that institute the society it aims to regulate. This is the subject matter of the next section (8.3).

Acknowledging that law is relational entails a recognition that law is – like technology – inherently multistable. This does not mean that anything goes. It is not a matter of radical relativism. Legal traditions stabilize in different ways, in tune with those that live under their rule. To provide guidance, orientation and reliability to human interaction, however, a legal tradition must at least help to re-establish the norms whose violation threatens to disrupt the social fabric. Norms in this sense are defined as the patterns of mutual double expectations that enable people to act, having a fair idea of how their fellows will respond. Norms enable trust and create room for reinvention, though this implies that norms also enable disruption and loss of trust. Precisely when norms are violated they create fear and need realignment to reinstate the tenacity of the normative framework that was ruffled. Once the state takes the stage, dispute resolution is slowly confiscated by the state making the legal solidity of the normative order dependent on its own decisions in court. If we then leapfrog to the modern state that claims internal and external sovereignty we will see a new affiliation between law and state. Not merely dispute resolution but also legislation becomes the monopoly of the sovereign. One can hardly overestimate the impact of this grasping of power: the power to enact general orders backed by threats, including the power to adjudicate with a final decision any said violation of these orders. Such a monopoly, reinforced by the monopoly on violence and the exclusive right to punish (*ius punienda*), enables tyranny and dictatorship. It is this envious monopolistic power of the modern state that calls for the notion of individual rights, for the invention of a social contract that both limits the powers of the state and tasks it with the care for the *res publica*, the public good. Law becomes a complex instrument that is used to rule the nation while at the same time reigning in the absolutist power claims of the sovereign. Historically, the absolute states of the 17th and 18th centuries in Europe precede both the Rule of Law and democracy. Even before the advent of a democratic legislator the Rule of Law established a pertinent check on sovereign powers. As discussed above, this was first a matter of formal procedural safeguards, forcing the sovereign to abide by its own rules, while not providing a stable framework to guarantee that such rules express substantive justice. In the course of the 19th century, legalism appears in the common law together with formal procedural conceptions of the Rule of Law, the *Rechtsstaat* and the *État Legal*. When the powers of the state increase with the rise of the welfare state, which takes an active approach to the construction of the common good, this narrow understanding of the Rule of Law does not provide the protection needed to counter the totalitarian urges of the state. To achieve and increase the public good, the state wants to know everything on each of its citizens, and dictate in ever greater detail how they should behave in order to reach ever new instantiations of welfare. This finally led to the idea of legality, the notion that the state is not free to act as it sees fit, but must clarify how its actions are compatible with a legal framework that provides citizens with fundamental rights against the state. This entails a substantive procedural conception of the Rule of Law and the *Rechtsstaat*, culminating in France in the idea of the *État de droit*, instead of the *État legal*. This confirms that law (*droit*) is not equivalent with enacted written law, but depends on a set of checks and balances that form the implied philosophy that should inspire the interpretation of written law,[250] sustained by the institution of countervailing powers. Law, then, becomes the mediation between sovereign and subjects, government and citizens, ultimately grounding democracy in the sound territory of legality that both institutes and restricts even the rule of democratic majorities.[251]

This particular mode of existence of the law is a historical artefact. It cannot be taken for granted; its existence is complex and layered and depends on continuous hard work to be sustained. Notably, it is grounded in the proliferation of the written word that was precipitated by the ICI of the printing press. Modern law is rooted in text. In the next section I will investigate how this particular affiliation between law and text determines a whole range of characteristics that we tend to attribute to law as a system of normative rules, as a social institution or as a 'regime of veridiction'.

8.3 NO SUCH THING AS TECHNOLOGICALLY NEUTRAL LAW

8.3.1 The Technological Embodiment of Law

This section is not about technology neutral law, which I will discuss in the chapter on Legal Protection by Design. *Technology neutral law* is basically a normative appeal to enact laws that do not favour a particular technology as this would obstruct innovation, or to refrain from enacting laws that apply only to specific technologies as this would make the law less sustainable in the long run, or an appeal to take into account how specific technologies diminish the effectiveness of a particular fundamental right by compensating these effects with legislative measures. Technology neutral law assumes a stable relationship between law and its *own* technological embodiment, whereas this is what needs argument and investigation in the onl*ife* world. This investigation will be done under the heading of *technologically neutral law*, raising the question whether, and if so, to what extent, modern law is inscribed in a particular technology. If the answer is positive, law is not technologically neutral and necessarily shares the affordances of its embodiment.

In the previous section I have argued that neither law nor technology are neutral instruments, while neither qualifies as an independent force or institution. Instead, both are seen as relational and co-constituting both those who shape or use them and the goals they aim to achieve. The implication is that where law attaches itself to a particular ICI, it will bear the brunt of such alignment. An ICI is an information and communication infrastructure; it involves more than an information and communication technology (ICT) because the notion of infrastructure denotes 'the basic equipment and structures (such as roads and bridges) that are needed for a country, region, or organization to function properly'.[252] It cannot be defined in terms of technology *an sich* (if there even were such a thing) as it refers to the capillaries, arterioles and venules that enable the exchange of information on which a complex body with interdependent systems and components depends. Without an ICI, human society is not thinkable. However, early ICIs were less technologically mediated than those of literate societies.

In an oral culture the ICI is structured around language, which is a technique, but not a technology. This is not to say that language has no material embodiment, but this embodiment is mostly part of the human body. It concerns the various organs involved in speaking and hearing, but also memory and imagination as they develop from the capacity to remember and to anticipate, all enabled by the plasticity of our brains and the interconnections with memories and projections inscribed in other parts of the body. As indicated in Chapter 3, the ICI of an oral culture largely depends on face-to-face communication, while memory is enabled by mnemonic techniques that enable transgenerational 'storage' of information. This storage, however, must be enacted reiterantly, otherwise the information in it is lost. Basically, the amount of information that can be accumulated is restricted to what can be re-enacted by the human body during its lifetime. If we understand law as the relational construct that enables the consolidation of the patterns of mutual double expectations between people that share jurisdiction, oral law is bound to depend on ritual confirmations of the norms that hold together the social fabric of those living together. In case of conflict the normativity is supported by (the threat of) feud and by voluntary types of dispute resolution. Since oral societies are societies without a state, dispute resolution relies on third parties that have only persuasive authority.[253] The 'legal' norms that consolidate mutual expectations – undifferentiated from religious, moral and political norms – are not written down. They are not part of an external mind; they cannot be objectified and reflected upon as with legal norms in a written culture. They regulate action as it were from under the skin and, as such, they are harder to contest.[254]

Since law depends on human language, and is entirely dependent on communication to establish and consolidate its normative framework, it will have to respond to transformations in the dominant ICI. When law inscribed itself in the ICI of the (handwritten) manuscript, it shared the affordances of the script. The legal dimension of society acquired an extended mind in written manuscripts and this favoured the emergence of a class of legal scribes that held a monopoly on the legal knowledge that was consolidated in the relevant documents. The era of the manuscript entailed much larger societies than that of an oral culture. The reach of written text is far more extensive in time and space than that of the spoken word. But reading and writing are not democratized. Often neither the ruler, nor his subjects were interested in reading and writing. They had professionals for such labours, scribes, who registered land and perhaps at some point carved out some laws on stone tablets to help consolidate normativity throughout the polity. And, still later, we can observe the appearance of lengthy written texts that began a life of their own as primary texts of a religion or even a legal tradition. Glenn has written a masterwork on the emergence of seven legal traditions, especially where he traces this particular phase in the life of the traditions as drawing on a primary text that acquires persuasive authority.[255] Over the course of centuries this led to a set of authoritative commentaries on the initial, primary text, which is often seen as a revelation. The commentaries were crucial, because, with the advent of the script, interpretation became critical. Since text cannot speak for itself, others must take on the task of translating its normative message for distant times and spaces. Finally, over the course of further centuries, this was followed by consolidated commentaries on the commentaries. *The Torah*, the *Mishnah*, the *Talmud* within the talmudic tradition; the *Koran*, the *Sunna*, *Ijma* of the Islamic tradition, and even the *Corpus Iuris Civilis* of the civil legal tradition, they all followed this same scheme. We can see it in the layout of a page in the *Digests*: the primary text in the middle, the glosses and commentaries take secondary position, while enveloping the primary text, steeping it in interpretation. The powers of the state in the era of the script are limited. Not limited by law, but by the affordances of the ICI. It is only with the rise of the modern state, at the end of the Middle Ages, that the monopoly of internal sovereignty emerges as a direct and powerful influence in the lives of its subjects. And this was only possible with the proliferation of the printing press.

8.3.2   The Hallmarks of Modern Law

Perhaps to some the idea that modern law is dependent on and shares the affordances of the printing press is an uncomfortable thought. It implies that matter matters, that law cannot dictate its own terms, and, ultimately, it signifies that under the next dominant ICI, law as we know it may be gone. This is a cause of concern in so far as we value some of the characteristics of modern law; we have no reason to assume they will be part of the next ICI. However, before investigating their potential loss in the onli*fe* world, let me trace the affordances of modern law as contingent upon those of the printing press.

First, let's reconfirm that this is not about technological determinism. Just like we cannot disentangle the law from its environment as if it were merely a neutral instrument, we should not attribute autonomous force to the printing press. However, that being said, we don't want to be naïve and suggest that a technology does not involve both constraining and enabling affordances for those using it or interacting with it. The point is to flesh out what the technology makes possible and how it restricts. Much has been written about the affordances of the script and the printing press. Actually, the findings are scattered in research findings of media studies, cultural anthropology and philosophy of technology.[256] What may be surprising is the lack of research on the side of the law, apart from some work on the law of evidence and the implications of the web for legal precedent.[257] Glenn's investigations into pre-literate legal traditions seem on the spot, and his assessment of the civil law tradition as one firmly rooted in the authority of text is informative. Also, Lessig's critical insights into the normative role played by law's technological architecture have contributed prodigiously to a proper understanding of law's inadequacy in the face of computer coded ICIs. I would, nevertheless, be interested in a more thorough investigation of the relationship between sovereignty and the various manifestations of the Rule of Law on the one hand, and the proliferation of printed text on the other. This cannot be a merely historiographical undertaking or a matter of social scientific research into the causation of modern law and the modern state. The relationship is not one of causation, but one of affordances and co-constitution. It requires philosophical inquiry with keen attention to the empirical realities of the rise of sovereignty and the institution of the Rule of Law. In other work I have made a modest beginning in such research.[258] Here I follow up with a set of seven affordances of the script and the printing press and indicate how they enabled the development of modern law, the rise of the state and, finally, the institution of the Rule of Law.

First, written law externalizes legal norms by inscribing them in stone, clay tablets, scrolls and books. This gives the rules an *independent existence capable of surviving their author (legislator) and even their interpreter (court)*. Written law thus generates continuity and durability. Second, the distantiation between author, interpreter and addressee of the law implies that *interpretation becomes the hallmark of law*, even before the advent of modern law. Third, the externalization of law on material carriers enables a far wider scope of application. This entails, as noted above, that the polity can be extended, enabling *a shift from local to translocal law*. The script thus enables the formation of proto-states and empires run by means of law as an instrument for unification and centralization. Such empires must not be confused with sovereign states; their hold on the lives of the inhabitants is relatively weak. The rulers depend on a class of scribes, capable of explaining and interpreting the written law, advising the courts. This, fourth, allows these scribes to *form a buffer between ruler and subjects maintaining a relatively coherent interpretation of the authoritative texts* – whether legislation or religious text with legal implications.[259] However, their influence is not based on formal authority.

Fifth, with the proliferation of the printing press, the reach and force of written text is at once multiplied and, steadily, also democratized. *Lawyers become integrated as civil servants into the administration headed by the king, thus enabling the formation of a bureaucratic state.* This extends and intensifies the role played by the state as initiator of legal norms, facilitating the emergence of monopolistic claims as to the creation of law by the state. The science of police, which appeared in 18th-century Germany and connects with the old meaning of police (government, public administration), shows how text-based science informs the institution of the modern state, contributing to an effective sovereign rule. Suggesting that the proliferation of text and the ensuing systemization of knowledge have triggered the development of internal sovereignty by no means implies a mono-causal explanation of the modern state. Quite the contrary, a complex construct such as the monopolistic nation-state cannot be explained in terms of singular causes, let alone traced back to technological innovation as its sole cause. For printed matter to have any such effect, the deal struck during the negotiations of the 1648 Peace of Westphalia was pre-conditional. By welding internal and external sovereignty together, based on an internal monopoly on violence and an external respect for states as legal subjects and equal players, the hierarchical model of bureaucratic administration could develop without external interference. The Treaties of Westphalia thus allowed states to focus their attention on internal economic and social welfare, culminating somewhere in the 17th and 18th centuries in a sustainable, enforceable rule *by* law by the sovereign.

Sixth, the proliferation of printed text that reinforces the need for reiterant interpretation greatly enhances the role of the lawyers as stewards of a coherent web of legal texts (legislation, administrative and judicial decisions). Eisenstein has traced the increasing rationalization and systemization of scientific knowledge as an affordance of the printing press, as something made possible and even necessary by the growth of available and contradictory content. The employment of tables of content, indexing and the use of taxonomies is induced by the need to think in terms of headings, categories and search terms to keep track of and still make sense of the growing totality of knowledge claims. This has similar consequences for the law. Though the enactment of written law at the end of the Middle Ages in part concerned the codification of customs, their systematic formulation – often coupled with some infusion of Roman law – went further than mere confirmation. The written articulation of a legal custom transforms its nature, if only because the unified text necessarily translates the complexity of unwritten legal norms into a particular interpretation thereof; which subsequently calls for renewed interpretation, every time it is applied. A prime example of codification at the heart of the early modern state is the *Constitio Criminalis Carolina*, unifying the criminal law within the Holy Roman Empire in 1532, which instituted the inquisitorial system of criminal law – attributing a monopoly to the state for charging a person with a criminal offence. Such centralization is not possible based on hand-written manuscripts; it requires a large body of civil servants that can be instructed by means of printed text.

Though lawyers had first been hired as civil servants in service of the rule *by* law, their resistance against interference by the king slowly but steadily gains traction. Rule by law concretely meant that the courts issued their verdicts in the name of the king, and could be overruled by the king as he pleased. In a famous remonstration, in 1608, Chief Justice Coke spoke against the attempt by King James I to interfere in the application of the law:[260]

> Then the King said that he thought the law was founded upon reason, and that he and others had reason as well as the Judges: to which it was answered by me, that true it was, that God had endowed His Majesty with excellent science, and great endowments of nature; but His Majesty was not learned in the laws of his realm of England, and causes which concern the life, or inheritance, or goods or fortunes of his subjects, are not to be decided by natural reason but by artificial reason and judgement of law, which law is an art which requires long study and experience, before that a man can attain to the cognizance of it.

Here we see how *the complexity of the domain of legal knowledge is cause to redirect the king back to his own realm, claiming a monopoly of interpretation for those trained in legal knowledge.* Coke actually spoke of 'artificial reason and judgement of law', acknowledging that neither moral intuition nor the power to govern could keep up with the growth of legal knowledge. In his *Spirit of the Laws*, Montesquieu remarks that a moderate government fares well with a complex criminal law, as this provides a buffer between ruler and ruled. In short, somehow, the legal profession managed to install the enormity of textual legal knowledge in between the king and his subjects, thus initiating the Rule of Law. This was, however, only the first implication of the expanding domain of legal knowledge. The second implication regards the fact that the king may come to violate his own law, and cannot be trusted to be judge in his own case. Based on the same argument, the courts will, at a far later point in

history, be granted the power to judge against the state, thus finally
bringing the sovereign under the Rule of Law. This is possible by an
internal division within the sovereign, creating the system of checks and
balances that enables a court to employ the monopoly of violence – the
power to enforce – against the public administration or even against the
democratic legislator itself. It goes without saying that this is no small
feat and cannot be taken for granted, and to sustain the ensuing tension
between democracy and the Rule of Law requires hard work.[261]

Seventh, the Rule of Law emerged in the wake of modern law and the
modern state, feeding on two of the most important interrelated
affordances of the printing press. On the one hand, referring to the
second affordance, *the need to interpret* a written norm in the light of the
web of applicable legal norms and in the light of the case at hand,
requires *suspending judgement*. Interpretation must take into account the
legal effect that a decision will have on similar cases, while paying keen
attention to how the same norm has been applied in preceding case law.
This takes time and forces the court to suspend any immediate intuitive
evaluation; it generates a professional hesitation that is real, precisely
because the legal effect of the decision will always implicate both past
and future decisions. On the other hand, the flood of potentially
contradictory texts *threatens* the reader with a *loss of meaning*, with an
impossibility of coming to any conclusion. The hesitation may lead to a
paralysis, to an inability to either act or decide. This is where sovereignty
comes to the rescue. Its unilateral powers feed on a system of unified
texts that are used as instruments to steer the magistrates and, ultimately,
the subjects of the law. Through the lending of sovereign power to the
decision of an independent court, the hesitation is confronted with a
deadline and a final, unilateral decision is made. Paradoxically the threat
of a loss of meaning leads to a *need for closure*, as the French would say.
For the parties to get on with their lives, an authoritative decision for the
case at hand must be made. The legal conflict must be terminated such
that the legal status and the rights and obligations of the parties become
clear and enforceable. This is not only relevant for the parties themselves,
but also for all those who share their jurisdiction. To know how their
actions will be interpreted, under what conditions they are liable and how
the courts will interpret their actions and the applicable law, the case
must be decided and terminated. The law has a clear role to play in
relation to the double mutual anticipation between those who share a life
world. It is interesting to note that the legal maxims *litis finiri oportet*
(the struggle must be ended) and *res judicata est* (the highest court has
spoken, the verdict is final), stem from the late medieval reception of
Roman Law. These maxims were in fact not a part of Roman law as in

force during the Roman Empire, since this was an empire without modern sovereignty, without the bureaucracy enabled by the printing press. The twofold affordances of the printing press – the need to interpret and the threat of a loss of meaning – coalesce with the sovereign's urge to impose its will and with its capability to enforce its decisions. Thus, the Rule of Law in the end consolidates these affordances by requiring the sovereign to enforce an obligation to hesitate before taking an enforceable decision, while taking note that the Rule of Law enables the enforcement of decisions even against the sovereign.

8.3.3 The Challenges of Law in the Onlife World

The onlife world will contain a number of challenges for the law; for instance, concerning types of abuse that do not fall within the scope of existing legal precepts, requiring new legislation or extensive or analogous interpretation by the courts. Some of these challenges will be discussed in the next chapters. Here, I want to investigate how the onlife world affects the mode of existence of law, in relation to the mode of existence of technology. In the previous section I defined modern law and the Rule of Law in terms of seven affordances of the script and the printing press. I will now briefly test how these affordances fare in the onlife world.

First, the script externalizes legal norms by inscribing them into matter. This externalization creates visibility and thereby enables criticism; tacit norms are translated into explicit norms. The ICI of the onlife world is built on hidden complexity; its computational mechanisms are invisible and therefore hard to criticize. Second, the script entails a distantiation in time and space that necessitates interpretation in order to tune the unified norm to its changing contexts. This raises the possibility of disagreement about the right interpretation, which makes the act of interpretation explicit and turns the law into a platform for argument and contestation. The onlife world returns to tacit, invisible interpretations, which are performed by machines that have no use for meaning. It becomes more difficult to engage in argumentation and contestation if the ICI does not operate on the basis of reasons and arguments but on the basis of algorithms or neural nets. Third, compared with an oral society, text enables an extension of the polity and the emergence of translocal law. This potentially reduces the social pressures from kinship relationships, and often enables the co-existence of multiple jurisdictions, notably local, feudal and royal jurisdictions. Such multiplicity creates some freedom – to engage in forum shopping and to have one's case heard by third parties that are less implicated in local interests. The emergence of impartiality as a critical attribute of the Rule of Law may feed on this affordance. The onli*fe* world may nourish an even greater freedom from local constraints. In so far as hyperconnectivity facilitates 'friending' people one would otherwise never meet and building personal and professional communities that reduce pressures from one's local peers to conform to their norms, the onli*fe* world may be an emancipatory, liberating experience. Whether this also amounts to new forms of translocal law is another issue. The early cyberlibertarians of the 1990s expected paradise from what they called Internet freedom, proposing that the state had no business and law no jurisdiction in cyberspace.[262] However, it soon turned out that freedom easily leads to a wild west, where the might of the strongest dictates the law for the weaker, while the state found new ways to assert its monopolies in the realm of the web, with the added advantage that much of its actions were invisible and surveillance could be operated in far more detail. Fourth, the era of the manuscript generated a class of scribes that managed a monopoly on legal expertise, due to their ability to read and write. They thus formed a buffer between ruler and ruled in the age of the great empires. Being restricted to an advisory position, they were in a position to mitigate the autocracy of the magistrates that were appointed on the basis of their political affiliation or economic power. In the onli*fe* world it would seem more likely that computer engineers and programmers perform a similar role. However, those who build the ICI of pre-emptive computing are often in charge or in the service of large commercial enterprises, entailing a private interest in their own business. We can hardly expect them to provide independent advice. It may be true, though, that the hacker community, and those developing privacy enhancing technologies, could take this role in the context of the onli*fe* world. The problem may be, however, that the backbone of the onli*fe* world is formed by a curious amalgam of private enterprise and public bodies that combine competition and strife with invisible alignment and exchange of intelligence. Since many computer engineers and programmers are part of this amalgam we cannot expect that, as a professional body, they form a relatively independent buffer between government and corporations on the one hand and citizens and consumers on the other. Fifth, the era of the printing press made possible the rise of the bureaucratic state, supported by the class of legal scholars that became part and parcel of the early modern state in their capacity as civil servants. This ushered in the era of the rule by law, where regulation by means of written codes and statues became a crucial way to govern the population. Though the law was now a mere instrument in the hands of the sovereign, its alignment with printed text made it an unreliable instrument. The ambiguity of human language in combination with the proliferation of legal text turned the lawyers into stewards of the expanding domain of legal knowledge. In the end they regained their position as buffers between ruler and ruled, though now in an infinitely more complex world, where the ability of the sovereign to determine the lives of his subjects was far greater than in earlier times. In the on*life* world it seems that those who rule seek out other disciplines than law to steer their subjects or to lure their (potential) customers. It is important to note that neither behavioural economics, nor policy science or computer engineering depend on text in the way that the law did. There is a preference for quantitative research, data science and a pervasive tendency to view both policy science and business administration in terms of cybernetics, the science of how to control one's environment. This links up with the regulatory paradigm, discussed above. Sixth, there is an insurmountable tension between being employed as magistrates that speak the law of the king, and being trained as lawyers who seek to reconstruct the multiplicity of authoritative legal texts as a coherent domain of legal knowledge. This tension makes lawyers the stewards of the growing province of legal text, providing them with a factual and, finally, a legal monopoly on the interpretation of the law. Sustaining this tension enables the establishment of the Rule of Law, balancing and compatibilizing the demands for legal certainty, justice and purposiveness on the one hand, and democratic government on the other. Computational thinking thrives on excluding ambiguity and on achieving control of the environment by means of data-driven feedback mechanisms. Does this afford something like the Rule of Law? Or, does it afford anything similar, capable of protecting us from being dependent on an enlightened despot that may turn off the light any time?

Finally, seventh, the printing press affords a suspension of judgement, a cautious reflection on the meaning of a legal precept in the light of the case at hand, and vice versa. And, precisely because of the threat that judgement will be suspended forever, closure is imposed unilaterally after having taken the time to explore uncertainties and ambiguities. Does the ICI of the on*life* world afford this odd and paradoxical need to hesitate coupled with the need to decide in a binding, conclusive way, both on the case at hand and on the applicable law? All this in one sweeping movement, one procedure, one – fair – trial? Or doesn't it?

8.4 CONCLUSIONS: LAW AND THE AFFORDANCES OF THE ONL*IF*E WORLD

Law – as we know it – requires deliberation as well as binding decisions. This core idiosyncrasy, a critical quality of the Rule of Law, is tied to the linearity of the reading mind, to its acquired habit of sequential process-ing, as explained and elaborated by Maryanne Wolf in her work on the reading brain. This chapter proposes that if we stop reading and start behaving like digital natives, we may lose the need to reflect, to consider, to hesitate, to delay our judgement. If we are no longer forced to confront contradictory texts, why should we hesitate? I am not sure that inter-actions with the smart ICI of the *onlife* world afford much self-conscious deliberation. This raises a final, twofold concern that relates to, on the one hand, the possibility that the affordances of the *onlife* world will lead to an instrumentalization of the law, and, on the other hand, to the possibility that the ICI of pre-emptive computing takes a deterministic turn.

The instrumentalization of the law, offset by the affordances of the *onlife* world, could reduce the law to an instrument to influence societal players, maybe even to influence and discipline artificial agents. This may lead to a further engagement with techno-regulation and techno-nudging, approaching people as mechanisms that can be tweaked into desirable behaviour after figuring out on what bias they operate. Once we learn how to use affective computing and synthetic emotions to keep robots and other data-driven agents in check, we might be tempted to try this on our fellows. We already have computer programs capable of recognizing facial expressions, where researchers claim that their soft-ware can detect genuine or faked pain in a far more accurate way than humans do.[263] Does this mean that health insurance coverage will come to depend on a computer assessment of one's health symptoms? Is this a problem, or should we be grateful that fake claims are more efficiently and effectively rejected? The problem is that the research design asks people to deliberately fake pain and then tests whether either machines or humans are good at figuring out who is faking and who is not. To extrapolate the results of the research to real-life situations we would need to know whether people who fake pain in a laboratory situation display the same facial behaviours as those faking pain while navigating their *onlife* world. We also need to consider how this type of research relates to the findings on placebos that actually 'work', whereby the neural correlates of such 'working' have been detected in the brain. What about so-called psychosomatic symptoms,[264] that a computer might either not detect or might qualify as fake, whereas the patient is actually suffering? Based on a pluralist understanding of technology, affective computing can, in principle, be designed and used to contribute to a better understanding of the constitutive relationship between body and mind. The multistability of the technologies involved implies that this can be done without attempting to manipulate people into behaving as healthy productive members of society. However, the regulative paradigm has little critical potential against such manipulation; its adherents might actually cherish the attempt in so far as it works. Though, probably, they would prefer to do this under the heading of nudging or behavioural economics, instead of admitting to manipulation. In so far as the onli*fe* world is designed and engineered in a way that is conducive to pre-emptive computing as an instrument for achieving policy objectives that can replace legal precepts whenever these are less effective or efficient, the mode of existence of the law will be reduced to the instrumentalist modus. Its employment can then be traded against more innovative tools to attain public welfare, or whatever other policy goal takes precedence.

Though we cannot assume that technology is deterministic, we should also not rule out the possibility that a particular technology has a deterministic effect on human action. The point of a pluralist conception of technology is, precisely, that whether a technology overrules human intent is an empirical question. If data-driven agency becomes a pervasive part of our environments our intent may be pre-empted instead of overruled, which seems to me even more deterministic than being forced despite having resisted. In the case of a pre-emption of our intent the law loses its specific mode of existence, blending into the architecture of autonomic decision-making based on a digital unconscious, rather than requiring of such decisions that they are made transparent as well as contestable. It is not so difficult to imagine the growth of a deterministic ICI that keeps itself one step ahead of our inferred preferences or inclinations. Especially where the onli*fe* world becomes saturated with invisible detection and decision mechanisms that manage to redress our *behaviours* instead of addressing us with regard to our *actions*. From the perspective of the Rule of Law the challenge would be to bring the addressee back into the equation; *my behaviour should not be redressed without first addressing me about it*, enabling me to take responsibility for my behaviour as my action, thus initiating and confirming person-hood. An ICI that finds this cumbersome may circumvent such 'address-ing', which is fundamental for the mode of existence of the law. It may rightly fear that addressing someone as a person will afford resistance, recalcitrance and contestation. Does this imply that I am attributing intentions to an ICI, perhaps even anthropomorphizing? No, on the contrary, the analysis takes into account that the ICI has agency charac-teristics and will develop a mind of its own. It is up to us to design and engineer this mind in a way that does not pre-empt us such that we become the cognitive resource of the ICI instead of the other way round.

9. The fundamental right of data protection

9.1 WHY SHOULD DATA PROTECTION BE A FUNDAMENTAL RIGHT?

In the global context two conceptions of data protection vie for hegemony. The one defines data protection as a *subset of* or *means to achieve* privacy, usually speaking of informational privacy as equivalent with data protection. This seems the point of departure for the legal framework of, for instance, the USA. The other conception defines data protection as a fundamental right on its own account that must be distinguished from privacy, although there is overlap. This is the point of view within the EU jurisdiction, where privacy and data protection have been codified as distinct rights in the Charter of Fundamental Rights of the European Union (CFREU).[265] Within Europe, the legal framework for privacy is based mainly on Art. 8 of the European Convention of Human Rights (ECHR), which speaks of the protection of home, family life, private life and correspondence. The ECHR is the human rights treaty of the Council of Europe, which has also issued a Convention on automatic processing of personal data (Convention 108, recently updated). All member states of the EU are party to the ECHR, which means that they are all obliged to adhere to its standards, while citizens have a right to complain about violation of their rights to the European Court of Human Rights (ECtHR) after exhausting national remedies. Art. 8 has generated a prolific case law, part of which regards issues of data protection. The CFREU is complemented by various legal instruments that regard data processing, notably the Data Protection Directive (DPD) of 1995, the ePrivacy Directive of 2002 (critical amendments in 2009) and the eCommerce Directive of 2000. Within the EU, data protection is tied up with the functioning of the internal economic market, and closely aligned with the idea of the free flow of information between the member states. The Court of Justice of the EU (CJEU) has issued a small number of preliminary rulings on issues of data protection, notably in relation to violations of data protection rights due to copyright enforcement, freedom of expression and data retention obligations for the sake of public security and criminal investigation.

Having inquired into the increasingly animated environment of the onli*fe* world, I have made an analysis of a small set of threats in the first part of the book. The focus has been on threats caused by the emergence of a new ICI that depends conclusively on data-driven agency, instead of merely addressing potential abuse or misuse. As argued, the major challenge is not what will happen in case of malicious intent or undue negligence, but what will ensue if data-driven agency informs the majority of decisions taken by our artificial environments – assuming good faith. These threats cannot be reduced to privacy, and apparently we need to review our concept of privacy to cope with the era of 'every-wared' artificial intelligence. EU data protection law seems to tackle these issues upfront; it provides clear – though not rigid or unambiguous – guidelines on how to deal with personal data, taking into account the anonymous profiles that can be constructed and the decisions they may generate. Thus, it should not be confused with the rights it helps to protect, such as privacy, non-discrimination, due process and the presumption of innocence. These rights are not necessarily involved with personal data or pre-emptive computing (they entail more than data protection), and they are not fine-tuned to specifically deal with data-driven environments (they entail less than data protection). Data protection law institutes countervailing powers, meant to redress the implications of the threats discussed. As with any law, the right to data protection will not solve all the problems nor rule out new developments. It does, however, provide a framework for rebalancing unjust inequalities (aiming for justice), setting enforceable standards for the industry that can be relied upon as a level playing field (aiming for legal certainty), while helping to regulate the added value that may be created by the use of data-driven agency (purposiveness). Having legal effect, an individual right to data protection has other affordances than moral rights or ethical codes of conduct. Moreover, it operates at another level than techno-regulation or socio-economic nudging and it abides by another 'regime of veridiction' than that of the market or political games.

In this chapter I argue that we must reinvent Odysseus' smart system of checks and balances to have our cakes and eat them too; we need to reinstate the purpose binding principle as the centrefold image of data protection, next to consent and transparency – in order to enjoy the benefits of data-driven agency in a safe way.

9.2   DATA PROTECTION AND OTHER FUNDAMENTAL RIGHTS

9.2.1   Data Protection and Privacy

The problem with privacy is its iridescent nature; the concept means different things in different contexts and its elusive character makes it hard to provide hard and fast rules for its application. The concept is exemplary as an essentially contested concept, its content being value-laden, and therefore vague and ambiguous, requiring sound knowledge of case law to grasp the legal effect of an infringement. Art. 8 ECHR defines the right to privacy in terms of the protection of the home, family life, private life and correspondence. The ECtHR has given a broad interpretation to its scope, to prevent circumvention, but privacy is not an absolute right. Art. 8 also stipulates the cumulative conditions that justify an infringement: first, the infringing measures must be in accordance with the law, meaning that they are both foreseeable and provide sufficient safeguards; second, they must be necessary in a democratic society, meaning that there is a 'pressing social need' for the measure; and third, they must have a legitimate aim, such as public security or criminal justice. The ECtHR explains the second condition, notably the necessity, by asking if there was a pressing social need, and if so, by testing whether the infringement was proportional to this need. For instance, a measure to detect tax fraud (a legitimate aim) that is based on a legal statute with explicit safeguards, such as the possibility of appealing against the measure and limitation on the volume and temporal range of the infringement (in accordance with the law) may still be disproportional. For instance, if the infringement implies that the parking behaviours of all car owners is checked. Though such a measure may be effective in the sense of helping to detect some cases of fraud that might otherwise have gone unnoticed, it is not *necessary* in a democratic society, because the impact on the private life of car drivers is far too extensive in relation to the social need that is served.[266] Those trained in privacy law will have a fair idea of this type of case law, but it is not so easy to induce general rules with regard to data processing on the basis of the right to privacy. Though data protection law has its own ambiguities (otherwise it would not be law but administration), it has been articulated in a more rule-based manner, basically containing a set of rights for so-called data subjects (those to whom personal data relate) and obligations for data controllers (those who determine the purpose of data processing).

In the US context, a second problem with the right to privacy is that it has the character of a liberty; it is a right that requires others to abstain from infringing one's privacy. Instead of an obligation for others to provide privacy, there is only an obligation to refrain from taking, damaging or otherwise interfering with it. If one didn't have it in the first place, it cannot be infringed.[267] This easily leads to the conclusion that an ICI with default settings that afford no meaningful privacy cannot infringe a person's privacy, because she never had it. The third party doctrine in US privacy law may be traced back to this view: if you share data, you cannot complain that it is now shared with third parties, because you had given up a legitimate privacy expectation by sharing the data.[268] From a European perspective, privacy is rather seen as a freedom, which implies that it cannot be defined in advance, because one would have to foresee all potentially infringing actions. Once a freedom is defined its protection is necessarily limited and this may result in an injustice or fail to achieve the end of protection whenever new situations come up that fall outside the scope of the definition.[269] This does not imply that the protection is unlimited, but that the scope must be interpreted widely rather than narrowly. So, whereas in the US context privacy as a liberty may reduce the protection we need, privacy as a freedom in the EU context may create some legal uncertainty. As discussed in Chapter 8, the end of legal certainty does not necessarily overrule the ends of justice and purposiveness if their demands turn out to be incompatible in a specific case. For a human right, justice may be more important than legal certainty, though at some point its effectiveness will also depend on its alliance with legal certainty.

This brings me to the core of the fundamental right to privacy, which is the *freedom from* unlawful interference over and against the government. This is a prerequisite for the *freedom to* develop one's identity. Privacy thus framed is an opacity right. It guarantees citizens a sphere of unmonitored freedom, where the government has no business, unless justified by a legitimate aim, based on law and necessary in a democratic society. By default, opacity shields individual citizens from the scrutiny of governmental spying. The other side of this constitutional protection is that state interventions should be transparent by default, to enable accountability of the government towards its constituency. Individual opacity and governmental transparency are two sides of the same coin, and core to constitutional government. The duality aligns with the legality principle; whereas governments can only act based on a legal competence and in a general interest, citizens are free to act strategically in their own private interests, unless expressly forbidden.

Within the EU legislative framework data protection does three things: first, it extends the transparency right to all parties responsible for the processing of personal data, whether or not they are part of the government; second, it mitigates the opacity right in stipulating that if data controllers stick to specific conditions the default is that they may process personal data; and third, it provides for a limited set of rules that give clear indications of the conditions for lawful processing, instead of depending on a single ambiguous concept. One could say that the fundamental right to data protection gives private and public parties a positive right to process personal data, provided this is done in accordance with the rules of data protection law. Whereas privacy is a freedom or liberty of an individual citizen, data protection seems to attribute a right to data controllers. The first can be termed a negative right, depicting what cannot be done, an obligation of non-interference; the second is a positive right, denoting what can be done under what conditions. One of these conditions is that the processing of personal data must always be based on one of six legal grounds: consent, contract, a legal obligation, the vital interests of the data subject, public tasks or the legitimate interests of the data controller. The right to data protection thereby creates a different balancing act between justice, legal certainty and purposiveness than the right to privacy, with a more pronounced focus on legal certainty, although we must take into account that merely abiding by data protection legislation does not provide exemption from a violation of privacy rights. The fundamental right to data protection in fact entails a surreptitious extension of the legality principle to the private sphere by means of, first, an extension of the transparency right against private data controllers, and second, a requirement that the processing of personal data is only allowed if there is a valid legal ground. In short, data protection reconfigures the addressees (both private parties and public authorities), the content (addition of a specified set of transparency rights against the data controller), the form (rule based rights and obligations instead of a freedom or liberty) and the scope (only but always applicable when personal data is processed) of data protection as compared to privacy.

Privacy is strongly entwined with notions such as identity and autonomy. Both terms are notoriously contested, vague and ambiguous. As with the notion of privacy itself, we are in the realm of freedom that cannot easily be defined without reducing protection. Data protection, instead, connects with notions such as informational self-determination and control, which seem more straightforward and directed to the positive freedom of the data subject. Some conceptions of data protection actually view individuals as sovereigns reigning over their data. In this chapter I will argue that this is not the core of data protection, but it is interesting to note that the idea of data protection as control has produced a certain endowment effect. In the view of behavioural economics the endowment bias predicts that if people believe they possess something they will fight to keep it, or ask a higher price for alienating it than they would be willing to pay if they thought it was not yet theirs. This is how some authors explain the advance of human rights: if people believe they have such a right they will fight for it, whereas otherwise they might have no hopes of ever gaining such rights.[270] From a legal perspective personal data are never possessed by a person, though she may indeed be the referent of the data and have specific rights in them for that reason. Data are not rivalrous; you having my name does not mean I lose it, my having your address does not imply you no longer have it. The only reason to have a name is for others to be able to address and locate me; without sharing the name it makes no sense. The reason we need data protection is that putting data together has huge implications for a number of rights and freedoms. This is notably so when behavioural data are correlated. It is, therefore, important to have a right to data protection, without equating it with individual control, although some type of control – depending on the context, the type of data and the data controller – is definitely necessary.

9.2.2 Data Protection and Non-discrimination

The legal rights to non-discrimination and equal treatment must be distinguished from more general moral or social norms that reject social sorting or stereotyping per se. Schauer has written a wonderful book on the utility of stereotyping,[271] taking into account our limited cognitive capacities and the need to generalize when dealing with others. He does not imply that just any kind of discrimination should be allowed, but explains why both individual people and organizations are wise to generalize and stereotype to reduce the complexity of the life world. Luhmann and Habermas spoke of *Kontingenzbewaltigung*, which could be translated as the management of contingency. Although the term was coined in the context of religion,[272] it applies equally to the shared and interactive stereotyping by which we create a *Welt* that is less confusing and volatile than it would be if we had to sit down and consider all the differences that make a difference in daily life. This kind of complexity reduction is not an epistemological effort, but an act of creation that provides structure, stability and foreseeability to our shared *Welt*. The etymological roots of the verb to categorize refer to the Greek *kategorein* which translates as 'accuse, assert, predict'.[273] By categorizing we assert structure and predict how things hold together, which also enables us to accuse, based on inferences made from the categorizations we share. In Chapter 5 we looked extensively into the threats of digital sorting enacted by pre-emptive computing, concluding that such sorting has direct consequences for our manipulability. This relates to the right of privacy in the broader sense of the freedom from unreasonable constraints on the building of one's identity; it depicts the so-called autonomy trap. The connection between prediction and accusation will resurface when discussing the presumption of innocence.

The legal right to non-discrimination is a far more narrowly defined prohibition of differential treatment based on a limited set of prohibited grounds, or an obligation to treat people equally despite all kinds of differences between them. As discussed in Chapter 5, in section 5.3.4, these are human rights, codified in numerous human rights treaties and in Arts. 21 and 23 of the CFREU. Building on the right to non-discrimination, Art. 8 of the DPD establishes a default prohibition on the processing of personal data 'revealing racial or ethnic origin, political opinions, religious or philosophical beliefs, trade-union membership, and the processing of data concerning health or sex life'. These types of data are usually called sensitive data. It is important to note that this qualifies a set of data as subject to a special regime; the prohibition concerns only the sensitive data enumerated, and does not depend on what a particular person, company or government agency finds sensitive. For instance, many people are sensitive about their financial data, which is not protected under this provision, whereas others may have no qualms about their religious beliefs being shared, which is protected by the prohibition. Art. 8 DPD formulates a small set of exceptions: explicit consent; compliance with rights and obligations in the context of employment; protection of the vital interests of the data subject; and if the processing is done by a non-profit organization and concerns only its members. Exceptions also apply in the context of medical research and healthcare, and criminal convictions and administrative sanctions. All exceptions are qualified by requiring extra adequate safeguards.

The right to non-discrimination concerns both direct and indirect discrimination. As explained in Chapter 5, indirect discrimination refers to making a difference on neutral grounds that results in an outcome that discriminates on one of the prohibited grounds. For instance, by discriminating against people who do not eat pork (a neutral ground) it is possible to target Muslims (a prohibited ground). In Chapter 5 we observed two reasons why the onlife world presents new concerns about unlawful discrimination. First, direct discrimination is not easily perceived, because of the invisibility of data sharing across contextual boundaries. If a sensitive piece of data falls within the scope of an exception and is subsequently shared with third parties 'behind one's back', it is next to impossible to trace and track both the existence of such invisible sharing and to stop it by exercising one's rights. Second, it becomes far more difficult to detect indirect discrimination, because the algorithms that adapt the environment can engage in masking. That is, they can figure out which data points correlate with sensitive data, and process only the correlated non-sensitive data. That way, the same result can be achieved, though the prohibition of Art. 8 DPD has been bypassed.

To the extent that the adaptations of the smart environment are intuitive and surreptitious, it becomes an enormous challenge to scrutinize them for either direct or indirect discrimination, especially if we consider the amount and types of third parties involved. The good news is that techniques are being developed to test data mining operations in terms of direct or indirect discrimination, called 'discrimination-aware data mining'. Though the uptake of such techniques is nowhere near offering an effective protection yet, they show that we can learn to use the technologies we are up against to defend ourselves against their unlawful usage. This learning process is crucial for sustaining legal protection, since written law by itself cannot provide effective protection because of the seemingly impenetrable complexities of the computational layers that surround us. However, technologies that can in principle develop into full-fledged protection will only be taken up if their use becomes an enforceable legal obligation. We will return to this point under the heading of Legal Protection by Design (LPbD) in the last chapter.

Like all human rights, the rights to non-discrimination and equal treatment apply in the relationship between a government and its citizens, though in some cases a horizontal effect extends the application. In that case, the obligation to comply still rests on the government, meaning that it must create a legal framework to make the substance of a specific human right enforceable against others than the government. The prohibition on processing sensitive data, however, applies directly to all data controllers, not just to the government.[274] On top of that, the prohibition on the processing of sensitive data is not dependent on whether that data is actually used to engage in prohibited discrimination or unequal treatment. The prohibition does not redress harm caused, but filters out some of the techniques that enable discrimination. A legal claim against the processing of sensitive data does not require evidence that harm has been done or damage caused. By *indiscriminately* prohibiting such processing, data protection law aims to prevent the accumulation of resources to engage in discrimination, while taking into account that in specific circumstances exceptions are necessary. There is something of Odysseus' clever dealing with the Sirens here. We know that we could have all this data collected and find some wonderful business models for the data, but since we also know that this could lure us – or a despotic government or an unscrupulous private enterprise – into discrimination, we prevent the collection itself. Not merely its abuse.

Obviously, scepticism is warranted on two accounts. First, the exceptions still create room to process unprecedented amounts of sensitive data. Notably the first exception, that speaks of explicit consent, justifies the processing of massive amounts of sensitive behavioural data, for instance in the context of the quantified self movement, where people willingly collect and share data about their own biometrics, health, and so on.[275] In particular, the service providers who develop the Apps to make this possible have the opportunity to process sensitive data that can be linked with a host of other data, thus enabling masking and other dubious practices. In the case of health data we can imagine how this may disrupt not only medical research but also medical and life insurance policy. Insurance is based on an uncertainty that validates solidarity as a form of self-interest; once it becomes cheap and viable to personalize health risks the uncertainty reduces and the solidarity may break down. Or it becomes real – but some of us may not want to bet on that.

The issue of discrimination should also be discussed in relation to the notion of open data, which cleverly lures us into a positive evaluation of massive data sharing. This may be due to the use of the term 'open', which has an attractive ring, and anyway, how could any democrat be against 'open'? Open data, however, becomes part of Big Data Space and will stew and broil in the distributed digital unconscious of our preemptive environment. One can imagine that upfront prohibitions to even collect sensitive data cause great irritation in the solutionists of Silicon Valley and those dedicated to the common good of eternal good health. However, as Gina Neff neatly summarizes, 'Big Data won't cure us'. Just two quotations suffice to explain what she means:[276]

> One physician simply said: 'I don't need more data. I need more resources'.

> In another setting, we observed nurse-practitioner case managers in a Medicare demonstration project working with a simple algorithm parsing patient-entered health data. Combined with case management, these data provided a look into the daily health of chronically ill elderly patients and a pathway for the care when it was needed. The data in that project were tightly tied to medical expertise within an existing clinic where a trusted person could initiate a chain of care responses. Although widely recognized as a clinical success, Medicare pulled the plug on the project for financial reasons – expertise is expensive.

This nicely shows what can be done with Big Data, and what priorities this requires. The illusion that Big Data has no costs is dangerous in so far as it invites indiscriminate data collection in a collective effect to 'do good'. The road to hell is paved with good intentions, as we know. Not necessarily, but it happens. Data protection law masters the delicate balancing act required between the need for legal certainty (stipulating that by default sensitive data cannot be processed), justice (preventing invisible prohibited discrimination) and purposiveness (helping to build a trustworthy infrastructure for gaining the potential benefits of Big Data).

9.2.3 Data Protection, the Presumption of Innocence and Due Process

One of the major advantages of recognizing the right to data protection as a distinct right from the right to informational privacy is that it qualifies data protection law as covering much more than the protection of private life, the home, family or confidential communication (as well as much less). Data protection is focused on a new phenomenon, called data, aiming to regulate the consequences of its processing. Though there is doubt as to whether data protection should make its entire framework dependent on one particular type of data, namely personal data, the emergence of digital data warrants a targeted legal framework. Before moving on to the presumption of innocence and due process I will briefly engage with two questions: first, why would digital data be a new phenomenon; and second, why should it warrant a specific legal approach? These questions have been answered one way or another in the preceding chapters, but it may be helpful to reiterate, specify and expand the answers at this point.

The invention of the mathematical theory of information, in conjunction with the invention of tubes, transistors and integrated circuits, has revolutionized the ICI of modern societies to an extent that can hardly be fathomed.[277] Mathematicians and electrical engineers have rebuilt our *Welt*, or perhaps, they have pulled the carpet from under its feet to rebuild something altogether different, like an on*life* world. The so-called information revolution is built upon a mathematical theory of information that involves a ubiquitous translation of thought, text, knowledge, communication, behaviour, and whatever, into a digital format that enables breaking the flux of life into discrete machine-readable bits and bytes. These are called data. Though data translates as 'givens', these givens are *made*. Though some speak of data as made of mental stuff, they are embodied in vacuum tubes, punched in cards, and conducted in transistors or integrated circuits. The embedding shapes the data as much as they shape their embedment. The fabrication of digital data is an act of interpretation and categorization that has reconfigured what counts as information and given rise to an entirely different understanding of the basic building blocks of knowledge, due to the generative nature of their recombination.[278] The critical mutation (as French philosophers might say) was the development of an information system devoid of meaning, independent of semantic reference, capable of seamless interoperability. Within the context of the mathematical theory of information, meaning becomes a by-product, an added luxury, perhaps an attractive illusion to keep us going as resources for the mindless system. This is not a joke, not an exaggeration, nor an extreme position. Just as some neuro-scientists or philosophers of mind declare consciousness and human intention to be so-called epiphenomena, *caused by* but not *required for* intelligent action,[279] the mathematical theory of information that 'informs' the ICI of the onli*fe* world is agnostic as to the meaning attribution it may generate. Data-driven agency, based on AI and ML, produces wonderful results but remains a mindless agency, even when capable of second order preferences and higher order decision-making. This brings me to a caveat. For humans, information involves meaning.[280] For the computational layers of our smart environment, data is either information or noise, depending on how it gets connected – but the smart environment has no need for meaning. Meaning cannot be taken for granted and critically depends on how data is woven into the fabric of our *Welt*, suspended in mid-air between individual enaction and the artificial world we depend on. Considering the amount of data flooding the digital unconscious compared to the information that individuals can connect with, we should admit that most of the information that is around now is meaningless, but highly influential. This curious combination makes us prone to manipulation. Data, not information, is the new phenomenon that is rapidly reconfiguring our relation with the realities it co-constitutes.

Digital data is the core unit of the digital unconscious and the building block on which AI thrives. Data protection makes a difference for privacy and non-discrimination, because it takes into account how these building blocks redefine our lives. This has enabled the legal regime to tweak conventional conceptions of privacy and non-discrimination in a direction that is better adapted to the new technological landscape. But more is at stake. Focusing on the data clears the way for protecting still other fundamental rights that may be jeopardized by the invisible visibilities of predictive analytics. The Greek roots of 'categorize' connect prediction with accusation. Let's move on to the usage of data to frame future criminals, reminding ourselves that, although governments usually claim to need access to Big Data to profile international terrorists, the more mundane passage to Big Data Space concerns the detection of tax or social security fraud. By now, a quasi-religious belief in the benefits of Big Data Analytics has fuelled magical expectations regarding the pre-emption of criminal intent. Though some have remarked that 'prediction is very difficult, especially when it's about the future',[281] governments have been moving forward by investing in expensive early warning systems that raise both privacy and security issues. The more pressing concern, however, is that they may unwillingly confirm that 'the best way to predict the future is to create it'.[282] This goes with another aphorism that modulates the famous Thomas Theorem: 'If men define a situation as real, it is real in its consequences'.[283] The contemporary revision states: 'If machines define a situation as real, it is real in its consequences'.[284]

In Chapter 5 we discussed why criminal profiling may not be effective and how it relates to the presumption of innocence. Here, the question is whether data protection law has added value in preventing the erosion of the presumption. In Art. 8 (5) the DPD states that the processing of personal data relating to offences, criminal convictions or security measures, is only allowed under specific conditions, with suitable and specific safeguards applied. It is crucial that such obligations are enforceable, because leaking or sharing information about criminal convictions can have a major impact on the effectiveness of the presumption of innocence in the broader sense. The problem with current EU data protection legislation is that it exempts the activities of the state in areas of criminal law, although some regulation is in place, also at the level of the EU.

Nevertheless, in relation to pre-emptive computing, EU data protection law has codified an important right that relates directly to both the presumption of innocence and due process requirements. This right is directed to the implications of profiling and could be helpful in addressing data-driven agency as it apparently addresses the digital unconscious up-front. Under the heading of 'Automated individual decisions' the DPD stipulates in Art. 15 (1) that:

> Member States shall grant the right to every person not to be subject to a decision which produces legal effects concerning him or [which] significantly affects him and which is based solely on automated processing of data intended to evaluate certain personal aspects relating to him, such as his performance at work, creditworthiness, reliability, conduct, etc.

The latest version of the proposed General Data Protection Regulation (pGDPR) is even more to the point.[285] It defines profiling as:

> any form of automated processing of personal data intended to evaluate certain personal aspects relating to a natural person or to analyse or predict in particular that natural person's performance at work, economic situation, location, health, personal preferences, reliability or behaviour.

It then stipulates:

> Profiling which leads to measures producing legal effects concerning the data subject or does similarly significantly affect the interests, rights or freedoms of the concerned data subject shall not be based solely or predominantly on automated processing and shall include human assessment, including an explanation of the decision reached after such an assessment.

Instead of providing protection only for profiling 'based solely on automated processing', the pGDPR takes a more nuanced approach by speaking of 'based solely or predominantly on automated processing'. This provision clearly addresses 'measures producing legal effects' or measures that 'similarly significantly affect the interests, rights or freedoms of the data subject'. Though there are exceptions to the *prohibition of* (pGDPR) or to the *right not to be subject to* (DPD) decisions based on profiling, the default is apparent. Data-driven agency involves a plethora of automated decisions, which would escape scrutiny if this were to be allowed by default. In the context of criminal justice a similar default applies in the current and proposed framework, with only one exception; data-driven decisions are allowed if the decision is 'authorized by a law that also lays down measures to safeguard the data subjects' legitimate interests'. This places the burden of inventing the right types of safeguards on national legislators, while testing their adequacy will depend on their counterparts, the courts.

A prohibition of decisions based on profiling should mitigate the erosion of the presumption of innocence. The question is, however, whether citizens have the means to figure out when the presumption is being undermined. This relates to the notion of due process, as discussed in Chapter 5 (section 5.4.2), taking the broad perspective of 'the capability of contesting adverse decisions'. Due process thus understood aligns with transparency rights that promote a person who is the object of an investigation to the position of a subject with standing in court. With regard to profiling, specific transparency rights have been developed. The DPD states that data subjects should have the right to obtain from the data controller 'knowledge of the logic involved in any automatic processing of data concerning him at least in the case of the automated decisions referred to in Article 15 (1)'. The pGDPR wisely reframes this as: 'meaningful information about the logic involved in any automated processing'. This acknowledges that merely providing the algorithm will not do. The disadvantage may be that neural networks and other forms of bottom-up profiling cannot be used in so far as they render the provision of meaningful information impossible. In the case of decisions that significantly affect a person, or even adversely affect a person, this is not a disadvantage but an advantage; it forces data controllers to make sense of the decision and to provide reasons that can be contested by whoever is incriminated.

As was to be expected, no such transparency right is to be found in the legislation that applies to profiling in the area of criminal law. This is unacceptable. Precisely when the presumption of innocence in the narrow sense is at stake we are kept in the dark. This reminds me of an earlier era, when a defendant was not briefed on the charge until the very last moment, because otherwise he might find ways to defend himself. Although it can be reasonable not to tell a person that she is being profiled as a potential suspect during the course of an investigation, it is imperative that the usage of AI is tested and scrutinized by countervailing powers and made contestable in a court of law. This is the only manner by which the viability, effectiveness and proportionality of criminal profiling can be exposed in relation to the presumption of innocence. If machines target people as potential criminals, these people may end up becoming criminals. Which could indeed validate the idea that the best way to predict the future is to create it.

A dystopian reader may find that upholding prohibitions of profiling and obligations for profile transparency will be a mission impossible in an on*life* world. I would suggest, instead, that we pour wax in the ears of those who are lured by the animistic magic of pre-emptive computing, and tie those who want to engage with it to the mast of the legality principle. Protection against the wrong defaults is as artificial, as critical and as important as Odysseus' ship, the wax, the ropes and the mast. Let us sail clear of the Scylla of data fetishism and the Charybdis of data denial. The latter refers to those who wish to maintain that data does not make a difference in fact, or should not make a difference to the law. In the next section I will return to the impossibility of a technologically neutral law and the need for a technology neutral law. First I will sum up the added value of data protection in terms of the purpose binding principle.

9.3 THE ADDED VALUE OF DATA PROTECTION: TRANSPARENCY AND PURPOSE BINDING

9.3.1 A New Roadmap for the Fair Information Principles: Property or Harm?

Most data protection legislation builds – more or less – on the OECD Guidelines for fair information principles (FIPs) that date from 1980. They recommend a relatively small set of principles to ensure fair processing: collection limitation, data quality, purpose specification, use limitation, security safeguards, openness, individual participation and accountability. The Guidelines combine the aim of promoting the free flow of information with appropriate safeguards against privacy risks for individual citizens. The OECD, being an organization that aims to promote economic cooperation, has a keen eye for the economic benefits of providing protection in order to stimulate the kind of mutual trust that invites unhampered transnational information flows. The bottom line of the principles is that data controllers should select before they collect, preserve the correctness and completeness of data, clarify the purpose and refrain from processing once the purpose is no longer relevant; they should provide for adequate security, be transparent, enable individuals to obtain information and to object to processing or ask for erasure, and they should implement a privacy management program that includes risk assessments and an organisational framework that ensures compliance with the principles. The Guidelines have been revised in 2013, but the principles themselves were not updated. Instead, extra attention was given to the accountability mechanisms and security breach notification.

The FIPs were articulated before the Internet took off, before the world wide web spread its wings and long before mobile smart devices, online social networking sites and cloud computing were even conceived. Artificial intelligence was still rule-based and embedded in stand-alone devices. The connection between AI and data (notably via machine-learning) was hardly made and the idea of softwared and firmwired anywares was not yet on the horizon. Nevertheless, the FIPs focused on the processing of data, and the mathematical theory of information that informs all of what came later had long since been developed.

Since the advance of data science and the ability to connect the dots across contexts, national borders and scientific disciplines, a number of questions have arisen as to the sustainability of the current FIPs. Is the emphasis on individual data and individual persons still relevant and feasible in the era of Big Data Space? Should the principles focus on data flows instead of individual data, and on particular contexts instead of individual persons? Is purpose limitation still feasible or even desirable? Some authors have pointed out that function creep is the holy grail of Big Data and the ultimate resource for creating added value.[286] Others warn against naïve overestimation of the fruits of data science, especially when combined with a blind eye for the harms and the risks.[287] The issues have, over and again, been framed in terms of the clichéd balancing act:[288]

> [H]ow can we ensure data protection while enabling the personal and societal benefits that come from the use of data?

How to have our cakes and eat them too? The point is how to approach the idea of a balance. Are we back to balancing private against public interests, as with individual liberty and collective security? Or should we understand individual freedom as a public good? As discussed in Chapter 5, framing privacy as a private interest has its drawbacks, especially if the other side of the privacy coin is left out of the equation; privacy is also a public good and a human right, neither of which should be reduced to a private interest. When speaking of a balance we must not forget the distribution issue: who is asked to give up a benefit in order for others to gain one.[289] However, a free flow of information and protection of fundamental rights are not always compatible and choices must be made. It seems that three types of approaches are emerging: one based on property in the non-legal sense, meaning that people should retain control over their data and be given the technical, legal and economic means to share, trade or monetize them, for instance based on licensing of specific data flows; another simply gives up on individual control and focuses on redressing eventual harm, to be assessed after the fact; finally a third position builds on EU-style data protection, based on collection limitation and purpose binding, the need for a legal ground and adequate transparency tools. As regards data-driven agency, profile transparency and profiling prohibitions seem the only targeted approach; they address not merely individual data, specific contexts or particular data flows, but the results of AI operations in so far as they impact an individual. The EU legal framework is the only approach that copes directly with decision systems based on profiling.

The property approach has found an excellent voice in the World Economic Forum, which has made a critical attempt to rethink personal data and the ecosystem it has fuelled, by discriminating between volunteered, observed and inferred data. As discussed in Chapter 3, this highlights the crucial difference between: first, the content that people deliberately post on their profile; second, the machine-readable behaviours captured by the service providers and third parties; and third, the inferences drawn from all this data to enable the creation of added value. Different legal regimes may apply to the same data, such as copyright protection as well as data protection rights for content posted on one's profile and data protection and privacy rights for the observed data until they have been anonymized, while the inferred data may fall within the scope of trade secrets and intellectual property rights on the side of the data controller, as well as data protection and privacy rights on the side of data subjects, to the extent that they are reconnected to a particular person. Those who propose to think in terms of a personal data ecosystem (PDE) suggest that a PDE could overcome the tiresome hassles of meaningless notice and consent, while offering people contracts to license the use – and even the monetization – of their data. To make the ownership approach work one does not really need legal ownership of the data, as a consent requirement suffices to give individuals the capability to license the use of their data. The idea is that by giving people something like a property right in their data, the endowment effect will make them aware of the value of their data, thus helping them to protect their privacy,[290] or, as one could object, helping them to trade individual privacy interests against short-term private benefits (which bias was that: the immediate gratification bias).[291]

As regards the harm-based approach, Microsoft has brought together a set of 70 global privacy experts, and after numerous discussions over the course of several years, released a report on *Data Protection Principles for the 21st Century*, vouching for further adaptations in the OECD Guidelines. The report feeds on a harms-based approach and proposes to, first, reduce the focus on data collection (let them collect it all, since we cannot stop them anyway), second, eliminate or substantially reduce purpose binding (as this flies in the face of bottom-up profiling and free re-purposing of data), third, restore the balance between privacy and the free flow of information (suggesting we have done too much to restrict innovation), fourth, make data users more accountable and fifth, adopt a broader definition of the 'harms' that inappropriate usage of personal data can cause (taking a harms approach, which is only applicable after the fact).[292] As others have noted, doing away with collection limitation and the purpose binding principle makes it difficult to decide what counts as inappropriate use.[293] Who is going to carry the burden of proof? What is to count as harm? Should we take a risk-based approach to harm, creating a strict liability in case of data leakage due to negligence? But what if the most pervasive risk resides in the availability of the digital unconscious and the ensuing manipulability? Is manipulability a harm or is only the manipulation itself a harm, and if so, can we detect manipulation without reaching behind the walls of trade secret and intellectual property rights? Or is manipulation not a harm, but only the monetary or physical damage in which it results? If collection in itself is not unlawful and repurposing in principle legitimate (who cares about purpose anyway), how to locate criteria for wrongful use? Considering all this, an extension of the definition of harm after eliminating the conditions for inappropriate use might not really be of help. Some have noted that moving from an approach based on consent to one based on harm entails an unwelcome type of paternalism, especially in combination with the proposed diminishment of the purpose binding principle.[294]

9.3.2 Legality and Purpose Binding: Legal Certainty, Justice and Purposiveness

The good thing is that everybody seems to agree that in a world that echoes a perpetual background noise of multifarious data flows, a legal regime entirely focused on individual data points will not work. The narrative is that all things are being datafied and anything is datafiable, while all data is being correlated and any data is correlatable.[295] Even if this is an overstatement, there is no way that individual persons can be made responsible for determining which of 'their' data can be shared by what service providers and third parties. Moreover, the consequences of matching and profiling based on anonymized profiles are far greater in an onli*fe* world saturated with data-driven agency, than the consequences of sharing a particular personal data.

When we look into the basic structure of the current data protection regime within the EU, this is explicitly acknowledged. Individual consent is just one of six legal grounds that justify the processing of personal data. Five other grounds refer to necessity, for instance in the context of a contract, or in relation to the legitimate interests of the data controller. In those cases individuals don't have a choice: if one buys a book online, some personal data must be exchanged for delivery and payment. If a person makes use of an online social network without paying for the service, the provider can make a case for monetizing the personal data to make a profit. In both cases, however, the requirement of necessity is of prime importance. Once applications that enable identification of payment based on attribute based credentials become widely available, the necessity to require certain data may no longer be obvious.[296] And, once a person is willing to pay a subscription fee, the legitimate interest of the service provider may no longer hold for the monetization of behavioural data. By requiring a valid legal ground, EU data protection legislation opens a playground for business models that can do without Big Data flows, thus also cutting down on investments into security and all kinds of fancy data science of which the added value is unproven. However, if necessity does not apply, consent could still be used as a valid legal ground, though under EU law consent can be withdrawn – making for an unstable relationship with the data – and even in the case of consent, the purpose limitation principle is in force, restricting any arbitrary re-use of the data.

This requires a closer look at the purpose binding principle that combines two obligations for data controllers. First it requires the explicit and prior specification of a legitimate purpose, and second it requires that data is only processed for that, or a compatible, purpose. The purpose binding principle was first articulated in the OECD Guidelines. They describe the second obligation, regarding use limitation, as follows:

> Personal data should not be disclosed made available or otherwise used for purposes other than those specified in accordance with Paragraph 9 [purpose specification] except:
>
> a) with the consent of the data subject; or
> b) by the authority of law.

This entails that repurposing is allowed in the case of consent or when stipulated by law. Under EU legislation this is not allowed. Personal data shall be 'collected for specified, explicit and legitimate purposes and not further processed in a way incompatible with those purposes [purpose limitation]'.

The EU data protection advisory body (the Art. 29 Working Party) has made a point of emphasizing the importance of the ensuing prohibition to re-use data for an incompatible purpose. This basically regards the legal regime for historical data, that is data that has been collected and probably served its purpose, but is kept stored for any number of reasons (administrative accountability, customer relationship management, for tax purposes marketing, or for 'improving the services' of the provider). In the case of data-driven agency, this type of data forms an important resource as part of the digital unconscious. Storing data in the cloud is relatively cheap, and performing all kinds of Big Data analytics on them is more feasible than ever. This makes cloud computing one of the major enablers of pre-emptive computing environments. As a Google employee observed in the *New York Times*:[297]

> Historically, we've been in a world where computing was a scarce resource. Now it is moving to being an abundant resource. Anybody who claims to have a crystal ball about where this is heading is kidding themselves.

Technically as well as in terms of cost, access to an unlimited amount of data is now feasible and the lure of keeping historical data around for future research is fascinating, unsettling and irresistible. Not because we would ever need all of it, but rather because deciding what data sets will be of interest requires expertise and will cost more than just saving everything. However, the more linkable data is available, the more feasible it becomes to re-identify anonymous data and to construct detailed profiles of individual persons or predictive models that apply to them. This certifies that the collection and storage of historical data is a major vulnerability, a source of endless security issues and a full-scale liability for a myriad of infringements of human rights.

Putting a brake on the re-usage of personal data, while also limiting its collection, is one way of preventing the datafication of everything and the threats it entails. This connects with the legal status of a data controller, who is defined as the entity that determines the purpose of processing. By thus addressing the issue of personal data processing in terms of its purpose, the constitutive as well as limitative role of the law becomes apparent, demonstrating the salience of the Rule of Law in its substantive, relational understanding. The obligation to determine a purpose and the liability for data usage within the scope of a compatible purpose are two sides of the same coin. On one side of the coin, the notion of purpose constitutes and configures the role of the data controller, by forcing it to determine a purpose for each processing operation. On the other side of the same coin, the need to determine the purpose creates awareness of the liability for usage beyond the specified purpose. In this manner the purpose ensures that sharing data with a controller has reasonably foreseeable consequences. The law has an addressee, the data controller, and a mechanism for redress, liability, while both are configured around the notion of purpose. The reason is not that we *can* always foresee the consequences of employing data-driven agency, but that we *should* be reasonably capable of foreseeing them for reasons of justice, legal certainty and purposiveness. This can only be achieved if we do not engage in actions that turn the sharing of data in the onli*f*e world into a game of Russian Roulette, because we have no idea how our data points will correlate with what profiles, once repurposed for whatever unknown objective. Justice requires that liability is distributed in a fair way, requiring that those who take a risk pay the cost if others suffer the consequences. Legal certainty requires that both the data controller and the data subject are capable of foreseeing the implications of their actions, for instance by attributing liability that will prevent one party from taking risks with the capabilities of the other party. Purposiveness demands that the protection against unforeseeable harm is effective and therefore attributed to the party that facilitates the taking of risk.

Instead of closing the stable door after the horse has bolted (the harm approach), and instead of putting all our money on access control (the property approach), we need a balanced way to tie data controllers to the mast, after they have collected the data, filling our ears with wax until the Sirens are out of sight. The legality principle, transformed and attuned to the need of effective data protection, institutes, first, the need for a legal ground in combination with, second, the requirement of a legitimate, specified and explicit purpose that, third, ties the data controller to the mast since the data controller is the entity that determines the purpose in the first place. Note that we are not speaking of self binding; Odysseus filled the ears of his sailors with wax because he knew that self binding does not work in the face of serious temptation.

9.3.3   The Issue of Jurisdiction: A Brussels Effect?

What if this argument does not convince the global community, notably those who stand to gain from access to a well-fed Big Data Space? Should we be realpolitikers and succumb to cynicism? This brings us to the nexus of constitutional law and international relations, noting that the latter is a social science close to political and policy science, tending to an external, objectivistic perspective (often presenting people as being either prey or predator).

In a daring article Anu Bradford claims that:[298]

> ... the rules and regulations originating from Brussels have penetrated many aspects of economic life within and outside of Europe through the process of 'unilateral regulatory globalization.' Unilateral regulatory globalization occurs when a single state is able to externalize its laws and regulations outside its borders through market mechanisms, resulting in the globalization of standards.

> Unilateral regulatory globalization is a development where a law of one jurisdiction migrates into another in the absence of the former actively imposing it or the latter willingly adopting it.

The claim is introduced with a wake-up call:[299]

> Few Americans are aware that EU regulations determine the makeup they apply in the morning, the cereal they eat for breakfast, the software they use on their computer, and the privacy settings they adjust on their Facebook page. And that's just before 8:30 AM.

Bradford shows how EU law gets exported by the simple fact that trade partners (states and transnational companies) are willing to adapt their practices to make them compatible with EU legislation, as this will give them access to the EU internal market. She thereby pits the so-called 'Delaware Effect' against the so-called 'California Effect', arguing that Europe is an example of the latter on a global scale. The Delaware Effect refers to a race to the regulatory bottom of incorporation standards of corporate enterprise, caused by differential standards between states within the US Federation. Having the most attractive regulatory framework for incorporation, Delaware won the race, thus winning a large share of corporate business enterprise in the US. We could compare this with a similar race to the bottom when companies shop around different jurisdictions to avoid taxation. Whoever wonders why so many technology companies have established their European headquarters in Ireland has missed out somewhere. The California Effect refers to the combination of California's large consumer market with its strict consumer and environmental law. This combination incentivizes companies to upgrade to California standards. In so far as it is easier or cheaper to keep one standard within the company, these standards are then also complied with in other states. The California effect applies, according to Bradford, if a jurisdiction has a large domestic market and is capable of enforcing strict rules over inelastic markets (notably consumer markets) as opposed to elastic markets (notably capital markets). Consumer markets are inelastic in so far as consumers do not easily migrate merely to buy products and services from less strictly regulated providers, whereas capital markets are elastic because it is far easier to move capital flows around the globe, in search of low tax or lesser transparency requirements. The Brussels Effect also results in an incentive for companies to lobby with their own government to raise the standards to similar protection, in order to level the playing field with local competitors. This is how EU law diffuses around the globe.

The conception of the Brussels Effect is part of the regulatory paradigm; it speaks of regulatory globalization in the objectivist language of impact and influence, without taking a normative perspective. It is critical to complement this approach with a legal perspective, looking into relevant case law on the cusp of internal and external sovereignty. Two cases are exemplary here. The first is the famous Yahoo case,[300] the second the equally ground-breaking case against Google's search engine on the right to be forgotten.[301] Both concern the question of whether national or supranational jurisdictions can still determine the purpose of their law and provide for the legal effect that ensures legal certainty. In the end, both cases also raise the question of whether justice has any meaning in the realm of international relations.

In the Yahoo case (2000), a French Court decided that Yahoo, an American Internet Service Provider, should prevent its French users from accessing a website that offered to sell Nazi paraphernalia. Under French law such offers constitute a criminal offence. However, Yahoo claimed that the US First Amendment protects against restrictions of free speech, meaning that Yahoo was not allowed to comply with the French decision. The suggestion was that since the Internet has no borders, Yahoo had to choose between applying either US or French law to all its users. Being a US based company it refused to bend to French law. Interestingly, during the course of the case it became clear that the technology to target French Internet users as such was available, meaning that Yahoo could comply with French law in France, while adhering to US law in the US. We can learn several things from this case. First of all, the case refuted the technological determinism that had led some to believe that once the Internet and the world wide web were used on a global scale it would no longer be possible to institute national law in cyberspace. This position was called exceptionalism,[302] because it declared cyberspace to be off-limits for state intervention, and thus for the law. That such a position was refuted should not come as a surprise, but the temptation to accept that things are the way they are because technology is the way it is, has a strong hold on public imagination, especially if partisan interests are at stake. Exceptionalism was refuted because technologies can be designed, developed and taken up in different manners. However, changing the direction of an emerging ICI requires a concerted effort. In this case additional technologies changed the affordances of online space, while their invention was triggered by the controversies that played out in court.[303] Such a turnaround, in turn, cannot be taken for granted; once a technology has been consolidated it acquires a tenacity that is not easily disrupted. Beyond technological determinism, the outcome of the case seems to confirm the importance of democratic legitimacy, local justice and legal certainty. Reidenberg argued that it is important that a polity can enforce its democratically agreed legal norms,[304] though some have pointed out that notoriously undemocratic polities will find similar ways to enforce their municipal law in cyberspace. In the end the democratic argument partly depends on the aims of justice and legal certainty. For society to thrive people must have an inkling of the consequences of their actions; if their own laws are overruled by those of other constituencies it will be difficult to foresee what they are up to, whereas they have no vote in the other constituency. This aligns legal certainty with democratic participation. As discussed under the heading of justice as equal treatment, distributive justice determines the equality of the treatment between those who share jurisdiction, but cannot decide the measure of what is distributed. Unless one takes a universalist approach, there is no objective criterion for this, as it depends on the purpose of a particular law – which is decided in the realm of politics. This aligns justice as equality with democratic decision-making. In that sense, the question of what is just is a local issue, as long as distributive justice is taken into account as well as the proportionality that plays out in corrective justice.

The case of *Google v. Spain* (2014) concerned a Spanish citizen whose house was auctioned due to financial problems, while the auction was announced in a local newspaper by order of the Ministry of Labour and Social Affairs. More than a decade later it turned out that the local newspaper had digitized its archives and published them online. When tapping into Google's search engine with a search after the name of the concerned citizen, the article in the newspaper came out on top of the search results. The citizen asked the newspaper to remove the item from its digital archive and required Google to remove the item from its search results. When they refused, he asked the Spanish Data Protection Authority to order erasure of the article, which order was given. Google then turned to the Spanish High Court, which submitted a so-called preliminary question to the CJEU, inquiring whether Google could be forced to tweak its algorithms in a way that would remove the item from its search results. The Advocate General (AG) of the CJEU advised against this, because he considered that Google is not a data controller, but a data processor that has no responsibility whatsoever for the content of the search results. The Court, however, decided that Google is a data controller, because its operations differ from those of the websites it crawls and it has a different and own purpose in processing the data. This means that the CJEU gets to the question of whether a person can require a search engine provider to remove her personal data, if the processing is no longer lawful. Three rights are at stake: (1) the right of the search engine to process the data, based on its legitimate interests; (2) the freedom of information of users of the search engine that would be deprived of the relevant information if it were to be removed; and (3) the fundamental rights of privacy and data protection of the concerned citizen. Without going into too much juridical-technical detail, we can conclude that the CJEU decided that *under specific circumstances* the legitimate economic interests of the data controller in processing the data, as well as the freedom of information of other users of the search engine, can be overruled by the privacy and data protection rights of the data subject. This can be the case when the data is prejudicial to the data subject and is either inaccurate, not kept up to date or kept longer than necessary, but also if it is inadequate, irrelevant or excessive in relation to the purpose of keeping the data.[305] In fact, the CJEU makes explicit that data being prejudicial to the data subject is not a necessary condition.[306] The court seems to rely on the so-called f-ground for the processing of personal data (stipulated in Art. 7(f) of the DPD), which allows the processing if it is a legitimate interest of the data controller. This ground is one of the six legal grounds that legitimate the processing of personal data, and one of the five grounds of necessity. The other one is consent. The f-ground is formulated as follows:

> [personal data may be processed if:] processing is necessary for the purposes of the legitimate interests pursued by the controller or by the third party or parties to whom the data are disclosed, except where such interests are overridden by the interests for fundamental rights and freedoms of the data subject which require protection under Article 1 (1) [which refers to protection of 'the fundamental rights and freedoms of natural persons, and in particular their right to privacy with respect to the processing of personal data]'.

A company whose business model depends on the processing of personal data, thereby has – in principle – a legal ground. This depends, however, on a balancing act, requiring keen attention to the way that the processing affects the fundamental rights of data subjects. In specific cases it may lead to a data controller being ordered to stop processing particular personal data. The judgment of the CJEU has created havoc, especially in the US, as this affects the legal obligations of large US companies that operate in the EU market. Under US Constitutional Law, the idea of a search engine removing information clashes with the First Amendment that sanctifies the freedom of information. Google has responded pragmatically. It has launched an online form for 'search removal requests under European Data Protection Law', promising to assess each individual request.[307] The search engine provider claims to have received 50,000 requests within the first weeks. Rumour has it that Google plans to alert its users with notifications when information has been removed as a result of citizens' requests.[308] This judgment shows that transnational companies, operating in the internal market of the EU, can be forced to comply with EU law. Just like China can force the hand of large US technology companies to abide by its administrative orders if they want to have a share of the Chinese market.

This case highlights once more that it is possible to find solutions that go against the grain of unlimited datafication. It is a critical case, because it denies that there is any such thing as an inevitable course of technological development. Moreover, it also ignores persistent claims that EU law cannot stand up to US companies, because they will either shrug their shoulders or leave Europe far behind. The case highlights the incredible complexity of weighting various fundamental rights in these kinds of cases, notably also the fundamental freedom to conduct a business (Art. 16 CFREU), that plays out in the f-ground as what stands for a legitimate interest. The CJEU thus balances privacy rights against the freedom of information and the legitimate business interests of the search engine. Finally, this case shows that new technologies have new affordances that were not at play before. The CJEU has not requested that the newspaper removes part of its content. It focuses on the new situation that a local news item that is relatively old, which would have been forgotten and hardly been accessible in the old days, is now available far outside its context of application, in a way that was never at stake before. The searchability of large data sets is a relatively new fact with an enormous impact. It connects directly to data-driven agency and the lure of the digital unconscious. The mere fact that a court of law has assessed the implications of such a new fact for the fundamental rights in question is good news. It indicates that though law is not technologically neutral, it should aim for technology neutrality. As will be explained in the last chapter, this may sometimes require technology specific law.

9.4　CONCLUSIONS: TO EAT OUR CAKES AND HAVE THEM TOO

If we can bake more cakes, it might just work. Eat some, bake some, have some. The point with cake is that it is meant to be eaten; this is not necessarily the case with privacy or other fundamental rights. It is rather that we want to have the added value of Big Data and protect our privacy too. The first may eat into the second, but often there will be ways to gain the added value without jeopardizing fundamental rights. If that is not possible, there are ways to employ Big Data that simply erase such rights and other ways that reinvent them, notably by limiting the infringements while requiring proportionality between the infringement and the benefits of sharing data. In the next chapter we will investigate how reinventing fundamental rights may be required when the ICI of pre-emptive computing becomes a competing or even the dominant ICI as compared to that of the printing press.

Here, we can sum up the findings on the fundamental right to data protection as follows. First, it is crucial that data controllers select before they collect, checking whether there is a necessity to collect (the five legal grounds other than consent). The same goes for data subjects when they have a choice to share data (the legal ground of consent); they should select before they leak, post or provide. The naïve intuition that more data is better should be discarded, because keeping data stored is costly due the hardware and the energy it takes to build, maintain and cool the servers. Keeping the data up to date and erasing it when no longer relevant is even more costly, because you need domain expertise. Databases containing historical data need to be cleansed before their usage is viable and reliable, even in the case of Big Data, and just putting it all in the cloud will generate incorrect inferences if updating and cleansing are skipped. Security is another costly issue that is part and parcel of data protection, though I have not focused on it. Notably, the EU framework requires security by design whenever possible and security breach notifications to inform those affected. Finally, we don't want the surface of the earth to be covered by data servers, or do we? Collecting all the behavioural data one can get one's hands on, is not feasible and keeping them is not sustainable, though I am sure some would invest in putting the data in outer space to continue collection. Let's spend that money on more urgent needs and stop dreaming of Big Data as the panacea for any and all problems we face.

Second, it is critical that the purpose of data processing is determined and explicitly specified, at the latest, at the moment of collection. Though it may be cumbersome to anticipate the usage and reflect on the necessity, this is what will prevent an unbridled datafication that will clog the system, while use limitation will also protect against hidden data processing and invisible re-usage. The fact that this is nevertheless common practice is not an argument against transparency and limitation, but a good reason to make the legislation more effective. The purpose binding principle ties up with the definition of the data controller and its accountability for compliance with the legal framework. If purpose binding were dropped as a requirement, why assume that the data controller has a purpose and why make it responsible and liable as the entity that determines the purpose? The harm approach is a viable and important way of dealing with data processing, but if there are no clear rules on which types of data processing are wrongful, focusing on the damage does not help much – unless strict liability is applied, but that might be an even greater challenge.[309]

Third, protection in an onli*fe* world is not just about the data. Knowing who is keeping which data for what purpose is important to have a fair idea of the proliferation of one's data trails, but knowing how one can be targeted is far more important. In a world animated by data-driven agency, profile transparency provided by the data controller is a critical precondition for exercising the right to object to autonomic decision-making. The EU legal framework has established various rights in relation to profiling, especially where decisions are made automatically or semi-automatically. This is the only set of data protection rights that confronts pre-emptive computing head-on. In the next chapter I will argue that we need to expand these rights with counter-profiling rights (not to be confused with anti-profiling rights), while also contending that we must urgently work on articulating these rights into the ICI of pre-emptive computing.

10. The end of law or Legal Protection by Design

10.1 WHY LEGAL PROTECTION BY DESIGN?

This book ends with Legal Protection by Design (LPbD) in a data-driven environment, weaving together some of the open endings of previous chapters. The argument is that without LPbD we face the end of law as we know it, though – paradoxically – engaging with LPbD will inevitably end the hegemony of modern law as we know it. There is no way back, we can only move forward. However, we have different options; either law turns into administration or techno-regulation, or it re-asserts its 'regime of veridiction' in novel ways. Moreover, I will briefly develop two types of design solutions that are not – yet – implementations of legal conditions; though I will argue that once they become operational they should be integrated into the legal framework. This would qualify them as instances of LPbD. That is how socio-technical innovation should drive legal protection and vice versa.

In this chapter I will briefly discuss why *technology neutral* law is a necessity, while *technologically neutral* law is an impossibility. This paves the way for a demonstration of how the upcoming obligation of Data Protection by Design (DPbD) qualifies as a form of LPbD that validates the fundamental right to data protection. This will be followed by two ways of engaging with the architecture of the onlife world that go beyond data protection: counter-profiling as a general strategy to figure out how one is targeted; and morphological computation in robotics to diminish dependence on central control models of intelligence. I will argue that counter-profiling could play a role in the onlife world that is similar to that of the free press, which implies that the freedom to counter-profile should probably be integrated into the framework of fundamental rights. Morphological computation, once it becomes state of the art, could become a necessary part of robotic design in so far as it enables smooth and safe interaction with humans based on the physical design of the robot, instead of being based on the data-driven computations in its central processing unit. To the extent that more morphological computation means less data-driven computation, it opens up new ways to achieve data minimization. It implies that at least part of our interactions with robot companions escape the storage and searchability of human behaviours within the digital unconscious.

10.2 LPBD IN AN ONL*I*FE WORLD

10.2.1 Technology Neutral Law: A Necessity

In other work we have evaluated the arguments that have been made for technology neutral law by regulators, business and legal scholars.[310] The arguments can be grouped together under three different objectives: first, the innovation objective that aims to prevent technology specific regulation as it might unfairly constrict the field or the development of specific technologies, thus interfering with the freedom to conduct a business; second, the sustainability objective that aims to prevent legislation from becoming outdated all too soon, because the changes in the technological landscape make it ineffective with regard to the goal it was supposed to serve; and third, the compensation objective that aims to redress erosion of the substance of a fundamental right which occurs as a side-effect of a new technology. Most debates on technology neutral law concern more than one objective, but it is important to distinguish them, if only to discern when they point in opposite directions. For instance, it may be that requiring consent for placing cookies on one's computer serves the third objective, while playing out against both the first and the second. It serves compensation because the use of tracking cookies threatens to render the rights of non-discrimination and privacy ineffective; by requiring prior informed consent it was hoped that the power imbalance created by the tracking mechanisms could be mitigated. However, if taken up in an effective way, the requirement contravenes the freedom to conduct a business in so far as business models are based on surreptitious tracing and tracking; once users are made aware of this practice they might want to withhold their consent and obstruct the business case for services based on the monetization of personal data. The requirement also contravenes the sustainability objective, since the legal norms were formulated in terms of one particular tracking mechanism (cookies), instead of tracking mechanisms in general (including browser fingerprinting, and so on). By being unnecessarily technology specific, other tracking mechanisms seem to fall outside the scope of the requirement.[311] Moreover, whereas session cookies and other cookies that are necessary to provide functionality and security were exempted from the consent requirement, most service providers found that by asking consent for all types of cookies in one stroke, they could practically force users to provide an all-in-one consent (since otherwise the site would not function). In the end none of the three objectives is served. This shows that technology specific legislation can easily become a burden on the industry as well as consumers, without adding any effective protection. Not because there is something wrong with technology specific legislation, but because the specificity was not articulated in the right manner. It was both under-inclusive (not covering all the relevant tracking mechanisms) and over-inclusive (allowing data controllers to seek consent by means of an all-in-one format, including consent for cookies that do not require consent).

In this chapter we focus on the compensation objective, to explain why technology specific law may sometimes be necessary in order to sustain the neutrality of the law with regard to emerging technologies. Neutrality means here that the mere fact that a new ICI is emerging should not diminish the substance and effectiveness of legal protection. This aligns with the approach Nissenbaum has developed in her decision heuristic with regard to contextual integrity,[312] investigating whether and how a new socio-technical practice infringes existing values. This entails taking a prudent but not a prudish position with regard to norms and values such as privacy or contextual integrity. The approach is prudent in so far as it focuses on existing rights or values, not necessarily advocating new ones. It is not prudish because it recognizes that to defend and preserve these values or rights, their substance and effectiveness must be evaluated in the light of the relevant new technologies, taking into account that the design of such technologies makes a difference for the values and the legal norms they enable or overrule. To some extent, we must accept that a new ICI may induce a reconfiguration of our norms and values; the point is that a reconfiguration should not go so far as to erase the substance of existing values merely because that fits new business models or more efficient administration. From the perspective of law in a constitutional democracy, we can add that legal norms are enacted or condoned by the democratic legislator and changing their scope should not be done without involving the constituency that is at stake.

As regards the example of mechanisms for online tracing and tracking we need to evaluate whether such mechanisms violate existing legal protection, such as the rights to privacy, non-discrimination, the presumption of innocence and due process. Having made an analysis of the threats of pre-emptive computing in Chapter 5, we can confirm that online tracing and tracking creates a manipulability across different contexts, by various private and public players, which ultimately translates into largely invisible infringements of these rights. The emergence of tracing and tracking, as well as their effects on these human rights, was not a decision of a legislator, nor did courts find justification for the practice. We therefore have to assume that these infringements, which are simply an affordance of a particular ICI, incentivized in the context of a particular political economy, must be redressed or compensated.

The next question is how this can be done and whether enactment of a new legal rule is sufficient to regulate (allow and restrict) the ICI that affords these infringements.

10.2.2 Technologically Neutral Law: An Impossibility

In Chapters 7 and 8 we saw that modern law has thrived on the affordances of the printing press. Text formats the extended mind of the lawyers; it feeds on an external memory and a systematized archive that comprises of codes, treaties, statutes, case law, doctrinal treatises and theoretical reflection. The proliferation of legal text has invited and enabled abstraction, complexity and systemization. It has generated the need for reiterative interpretation, paradoxically inviting both contestation and authoritative closure. Hesitation, doubt and consideration are situated in the heart of the law, instituting the antagonistic prerequisite for the competence to enact legislation and to issue a verdict. Written law externalizes legal norms, thus making contestation possible and final decisions necessary. This has led me to claim that law is not technologically neutral; its characteristics are contingent upon the ICI that mediates its verdict – its 'regime of veridiction' – and its mode of existence. As argued in Chapters 7 and 8, we cannot assume that the ICI of pre-emptive computing has affordances similar to those of the printing press.

This requires a rethinking of the legal embodiment of the law in an *onlife* world, since we cannot expect to regulate our new world via a law that is entirely inscribed via the ICI of a previous era. Re-articulation of the law in the emerging ICI will be necessary in so far as we wish to re-establish the fundamental rights developed in the era of the printing press. This does not mean that written law can be discarded. On the contrary, the externalization of legal norms that makes them contestable and enforceable should be preserved. But the nature of written law will somehow change. The spoken word did not disappear when we started writing, nor did unwritten law lose its bearing when written law became dominant, though some lawyers may deny that unwritten law has the force of law (law remains an essentially contested concept). What matters here is that the spoken word and unwritten law were transformed by their relationship with text. Before the script the notion of an unwritten law did not exist; before the arrival of 'the online' there was no such thing as 'an offline'. Mozart did not think of the performance of his music as being unplugged. We may expect similar transformations of our dealings with printed matter, due to the impact of pre-emptive computing. In that sense the hegemony of modern law, contingent upon the affordances of printed text, will end once we learn how to integrate legal norms in pre-emptive computing systems. This need not be the end of law if we develop new ways to preserve what differentiates law from administration and techno-regulation.

10.2.3   Legal Protection by Design

LPbD is a way to ensure that the technological normativity that regulates our lives: first, is compatible with enacted law, or even initiated by the democratic legislator; second, can be resisted; and third, may be contested in a court of law. This is what differentiates LPbD from techno-regulation. LPbD seeks a methodology capable of translating legal conditions into technical requirements, taking into account the fundamental requirements of 'resistability' and contestability. The 'resistability' requirement rules out deterministic environments, and the contestability requirement rules out invisible regulation. Moreover, LPbD, in being *legal*, must be *directed to* justice, legal certainty and purposiveness – even if these aims may be incompatible in concrete situations.

The reader may believe that LPbD is an attempt to apply affordances of the script and the printing press to an ICI that has very different affordances. Such an attempt is bound to fail. Obviously affordances cannot be applied; they can be detected and to some extent they can be tweaked or designed. The attempt is to detect, configure or design affordances that are compatible with specific legal norms that might otherwise lose their force, or to develop socio-technical systems that embody specific legal norms. This should always include attention to the 'resistability' and contestability of the ensuing normativity, and should always involve testing how the configuration or design of the affordances can best serve the goals of justice, legal certainty and purposiveness. Developing a methodology of LPbD entails a vertiginous challenge to traditional doctrinal research methods within legal scholarship and to the scientific methods of computer science, requirements engineering and electronics. No one area should colonize another, but LPbD is not a matter of different disciplines exchanging ideas. The point of departure is the task of articulating compatibility with a legal norm into an architecture, protocol, standard, hardware configuration, operating system, App or grid.

10.2.4 Data Protection by Design

LPbD signifies that the substance of legal protection, for instance privacy or non-discrimination, requires integration into the ICI of the onli*fe* world. The infrastructure will have to be engineered and organized in a way that is conducive to actions and behaviours that are compatible with the law. This is not a matter of nudging people into compliance; it is not a matter of techno-regulation. On the contrary, designing legal protection into an ICI means that mechanisms to steer people into certain behaviours must be made visible and contestable. This is what differentiates the regulatory paradigm from the 'regime of veridiction' of the Rule of Law. The point is that waiting for the technologies to consolidate, and imposing legal rules only after the socio-technical infrastructure has been shaped, will not be effective in the case of a novel ICI. Once the defaults are set it will be hard to change course. However, LPbD does not replace written law nor does it reject the achievements of modern law; rather, it should interface between written and unwritten legal norms on the one hand and the operations of data-driven agency on the other. LPbD thus draws its conclusions from the fact that law is not *technologically* neutral (as elaborated in Chapters 7 and 8), though it should be *technology* neutral (in accordance with the compensation objective).

Without much ado, the pGDPR has managed to integrate the implications of these findings in its stipulation that data controllers should implement data protection by design, to the extent that it is technically feasible. Before moving into the fascinating articulation of this written legal obligation, we have to face a potential objection. Some might object that the idea of technology neutral law is itself typical for modern law with its loyalty to distributive and corrective justice, and its emphasis on legal certainty. One could argue that once modern law is transformed by the emerging ICI of pre-emptive computing, it will be reconfigured by the novel affordances of its environment and take leave of the notions of distributive and corrective justice that inform the compensation objective, while also discarding legal certainty as a hindrance to technological innovation and scientific progress. This is correct. It is precisely where my concern is situated and clarifies that I am taking a normative position. Should we wish to preserve the legal protection of the Rule of Law in the context of a democratic society, we cannot take for granted that the upcoming ICI will afford such legal protection. We will have to take a stand for the substance of the norms and the values we wish to retain, and this will involve active participation in the design of the onli*fe* world.

Art. 23 of the pDPA stipulates:

(1).   Having regard to the state of the art, current technical knowledge, international best practices and the risks represented by the data processing, the controller and the processor, if any, shall, both at the time of the determination of the purposes and means for processing and at the time of the processing itself, implement appropriate and proportionate technical and organisational measures and procedures in such a way that the processing will meet the requirements of this Regulation and ensure the protection of the rights of the data subject, in particular with regard to the principles laid out in Article 5. Data protection by design shall have particular regard to the entire lifecycle management of personal data from collection to processing to deletion, systematically focusing on comprehensive procedural safeguards regarding the accuracy, confidentiality, integrity, physical security and deletion of personal data. Where the controller has carried out a data protection impact assessment pursuant to Article 33, the results shall be taken into account when developing those measures and procedures.

(2).   The controller shall ensure that, by default, only those personal data are processed which are necessary for each specific purpose of the processing and are especially not collected, retained or disseminated beyond the minimum necessary for those purposes, both in terms of the amount of the data and the time of their storage. In particular, those mechanisms shall ensure that by default personal data are not made accessible to an indefinite number of individuals and that data subjects are able to control the distribution of their personal data.

Note that the second paragraph defines data protection by default as a subcategory of data protection by design. Data protection by default is defined in terms of data minimization, the first and critical brake on the arbitrary collection of personal data. Processing data merely because we can do it and because it might come in handy later on is unlawful. Odysseus revisited; wax and ropes required. Personal data must not be collected, retained or disseminated beyond what is necessary for the purpose determined prior to first collection. Mechanisms must be put in place to prevent that data provided to a specific data controller is made available for an indefinite – undefined – public, and data subjects must be able to control further distribution. These mechanisms are the ropes and the wax; we are not speaking of individual self-binding that is contingent on decisions by those who stand to gain from access to Big Data.

Let us now have a better look at the overarching concept of Data Protection by Design. Though privacy by design has been around for some time, it has not been enacted as a legal obligation. Since privacy is a freedom and cannot easily be defined without reducing its protection, it does not lend itself to a legal requirement for privacy by design. Data protection by design makes more sense, because the right to data protection is more rule-based than the right to privacy. It basically demands that data controllers acquire and use technologies that are at least compatible with the rights and obligations of the pGDPR. This is a very smart way of organizing the market for data-driven systems, as it will force existing technology developers to include a new set of requirements at the starting point of their design process, while at the same time creating a market for new technologies that help to render data processing systems compatible with the pGDPR. In Chapter 9 we analysed the implications of the case of *Google v. Spain* on the right to be forgotten. What strikes me as critical is Google's immediate response. As recounted, within weeks Google arranged for an online form to enable users to request erasure of their personal data, promising that each request will be dealt with on a case-by-case basis once the implications of the ruling of the CJEU are clear. How all this will work out is unclear as yet. The cost of individual responses to requests to take down information may be prohibitive, so one can expect some kind of automation, which could exacerbate the problem as one cannot reason with the algorithms. The point is that Google does respond and that tools are being built to help users in exercising their rights. In the end the implementation of an individual right to be forgotten will force Google to automate decisions in a way that renders them both accountable and contestable.

In an animated environment that feeds on data-driven agency, legal protection will to a large extent depend on DPbD. This will entail a pervasive and sustained reflective equilibrium between the written legal norms of the pGDPR and the unwritten principles they imply, on the one hand, and the design of the 'softwired' hardware of ubiquitous computing on the other. At some points legal norms will have to be formulated with a keen eye to the fact that they should be translatable into technical and organizational requirements for the ICI of pre-emptive computing. This should, for instance, transform the emerging ICI into a more interactive environment.

As argued in the previous chapter, the most salient element of data protection with regard to the *onlife* world is the right to object to decisions based on machine-profiling and the right to obtain meaningful information about the underlying logic of processing. The challenge of translating these rights into technical and organizational requirements is intimidating. However, once the incentive structure to engage with these requirements is in place we might expect the unexpected and find that business models as well as innovative human machine interfacing technologies (HMI) will find ways to fabricate user empowerment. The incentive structure that could level the playing field for the industry is to be found in the fines foreseen in the pGDPR, which are proportional instead of symbolic (in the sense of ineffective). These fines – up to 5 per cent of the global turnover of the data controller – will bring data protection to the boardroom, they will help to translate data protection issues into technical and organizational requirements and they should help to create a market for data-driven systems that may give us enough of the Sirens as well as the ropes and the wax.

10.3 BEYOND DATA PROTECTION LAW

10.3.1 Counter-profiling

Two caveats, however, require attention. The first concerns the singular focus on data controllers. Data protection legislation seems to put all its eggs in one basket; the entity responsible for implementing the rights and obligations is foremost the data controller (with some additional obligations for the data processor). This makes the right to profile transparency contingent upon the data controller's compliance. Some authors have noted that this amounts to viewing the data controller as a trusted party,[313] whereas it is also the party that may have strong economic interests in non-compliance. It seems unwise to put the entire burden of checking for compliance on the shoulders of data protection authorities (DPAs), taking note of the fact that trade secrets and IP rights will make inspection of the backend system more difficult.

Let us return for a moment to the argument made in Chapters 3 and 5, on the critical role of double mutual anticipation, or double contingency, for human identity. Between humans, as well as between humans and their institutions, the anticipation is not made possible by opening the skull of another person to check what her brain is up to. We do not have any access to the internal workings of another's individual mind. Instead, we profile others by acting on how they interact, not merely by listening to what they say. Moreover, we check how their actions fit the action patterns of significant others, including the organizations and institutions that populate our *Welt*. In essence we are guessing, mostly intuitively, informed by a mix of perceptions and knowledge that does or does not pass the conscious mind. The epistemic trust this provides is based on experience with the source of our perceptions and knowledge. To achieve a similar reliable epistemic trust we need other sources than the information that data controllers are willing to provide, even if forced by law. Neither can we expect DPAs to do all the work, nor be sure that they are doing it well, unless we have other ways to verify and falsify how we are being targeted. In short, we must develop tools and skills to do counter-profiling with respect to data-driven agency. Counter-profiling must not be confused with anti-profiling. Quite the contrary, counter-profiling achieves a new balance by engaging in profiling; it means that the objects of profiling become subjects of profiling, conducting data mining operations on the behaviours of those that are in the business of profiling, whether 'those' are humans, computing systems or hybrid configurations. Double mutual anticipation actually implies double mutual counter-profiling. This is not an affair of isolated individual persons, however. To be effective it implies getting together with fellows that are similarly targeted, building platforms to share, store and mine the behaviour of profilers; in the end this will enable an individual person to develop a more or less intuitive but educated guess on how one is 'read'.

In a constitutional democracy the practice of counter-profiling could be safeguarded by the fundamental right to freedom of expression that includes the freedom of information, which protects a free press. In many ways, counter-profiling has the same function as the free press had in the era of books and newspapers. From the perspective of the Rule of Law, the right to freedom of information has horizontal effect and may include a positive obligation on the state to ensure that the right is effective.[314] This might even warrant investments of the state in an infrastructure that guarantees an independent free press.[315] To achieve this in an onli*fe* world would require technological mediation, for example in the form of platforms that facilitate people pooling their behavioural data, employing inference machines to infer the monetary value of the data and the manipulability of persons that match specific patterns.[316] Such platforms concern transparency on the front-end, where the data subjects find themselves. Front-end transparency will serve as a crucial complement to the legal requirement of backend transparency that concerns the data processing actually conducted by the data controllers and processors. At this moment there is no legal obligation to provide the socio-technical infrastructure for counter-profiling, whereas this seems to be a critical requirement for achieving the compensation that is called for by technology neutral law. The importance of such an infrastructure for the ICI of pre-emptive computing can hardly be overstated. If the onli*fe* world is to be a viable democracy such an infrastructure is as indispensable as a free press. To figure out how to actually fabricate smart technologies that enable counter-profiling is no mean feat; we need the kind of daring that drove Karen LaMonte to make the large cast glass sculptures that professional glass workers initially declared impossible:[317]

> Making sculpture, it's like trying to solve a riddle or figure out a puzzle. I had a vision of what I wanted to make, but there is no established technology to make it.

She did not take no for an answer when she was told that realizing her imagination was technically impossible. Obviously that is also what Silicon Valley stands for: imagination, daring and making 'things' work that nobody even dared to think of.

Enablers of counter-profiling, such as trusted platforms, social clouds, user-side reputation management systems and other forms of user empowerment, depend on a strong civil society. In composing legal code, lawyers and politicians will have to show acuity in enabling front-end transparency, for instance by qualifying obstacles to counter-profiling as infringements of the freedom of information and expression even in the case of non-governmental interventions. As inhabitants of an onli*fe* world we should not take no for an answer when it comes to inventing the 'hardwired softwares' for counter-profiling.

10.3.2 Morphological Computation

The second caveat concerns the focus on data. In fact, data protection puts all its eggs in two baskets. Even before we get to the issue of who is responsible for fair and lawful processing, we stumble over the point of entry for the applicability for the DPD or the pGDPR. The entire architecture of data protection is built on digital data. Personal data is the point of entry. Though that seems very wise in a data-driven environment, it also blinds us to potential solutions that turn away from data, back to atoms.

The software revolution has changed our world. We should expect that the upcoming hardware revolution that combines smart 3D printing, wearables, cloud robotics and modular interconnected hardware will have similarly substantial implications. At the very least it implies that our artefactual world is increasingly animated and capable of sharing our machine-readable behaviours via the cloud, thus generating a very precise knowledge at the aggregate and the individual level. Rules on lawfulness of data processing are important, but it seems crucial to also invest in artificial agency that is not – or is to a lesser extent – data-driven. Data that is not collected cannot be stored and searched; it cannot be matched or used to target manipulable individuals. Non-collection reduces our vulnerability. Select before you collect – a well-known principle in security research[318] – should inform the design of robots and other embedded systems that run our homes, transport, education, leisure time and office life.

In the field of soft robotics Pfeifer and others have begun to develop what they call morphological computation as a superior form of artificial intelligence for embodied agents. Whereas conventional computing requires digital representation, morphological computation depends on the material shape, texture, compliance and resistance of the robot. As discussed in Chapter 6, notably in section 6.3.2, morphological computation means that we can, first, prevent investing time and money in computational problems that are not related to the problem we want to solve, but only with its numerical translation; second, delegate problem solving to the shape and texture of the embedded system; and, third, morphological computation can prevent harm to human beings that encounter robots, by using compliant instead of rigid materials. In this section I want to briefly refer to the affordances of morphological computation in relation to the fundamental right to data protection and other fundamental rights.

Old-school robotics assumes that robots build internal, digital representations of the world they navigate, in order to plan their interactions. Their development is contingent on numerical modelling, acting in the world, tweaking the models on the basis of numerical feedback, followed by a persistent reiteration of the same cycle. This is what I have called data-driven agency. Morphological computation might enable the construction of artificial agents that navigate their physical and social world on the basis of direct interaction instead of via the computational bypass of the CPU. Viewing digital representation as a bypass might help to see the incalculable benefits of morphological computation that requires no such roundabout. It basically refers to computing a morphological design that helps an artificial agent to move around, to manipulate things and to communicate without depending on data-driven agency. Morphological computation introduces a novel paradigm. I believe it requires a revision of information theory, turning back from bits to atoms, acknowledging the pitfalls of equating data with information and cognition. Whereas 'data' and 'information' refer to material or immaterial entities, categories, types and tokens, cognition itself requires a cognizing subject.[319] If cognition is a matter of enaction (perception informed by action informed by perception), the issue of embodiment returns, requiring that we design robots in ways that emancipate them from our numerical models. Besides the benefits in terms of functionality and efficiency, morphological computation could also deliver robots capable of interaction without computational mediation, or, at least, robots that are less dependent on data models and the exchange of personal data. This could re-enable a relationship with individual robots that are capable of keeping part of their knowledge from entering the digital unconscious, thus preserving the privacy of their human companions. If they can deal with us in a fluent, affective and intelligent way without a non-stop numerical bypass, we might enjoy their company without sharing our behaviours.

10.4 CONCLUSIONS: THE END(S) OF LAW IN AN ONLI*FE* WORLD

Big Data is not a hype. It is here to stay. It is, however, a threat. It diverts attention from atoms to bits, and although this may help us to improve our life world, it may also take its place. Simulation is not what is simulated, digital data are not what is represented, and numerical computations do not necessarily solve real-world problems. Increasing dependence on ICT generates a bundle of security problems and safety issues and though they were not the focus of this volume, they should be taken into account when proselytizing the blessings of data-driven agency.

The ends of law are justice, legal certainty and purposiveness. A world focused on regulating, influencing or even enforcing behaviours has little to do with legal normativity. If one cannot disobey a law it is not law but discipline, as Hegel suggested. Trying to nudge people into obedience or into desirable behaviours does not take them seriously as individual human actors. We have accepted marketing and advertising, on the condition that we are made aware of the attempt to persuade us into purchasing. We need also to acknowledge that our governments will attempt to nudge us into compliance, possibly with the best of intentions. To retain and nourish individual autonomy, however, we must develop a more concrete understanding of the defaults of information and communication infrastructures that either protect us or deliver us to subliminal manipulations. We should require that our governments abstain from engaging in such manipulations, while protecting us from being tweaked into serving business models we don't even know about. An onli*fe* world thrives on data-driven agency that taps into a digital unconscious to which we have little or no access, capable of predicting and adapting the present, which may easily turn written law into a paper dragon. If we do not stand up to this, if lawyers do not involve themselves with legal protection by design, we might indeed face the end of law as a reliable framework to compatibilize fair distribution, proportional compensation and legitimate mutual expectations, while incentivizing economic welfare, facilitating the creation of added value and, finally, protecting the precious gem of individual human autonomy – however relative, fragile and contingent upon a shared life world.

Notes

1. Liptak, 'Supreme Court Says Phones Can't Be Searched Without a Warrant'. Clark, *Natural-Born Cyborgs. Minds, Technologies, and the Future of Human Intelligence.*
2. http://solidcon.com/solid2014
3. Kindly supported by the Netherlands Consulate in San Francisco, notably the Netherlands Office for Science and Technology (NOST), see http://nostsiliconvalley.org
4. Jacobs, *De computer de wet gesteld.*
5. On scenario studies, see e.g. Garreau, *Radical Evolution: The Promise and Peril of Enhancing Our Minds, Our Bodies – and What It Means to Be Human* at 78–9: scenario studies must conform to all 'known facts'; they must identify 'predetermineds' and subsequently 'critical uncertainties'; sometimes they identify 'wild cards'; they will reveal embedded assumptions; and finally it is useful to identify certain 'early warnings' that a specific scenario is about to be realized.
6. See www.fidis.net for several reports that include scenario studies.
7. E.g. Aarts and Marzano, *The New Everyday: Views on Ambient Intelligence.* For a less pre-emptive, more interactive approach: Aarts and Grotenhuis, 'Ambient Intelligence 2.0: Towards Synergetic Prosperity'.
8. Pew Research Center, *US Views of Technology and the Future: Science in the Next 50 Years*; Markoff, 'Police, Pedestrians and the Social Ballet of Merging'.
9. I capitalize the Rule of Law, not merely to pay my respects but foremost to prevent confusion with a particular rule/norm of law, cf. Waldron, 'The Concept and Rule of Law', p. 1 footnote 1.
10. Bijker, Hughes and Pinch, *The Social Construction of Technological Systems: New Directions in the Sociology and History of Technology.*
11. Goel, 'Facebook Tinkers with Users' Emotions in News Feed Experiment, Stirring Outcry'. Kramer, Guillory and Hancock, 'Experimental Evidence of Massive-Scale Emotional Contagion through Social Networks'.
12. Chopra and White, *A Legal Theory for Autonomous Artificial Agents.* Solum, 'Legal Personhood for Artificial Intelligences'.
13. See, however, Hildebrandt, 'Ambient Intelligence, Criminal Liability and Democracy'; ead., 'Criminal Liability and "Smart" Environments'; ead., 'Proactive Forensic Profiling: Unbounded Criminalization?'; ead., 'Criminal Law and Technology in a Data-Driven Society'.
14. Ibid.
15. E.g. Hildebrandt, 'Balance or Trade-Off?'
16. Solove, *The Digital Person: Technology and Privacy in the Information Age.*
17. Edward Snowden is a computer scientist who disclosed top-secret NSA documents, revealing extensive surveillance on phone and Internet communications by US intelligence. Cf. *The Guardian,* The Snowden Files, available at http://www.theguardian.com/world/series/the-snowden-files.
18. But see Sanger, 'U.S Accuses China's Military in Cyberattacks', Kaiman, 'China Reacts Furiously to US Cyber-Espionage Charges'.
19. Interesting work has been done from this angle: Bennett, 'Privacy Advocacy from the Inside and the Outside'; Acquisti, John, and Loewenstein, 'What Is Privacy Worth?'
20. Morozov, *To Save Everything, Click Here*; Cohen, *Configuring the Networked Self.*

21. This categorization is inspired by Karnow, 'Liability for Distributed Artificial Intelligences' at 155–161 and complemented with Pfeifer and Bongard, *How the Body Shapes the Way We Think: A New View of Intelligence*, cf. their notion of 'complete agents'.
22. See section 3.3.3.
23. Floridi and Sanders, 'On the Morality of Artificial Agents'.
24. E.g. Russell and Norvig, *Artificial Intelligence*.
25. This relates to the theory of cybernetics, Wiener, *Cybernetics: Or Control and Communication in the Animal and the Machine*.
26. Esposito, *The Future of Futures: The Time of Money in Financing and Society*, at 126ff.
27. Anderson, 'The End of Theory: The Data Deluge Makes the Scientific Method Obsolete'.
28. E.g. Ayres, *Super Crunchers: Why Thinking-by-Numbers Is the New Way to Be Smart*, and Mayer-Schönberger and Cukier, *Big Data*.
29. The original version, later coined as a 'self-fulfilling prophecy' by Robert Merton reads 'if men define situations as real, they are real in their consequences'. See Merton, 'The Self-Fulfilling Prophecy', who based his insights on Thomas and Thomas, *The Child in America*.
30. Ferber, *Multi-Agent System: An Introduction to Distributed Artificial Intelligence*.
31. Dreyfus, *What Computers Still Can't Do: A Critique of Artificial Reason*, also Brooks, 'Intelligence without Reason'; idem, 'Intelligence without Representation'.
32. Varela, Thompson and Rosch, *The Embodied Mind: Cognitive Science and Human Experience*.
33. Ihde, *Ironic Technics*.
34. Clark, *Natural-Born Cyborgs: Minds, Technologies, and the Future of Human Intelligence*.
35. Pfeifer and Bongard, *How the Body Shapes the Way We Think: A New View of Intelligence*.
36. Wolf, *Proust and the Squid*.
37. This book develops the analyses and arguments previously elaborated in e.g. Hildebrandt and Gutwirth, *Profiling the European Citizen: Cross-Disciplinary Perspectives*; Hildebrandt, 'Slaves to Big Data. Or Are We?' and Hildebrandt and De Vries, *Privacy, Due Process and the Computational Turn*.
38. Russell and Norvig, *Artificial Intelligence* at 28.
39. Duhigg, 'How Companies Learn Your Secrets'; Markoff, 'On "Jeopardy!" Watson Win is All but Trivial'; Fountain, 'Yes, Driverless Cars Know the Way to San Jose'; ENISA, *Give and Take: Good Practice Guide for Addressing Network and Information Security Aspects of Cybercrime*; The Economist, 'Data-Driven Finance. Go Figure. A New Class of Internet Start-Ups is Trying to Turn Data into Money'; Dobinson, 'Roundup', Intel Corporation, *Improving Traffic Management with Big Data Analytics*.
40. Fayyad et al., *Advances in Knowledge Discovery and Data Mining*.
41. Lohr, 'For Big-Data Scientists, "Janitor Work" Is Key Hurdle to Insights'.
42. The example is taken from Goel et al., 'Predicting Consumer Behavior with Web Search'.
43. Inspired by Wright, 'What's a Spurious Correlation?'.
44. Markoff, 'IBM Develops a New Chip That Functions Like a Brain'. Cf. IBM's website under cognitive computing, notably the project on neurosynaptic chips: http://www.research.ibm.com/cognitive-computing/projects/index.shtml#fbid=PyswxnwBKH1.
45. Mitchell, *Machine Learning* at 2.
46. Gitelman, *'Raw Data' Is an Oxymoron*.
47. Even if Big Data is equivalent with unstructured data, the datafication itself implies a translation that entails a form of modelling, while subsequent data mining operations like clustering result in more explicit modelling.
48. Mayer-Schönberger and Cukier, *Big Data* at 13. For an excellent criticism of such general beliefs in the benefits of Big Data, boyd and Crawford, *Six Provocations for Big Data*, with regard to objectivity and accuracy at 4–6.
49. E.g. Mayer-Schönberger and Cukier, *Big Data* at 134–5.
50. Cep, 'The Pointlessness of Unplugging'.
51. See http://ec.europa.eu/digital-agenda/en/onlife-initiative; and Floridi, *The Onlife Manifesto – Being Human in a Hyperconnected Era*.

52. Cf. Floridi, 'A Look into the Future Impact of ICT on Our Lives'.
53. This is not necessarily a Freudian subconscious. See e.g. Liu, *The Freudian Robot*. An early attempt to define the implications of Big Data in terms of a digital unconscious was initiated by Derrick de Kerckhove, see e.g. http://in3.uoc.edu/opencms_portalin3/opencms/en/activitats/seminaris/agenda/2012/agenda_004
54. Negroponte, *Being Digital* at 8.
55. http://www.spritzinc.com. See early comments: Wallop, 'Spritz'.
56. Hildebrandt, 'Location Data, Purpose Binding and Contextual Integrity. What's the Message?' at 35–6.
57. Gibson, *The Ecological Approach to Visual Perception*. David Norman introduced the concept in design theory, basically using it to refer to 'visible' affordances. I prefer Gibson's original concept, which also covers affordances that are not (immediately) perceived. Gibson's understanding of perception has been taken up in cognitive science and seems to fit well with Varela's 'enactive' understanding of cognition. Norman, *The Design of Everyday Things*.
58. Ricoeur, *Interpretation Theory*; idem, 'The Model of the Text: Meaningful Action Considered as a Text'.
59. Goody, *The Logic of Writing and the Organization of Society*; Ong, *Orality and Literacy: The Technologizing of the Word*.
60. Eisenstein, *The Printing Revolution in Early Modern Europe*.
61. Wolf, *Proust and the Squid*. See the section on 'Does an Alphabet Build a Different Brain?' at 60–9. Also Lévy, *Les Technologies de L'intelligence. L'avenir de La Pensée À L'ère Informatique*.
62. Wolf, *Proust and the Squid* at 15 and 17.
63. Gleick, *The Information*, Chapter 2 on 'The persistence of the word'.
64. McLuhan, *Understanding Media: The Extensions of Man*.
65. Cf. Manovich, 'Database as a Symbolic Form', who opposes the narrative structure of the old communication infrastructures to the non-sequential character of the database.
66. Tapscott, *Grown up Digital: How the Net Generation is Changing Your World*, at 97. Wolf, *Proust and the Squid*, at 16, 212–29.
67. I am using the terms *Umwelt* and *Welt* in the tradition of the late Husserl (*Lebenswelt*), Heidegger (*in-der-Welt-sein*), Merleau-Ponty (*Welt and Umwelt*), Plessner (*Welt and Umwelt*), interpreting them as close to Wittgenstein's *Lebensform*, see e.g. also Gier, *Wittgenstein and Phenomenology: A Comparative Study of the Later Wittgenstein, Husserl, Heidegger, and Merleau-Ponty*. See e.g. Ricoeur, 'The Model of the Text: Meaningful Action Considered as a Text'; Taylor, *Philosophical Arguments*; Van Brakel, *Interculturele Communicatie en Multiculturalisme*; Husserl, *The Crisis of European Sciences and Transcendental Phenomenology: An Introduction to Phenomenological Philosophy*; Wittgenstein, *Philosophical Investigations*; Heidegger, *Being and Time*; Plessner, *Die Stufen Des Organischen under Der Mensch. Einleitung in Die Philosophische Anthropologie*; De Mul, *Plessner's Philosophical Anthropology*. *Umwelt* is what allows for ostensive reference, whereas *Welt* is what is constituted by language and technologies that afford reference beyond the *Umwelt*. *Welt* is the dynamic web of meaning that constitutes our 'reality'. Cf. also Geertz, 'Local Knowledge: Fact and Law in Comparative Perspective' and Winch, *The Idea of a Social Science*. I will mostly use the singular, but we should acknowledge that most of us inhabit a variety of both *Umwelts* and *Welts*. For a number of reasons I omit a separate discussion of the so-called *Mitwelt* that supposedly constitutes the social world. I believe that the *Welt* is already a hybrid constitution that depends on language and the double contingency discussed in Chapter 3, section 3.3.3.
68. The importance of pattern recognition as the most crucial feature of cognition can already be traced in Herbert Simon's work on AI, cf. Frantz, 'Herbert Simon. Artificial Intelligence as a Framework for Understanding Intuition'. Simon, *The Sciences of the Artificial*, typical for first wave cybernetics. It returns in the second wave in Maturana and Varela's notion of structural coupling, cf. Maturana and Varela, *Autopoiesis and Cognition: The Realization of the Living*. In connectionism it reappears as the pattern that emerges from the initially

chaotic interaction between distributed nodes. Cf. Hayles, *How We Became Posthuman: Virtual Bodies in Cybernetics, Literature, and Informatics.*

69. Hildebrandt, Koops and De Vries, *Where Idem-Identity Meets Ipse-Identity: Conceptual Explorations.* The notion of 'double anticipation' is similar to Parson's and Luhmann's 'double contingency', which entails that one's actions are always contingent on those of others, see Parsons and Shils, *Toward a General Theory of Action*; Luhmann, *Social Systems*; Vanderstraeten, 'Parsons, Luhmann and the Theorem of Double Contingency'. It also connects to Dennett's 'intentional stance', which states that we might better anticipate another person if we assume that her actions follow from her intention to achieve certain goals, based on beliefs about the state of the world, see Dennett, 'Intentional Systems Theory'.

70. The difference between humans and animals is empirical to the extent that the difference may turn out to be much more differentiated than my use of the term mutation suggests. See, for instance De Waal, Macedo and Ober, *Primates and Philosophers*, on the social and moral life of primates and White, *In Defense of Dolphins*, on the social life of dolphins that seem to have developed a complex language. My point is not that humans are necessarily more advanced (or troubled) than any other type of animal or machine could ever be. I merely refer to our self-consciousness as a very specific way of co-constituting a world.

71. Much of this is contingent on bodily coordination instead of the calculations of a central control unit. Cf. Gigerenzer, *Gut Feelings: The Intelligence of the Unconscious.* This connects with the idea of morphological computation, e.g. Füchslin et al., 'Morphological Computation and Morphological Control'.

72. About language as typical for humans in Plessner's work, 'grounding' human eccentricity or the 'rootless homofaber', affording '*Selbstdistanz*', see Cheung, 'The Language Monopoly: Plessner on Apes, Humans and Expressions'. The idea is that animals 'are' a self, whereas humans are a self and aware of their self. The self is not described as a substance, but as a centrality that cannot be localized within the body – even if it constitutes the border between self and environment.

73. On the problematic assumption that a view from somewhere else can pretend to deliver objectivist knowledge see Nagel, 'What Is It like to Be a Bat?'

74. In using the term 'environment' I refer to the entanglement of *Welts* and *Umwelts* that we co-constitute and inhabit.

75. See Butler, *Giving an Account of Oneself* on the constitutive primary address, and Ricoeur, *Oneself as Another.* Whereas Ricoeur develops a narrative theory of identity, Butler stresses the opacity of the primal address. She argues that we cannot develop a final narrative about this beginning, because we were not yet around. Manovich, 'Database as a Symbolic Form' opposes the era of the database to that of the narrative, establishing that 'a database can support narrative, but there is nothing in the logic of the medium itself which would foster its generation'.

76. On the issue of 'the other mind' see e.g. Gallagher and Zahavi, *The Phenomenological Mind: An Introduction to Philosophy of Mind and Cognitive Science*, Chapter 9, discussing various versions of the idea that we develop a theory of what other people think or feel (inferring from their behaviours) and the idea that we simulate what other people think or feel (on the basis of our own thoughts and feelings).

77. Kephart and Chess, 'The Vision of Autonomic Computing' at 41.

78. Though this does not imply that our brains are mastering this complexity by means of complicated calculations of all potentially relevant variables, see Gigerenzer, *Gut Feelings: The Intelligence of the Unconscious*, on the intricacies of cerebral intuition.

79. Butler, *Giving an Account of Oneself.*

80. Ibid at 10.

81. Ratliff, 'Popcast'.

82. Müller et al., 'Amelioration of Psychiatric Symptoms through Exposure to Music Individually Adapted to Brain Rhythm Disorders – a Randomised Clinical Trial on the Basis of Fundamental Research'.

83. Kosner, 'The Appification of Everything Will Transform the World's 360 Million Web Sites'. Cf. the Warsaw declaration on the appification of society – 35th International Conference of Data Protection and Privacy Commissioners – September 23–26, 2013, available at http://www.priv.gc.ca/information/conf2013/declaration_e.asp

84. Pariser, *The Filter Bubble: What The Internet Is Hiding From You*. Sunstein, *Republic. com*.

85. Schwartz, *The Paradox of Choice: Why More Is Less*. Thaler and Sunstein, *Nudge: Improving Decisions about Health, Wealth, and Happiness*.

86. For a sketch of the dilemmas, see Powers, 'How Will I Die?'

87. Sontag, *A Susan Sontag Reader*. See Zittrain, 'The Generative Internet', who defines generativity as denoting 'a technology's overall capacity to produce unprompted change driven by large, varied, and uncoordinated audiences'.

88. Wolpert and Macready, 'No Free Lunch Theorems for Optimization'.

89. Hudson, 'Secrets of Self: Punishment and the Right to Privacy'. Hildebrandt, 'Autonomic and Autonomous "Thinking": Preconditions for Criminal Accountability'.

90. Might the reader not believe that such 'things' are in progress, see e.g. Vallverdu and Casacuberta, 'The Panic Room: On Synthetic Emotions'.

91. Damasio, *The Feeling of What Happens: Body and Emotion in the Making of Consciousness*; idem, *Looking for Spinoza: Joy, Sorrow, and the Feeling Brain*.

92. Picard, *Affective Computing* at 1.

93. Ibid.

94. Gleick, *The Information* and Chapter 2 on 'The persistence of the word'.

95. Davidson, 'Actions, Reasons, and Causes'.

96. Johnson, 'Kant's Moral Philosophy'.

97. Stirling, 'Science, Precaution, and the Politics of Technological Risk', Building on Wynne, 'Uncertainty and Environmental Learning'.

98. Westin, *Privacy and Freedom*.

99. Cf. Gurses and Berendt, 'The Social Web and Privacy: Practices, Reciprocity and Conflict Detection in Social Networks'; Rouvroy and Poullet, 'The Right to Informational Self-Determination and the Value of Self-Development: Reassessing the Importance of Privacy for Democracy'.

100. Nissenbaum, 'Towards an Approach to Privacy in Public: The Challenges of Information Technology'. About the privacy granted by the anonymity of public space see White, *Here is New York*: 'On any person who desires such queer prizes, New York will bestow the gift of loneliness and the gift of privacy' at 1.

101. Altman, *The Environment and Social Behavior: Privacy, Personal Space, Territory, Crowding*; Petronio, *Boundaries of Privacy: Dialectics of Disclosure*.

102. Agre and Rotenberg, *Technology and Privacy: The New Landscape* at 7.

103. Hildebrandt, 'Privacy and Identity'.

104. Berlin, 'Two Concepts of Liberty'.

105. Ricoeur, *Oneself as Another*.

106. Mouffe, *The Democractic Paradox*; Rip, 'Constructing Expertise: In a Third Wave of Science Studies?'.

107. This regards the so-called third party doctrine, first decided in *US v. Miller*, 425 U.S. 435 (1976).

108. Nissenbaum, *Privacy in Context: Technology, Policy, and the Integrity of Social Life*.

109. Goffman, *The Presentation of Self in Everyday Life* at 137.

110. Calhoun, *Habermas and the Public Sphere*.

111. In rational choice theory public goods are often defined as non-rivalrous and non-excludable, for instance fresh air, information, a lighthouse, the police. Though this seems to acknowledge the transpersonal character of public goods the definition rests on the assumptions of methodological individualism. A relational understanding of subjectivity may be at odds with such assumptions. In moral philosophy a public good is understood as what is good or beneficial for the public, constituency or population as a whole, being preconditional for the good life of the polity, for instance justice, safety, privacy, public health.

112. Arendt, *The Human Condition*, Chapter II, 'The Public and the Private Realm'.
113. E.g. Salganik and Watts, 'Leading the Herd Astray: An Experimental Study of Self-Fulfilling Prophecies in an Artificial Cultural Market'.
114. Arendt, *The Human Condition* at 41 and at 38.
115. Young and Quan-Haase, 'Privacy Protection Strategies on Facebook'.
116. On AB testing and e-selling Parvinen, Kaptein and Poyry, 'Data-Driven vs. Theory-Driven Approaches to E-Selling'. See e.g. the Google patent on research design for human interaction proof that integrates AB testing: DEO, Rajshekar and Ramakrishnan, 'System and Method for Creating and Implementing Scalable and Effective Surveys and Testing Methods with Human Interaction Proof (HIP) Capabilities'. See the outcry about Facebook's manipulations of its user's news feed, note 11 above.
117. This relates to Searle's distinction between brute facts (of nature) and institutional facts (that require constitutive norms to emerge as such, and language to take shape). Searle, *Speech Acts: An Essay in the Philosophy of Language*. I dare say that the difference is relative, because even brute facts are mediated by our cognitive interface, i.e. language.
118. Duhigg, 'How Companies Learn Your Secrets'.
119. Zarsky, '"Mine Your Own Business!": Making the Case for the Implications of the Data Mining of Personal Information in the Forum of Public Opinion', note 107 at p. 35; Schwartz, 'Internet Privacy and the State'.
120. Gigerenzer, 'Why Heuristics Work'.
121. Frankfurt, 'Freedom of the Will and the Concept of a Person' at 7.
122. The example is taken from Duhigg, 'How Companies Learn Your Secrets'.
123. Harcourt, *Against Prediction: Profiling, Policing, and Punishing in an Actuarial Age*.
124. Packer, 'Two Models of the Criminal Process'.
125. Dwyer, 'The Inference Problem and Pervasive Computing', at 3.
126. Section 5.2.1 supra. Dwyer refers to Petronio, *Boundaries of Privacy: Dialectics of Disclosure*, who builds on Altman.
127. Gigerenzer and Selten, *Bounded Rationality: The Adaptive Toolbox*.
128. Cf. Orito and Murata, 'Privacy Protection in Japan: Cultural Influence on the Universal Value'; Adams, Murata and Orito, 'The Japanese Sense of Information Privacy'; and Mizutani, Dorsey and Moor, 'The Internet and Japanese Conception of Privacy'.
129. Miyashita, 'The Evolving Concept of Data Privacy in Japanese Law'; Greenleaf, 'JAPAN'.
130. Greenleaf, Murata and Adams, *'My Number' Unlikely to Thaw Japan's Frozen Data Privacy Laws*. In the spring of 2014 Japan was approved as a participant in the Cross Border Privacy Rules (CBPR) System of the Asia-Pacific Economic Cooperation (APEC), which should be an indication that it provides effective informational privacy protection.
131. Davies and Ikeno, *The Japanese Mind: Understanding Contemporary Japanese Culture*, at 11. This quote is taken from their chapter on Japanese personal space *'Hedataru to Najimu'*. It concerns what we call physical or territorial privacy.
132. Cf. Wittgenstein et al., *Philosophical Investigations*; Solove, 'Conceptualizing Privacy'.
133. Altman, *The Environment and Social Behavior: Privacy, Personal Space, Territory, Crowding* at 6.
134. Glenn, *Legal Traditions of the World* about the emergence of subjective rights as a response to the powers of the state; Scott, *Seeing Like a State: How Certain Schemes to Improve the Human Condition Have Failed*.
135. My concept of culture is equivalent with that of *Welt* as discussed in the previous chapters. It roughly equates with Glenn's notion of tradition, see note 134, and with Geertz's notion of culture, Geertz, 'Local Knowledge: Fact and Law in Comparative Perspective'. This entails an anti-essentialist, performative understanding of cultural patterns and orientations.
136. See Descola and Palsson, *Nature and Society: Anthropological Perspectives*, on the difference between animistic, totemistic and naturalistic cultures.

137. Kasulis, in 'Japanese Philosophy' recounts that the history of Japanese thought tends to emphasize immanence over transcendence in defining spirituality.
138. Cf. Nakada and Tamura, 'Japanese Conceptions of Privacy: An Intercultural Perspective'; Capurro, 'Privacy: An Intercultural Perspective', who both stress that contemporary Japanese live in different worlds, e.g. that of *Seken* (traditional 'indigenous' worldviews) and that of *Shakai* (Western style worldviews). They explain how this involves a continuous shifting between different roles, which evidently also change from one generation to the next.
139. Davies and Ikeno, *The Japanese Mind: Understanding Contemporary Japanese Culture* at 127–33.
140. Macfarlane, *Japan through the Looking Glass* at 176–209. At 194–7 Macfarlane briefly discusses Karl Jaspers' framework of the Axial Age that introduced a schism between the material and the spiritual world, anticipating the separation of body and mind in the wake of the scientific revolution. Referring to Robert Bellah's *Imagining Japan* (Berkeley: University of California Press 2003) Macfarlane explains that Japan seems to be the only modern culture that has remained non-axial.
141. Kawano, *Ritual Practice in Modern Japan*, Chapter 1 on *kama* and *hotoke*.
142. Ibid. See also Descola, *Beyond Nature and Culture*.
143. Macfarlane, *Japan through the Looking Glass* at 182.
144. Kasulis, 'Japanese Philosophy'.
145. Nakayama, *Science, Technology and Society in Postwar Japan*.
146. Dreyfus, *What Computers Can't Do: The Limits of Artificial Intelligence*; idem, *What Computers Still Can't Do: A Critique of Artificial Reason*; Brooks, 'Intelligence without Representation'; idem, 'Intelligence without Reason'.
147. Pfeifer and Bongard, *How the Body Shapes the Way We Think: A New View of Intelligence*.
148. Ibid at 249.
149. Weiser, 'The Computer for the 21st Century'.
150. Clark, *Natural-Born Cyborgs: Minds, Technologies, and the Future of Human Intelligence*; Latour, *We Have Never Been Modern*; idem, 'The Berlin Key or How to Do Words with Things'.
151. Pfeifer and Bongard, *How the Body Shapes the Way We Think* at 253.
152. Ibid at 253–6.
153. A definition posted by Margaret Rouse in 2007 on WhatIs.com, see http://whatis.techtarget.com/definition/robot-insect-robot-autonomous-robot.
154. Füchslin et al., 'Morphological Computation and Morphological Control' at 19.
155. Hornyak, *Loving the Machine: The Art and Science of Japanese Robots*; Schodt, *Inside the Robot Kingdom: Japan, Mechatronics, and the Coming Robotopia*. See: http://factsanddetails.com/japan/cat26/sub163/item873.html: 'Japan is [the] world's leading manufacturer and consumer of robots. About half of the world's robot are made and used in Japan. About half of the world's 4,500 robot engineers are in Japan. In 2000, $5.7 billion worth of robots were produced in Japan'. See also Shinohara, *Robotics Research in Japan*.
156. Geraci, 'Spiritual Robots: Religion and Our Scientific View of the Natural World'.
157. Shinohara, *Robotics Research in Japan* at 11.
158. In the third formulation Kant actually speaks of 'every rational being' rather than 'humanity', which has led some authors to assume that rational agents other than humans could qualify as addressees of the categorical imperative. On the standard view see Stahl, 'Can a Computer Adhere to the Categorical Imperative? A Contemplation of the Limits of Transcendental Ethics in IT'.
159. Cf. Mary Shelley's *Frankenstein: The Modern Prometheus*, first published in 1818. The Czech play *Rossum's Universal Robots* by Karel Capek (1921), whose brother actually coined the term robot (meaning 'serf' or 'forced labor') is about an uprising of robots, who are depicted as mechanically more perfect than humans, but lacking a soul. Asimov's

laws of robotics also indicate that robots must be kept in check by their human masters, see note 191.

160. Cf. the philosophy of Watsuji Tetsuro (1889–1960). Wu, 'The Philosophy of As-Is: The Ethics of Watsuji Tetsuro'; Capurro, 'Privacy: An Intercultural Perspective'; Carter, 'Watsuji Tetsuro'. Watsuji studied in Berlin and has been influenced by Nietzsche, Kierkegaard and especially Heidegger.

161. Cf. Macfarlane, *Japan through the Looking Glass* at 76.

162. Thompson, *Between Ourselves: Second-Person Issues in the Study of Consciousness*, which includes a chapter by Yoko Arisaka, 'The Ontological Co-Emergence of "Self and Other" in Japanese Philosophy', 197–209.

163. Cf. the attempt to introduce neo-Confucian stratification during the Meiji period; Kasulis, 'Japanese Philosophy'.

164. Cf. Flynn, *The Philosophy of Claude Lefort: Interpreting the Political*.

165. Brown and Levinson, *Politeness: Some Universals in Language Usage*.

166. Langheinrich, 'Privacy by Design – Principles of Privacy-Aware Ubiquitous Systems'.

167. Haugh, 'The Importance of "Place" in Japanese Politeness: Implications for Cross-Cultural and Intercultural Analyses'; Haugh and Obana, 'Politeness in Japan'.

168. Macfarlane, *Japan through the Looking Glass* at 101.

169. Haugh, 'The Importance of "Place" in Japanese Politeness: Implications for Cross-Cultural and Intercultural Analyses', speaks of 'inclusion' and 'distinction'.

170. Mizutani, Dorsey and Moor, 'The Internet and Japanese Conception of Privacy' at 125; Macfarlane, *Japan through the Looking Glass* at 162.

171. Often considered to stem from Benedict, *The Chrysanthemum and the Sword: Patterns of Japanese Culture*. For a salient criticism of such reconstructions see Smith, *Japan: A Reinterpretation*; Murphy-Shigematsu, 'Multiethinic Japan and the Monoethnic Myth'; Dale, *The Myth of Japanese Uniqueness*.

172. Cf. Wu, 'The Philosophy of As-Is: The Ethics of Watsuji Tetsuro'.

173. Mizutani, Dorsey and Moor, 'The Internet and Japanese Conception of Privacy' at 123.

174. Ibid at 123.

175. Ibid.

176. Ibid at 121,126, 127.

177. Adams, Murata and Orito, 'The Japanese Sense of Information Privacy' at 4.

178. Ibid.

179. Cf. Macfarlane *Japan through the Looking Glass* at 141–2.

180. Goffman, *The Presentation of Self in Everyday Life*.

181. Adams, Murata and Orito, 'The Japanese Sense of Information Privacy' at 331.

182. Ibid at 335.

183. Davies and Ikeno, *The Japanese Mind: Understanding Contemporary Japanese Culture* at 111.

184. Ibid, citing, at 111, from J. Condon, *Cultural Dimensions of Communication* (Tokyo: Simul Press 1980), 369 (who cites Hamil, no Reference given).

185. Cf. Adams, Murata and Orito, 'The Japanese Sense of Information Privacy' at 335; Tamura, 'Japanese Feeling for Privacy'.

186. Young and Quan-Haase, 'Privacy Protection Strategies on Facebook'.

187. See e.g. Adams, Murata and Orito, 'The Japanese Sense of Information Privacy'; Miike, 'Japanese Enryo-Sasshi Communication and the Psychology of Amae: Reconsideration and Reconceptualization', referred to in Adams, Murata, and Orito, 'The Japanese Sense of Information Privacy'.

188. T. Doi (1973) 'The Japanese Patterns of Communication and the Concept of Amae', *Quarterly Journal of Speech* 59, no. 2: 180–85, quoted from Miike, 'Japanese Enryo-Sasshi Communication and the Psychology of Amae: Reconsideration and Reconceptualization' at 98.

189. Mizutani, Dorsey and Moor, 'The Internet and Japanese Conception of Privacy' at 124. Miike, 'Japanese Enryo-Sasshi Communication and the Psychology of Amae: Reconsideration and Reconceptualization' at 99.

190. Yamamoto, 'A Morality Based on Trust: Some Reflections on Japanese Morality' at 462.

191. See the short story 'The Runaround' by the famous science fiction author Asimov in his *I, Robot* at 37 (the story was first published in 1942).

192. Hegel, Wood and Nisbet, *Elements of the Philosophy of Right* at 124–6 (§ 99).

193. Biever, 'Roomba Creator'. See also e.g. Osaka, Ikeda and Osaka, 'Effect of Intentional Bias on Agency Attribution of Animated Motion'.

194. Edmundson, *An Introduction to Rights*.

195. France, *Le Lys Rouge* at 117.

196. Stengers, 'Reclaiming Animism'.

197. Wesel, *Frühformen Des Rechts in Vorstaatlichen Gesellschaften. Umrisse Einer Früh-geschichte Des Rechts Bei Sammlern Und Jägern Und Akephalen Ackerbauern Und Hirten* at 52: 'Was ist eigentlich Recht? Eine Antwort ist ähnlich einfach wie der bekannte Versuch, einen Pudding an die Wand zu nageln (translation MH)'.

198. Gallie, 'Essentially Contested Concepts'.

199. Rawls, *A Theory of Justice*.

200. Dworkin, *Law's Empire*.

201. Austin and Rumble, *The Province of Jurisprudence Determined*; Kelsen, *General Theory of Norms*; Hart, *The Concept of Law*.

202. Ost and Kerchove, *De la pyramide au réseau?*

203. See also Fuller, *The Morality of Law*; Hildebrandt, 'Radbruch's Rechtsstaat and Schmitt's Legal Order: Legalism, Legality and the Institution of Law'.

204. Dworkin, *Law's Empire*.

205. Assuming that a number of other legal rights and obligations are taken into account, see Chapter 9 below.

206. Austin, *How to Do Things with Words*.

207. Holmes, 'The Path of the Law' at 460–61.

208. See also Glastra van Loon, 'Rules and Commands', who developed an expectancy model of law.

209. Peirce and Turrisi, *Pragmatism as a Principle and Method of Right Thinking: The 1903 Harvard Lectures on Pragmatism* at 111.

210. Teubner, 'Rights of Non-Humans? Electronic Agents and Animals as New Actors in Politics and Law'.

211. Austin, *How To Do Things with Words*. I am avoiding a discussion of brute facts, because I am not convinced that the distinction holds, cf. Searle, *The Construction of Social Reality*. A legal theory based on institutional facts was expounded by MacCormick. In his later work, notably *Institutions of Law*, the main concern was how those who 'use' legal norms co-institute the law (meaning citizens), whereas Latour is focused on the practice of those who fabricate the law (meaning lawyers).

212. Latour, 'Biography of an Inquiry' at 1–2, referring to Souriau, *Les différents modes d'existence*.

213. Rabruch, 'Legal Philosophy'; Leawoods, 'Gustav Radbruch: An Extraordinary Legal Philosopher'; Paulson, 'Lon L. Fuller, Gustav Radbruch, and the "Positivist" Theses'.

214. Schmitt, *Political Theology: Four Chapters on the Concept of Sovereignty* at 5. The quotation that follows is taken from Vinx, 'Carl Schmitt'.

215. Radbruch, 'Five Minutes of Legal Philosophy'; idem, 'Statutory Lawlessness and Supra-Statutory Law'.

216. Radbruch, 'Legal Philosophy' at 116–17 (translation, MH).

217. Derrida, 'Force of Law: The "Mystical Foundation of Authority"'.

218. Radbruch, 'Legal Philosophy' at 107–8 (translation, MH).

219. Habermas, *Between Facts and Norms: Contributions to a Discourse Theory of Law and Democracy*.

220. Cf. Habermas' reconstructive *Diskurs Maxim*, notably in his *Between Facts and Norms*.

221. Radbruch, 'Legal Philosophy' at 117 (translation, MH).

222. Ibid at 111 (translation, MH).

223. Comaroff, *Rules and Processes: The Cultural Logic of Dispute in an African Context*.

224. Geertz, 'Local Knowledge: Fact and Law in Comparative Perspective'.
225. Radbruch, 'Legal Philosophy' at 91.
226. Ibid at 48.
227. Verbeek, *What Things Do: Philosophical Reflections on Technology, Agency and Design.*
228. Ihde, *Philosophy of Technology: An Introduction* at 47–8.
229. On the neuroscience of human use of tools and its relationship with language: Ambrose, 'Paeleolithic Technology and Human Evolution'. On philosophical anthropology and use of tools and language: Cheung, 'The Language Monopoly: Plessner on Apes, Humans and Expressions'. Cf. the seminal work of Ihde, *Technology and the Lifeworld: From Garden to Earth.*
230. Foqué and 't Hart, *Instrumentaliteit En Rechtsbescherming.*
231. Latour, *An Inquiry into Modes of Existence.* I endorse Latour's constructive realism that clarifies that reality is always co-constituted in the process of perception and enaction; the more constructed the more real. Which remains far from social constructivism and postmodern relativism. Cf. Latour, 'For Bloor and Beyond – a Reply to David Bloor's Anti-Latour'.
232. Kranzberg, 'Technology and History: "Kranzberg's Laws"' at 544.
233. It is not merely autocratic dictators that can be accused of endorsing a rule by law without developing their reign into the Rule of Law, e.g. Lugosi, 'Rule of Law or Rule by Law'.
234. With the rule by law, the adage is rex est lex loqui, whereas with the advance of the Rule of Law Montequieu's famous adage gets traction: iudex – non rex – lex loqui, cf. Schönfeld, 'Rex, Lex et Judex: Montesquieu and La Bouche de La Loi Revisted'.
235. Parker et al., *Regulating Law.*
236. Black, 'Critical Reflections on Regulation' at 20.
237. Action can be defined as meaningful behaviour, implying that action implies a self-conscious subject capable of reflecting upon her own behaviours and developing intentions about them. This also implies that behaviour is described from an observer's position and need not refer to an agent (even stones, the weather and the sun 'behave' in certain ways). See e.g. Winch, *The Idea of a Social Science*, on 'meaningful behavior' at 45–65 and Gier, *Wittgenstein and Phenomenology* at 135–53 on 'behaviorism and intentionality', on the difference between behaviour from a purely external perspective and the attribution of meaning to one's own behaviours.
238. Lessig, *Code Version 2.0*; cf. Gutwirth, De Hert and De Sutter, 'The Trouble with Technology Regulation from a Legal Perspective: Why Lessig's "Optimal Mix" Will Not Work'.
239. Calabresi and Melamed, 'Property Rules, Liability Rules and Inalienability: One View of the Cathedral'.
240. Thaler and Sunstein, *Nudge: Improving Decisions about Health, Wealth, and Happiness.*
241. Moravec, 'Pigs in Cyberspace'.
242. Kurzweil, *The Singularity Is Near: When Humans Transcend Biology.*
243. Heidegger, *The Question Concerning Technology, and Other Essays*; Ellul, *The Technological Society.*
244. On the so-called 'command theory of law', that explains the validity of the law entirely from its mode of existence as 'orders backed by threats': Austin and Rumble, *The Province of Jurisprudence Determined.* A supposedly more 'sociological' understanding of law: Hart, *The Concept of Law.*
245. Kelsen, *General Theory of Law and State.* Legal positivist Kelsen went so far as the claim that the state is entirely constituted by law. Others might claim, e.g. on historical grounds, that the modern state was founded upon a rule by law, notably Berman, *Law and Revolution: The Formation of the Western Legal Tradition.*
246. Nonet, *Law and Society in Transition: Toward Responsive Law.*
247. Norman, *The Design of Everyday Things.* On the role of cultural conventions in perceiving an affordance in the realm of computer interfaces: Norman, 'Affordance, Conventions, and Design'.

248. Ihde, *Technology and the Lifeworld: From Garden to Earth* at 144–51.
249. Zittrain, *The Future of the Internet – And How to Stop It*.
250. On the implied philosophy of the law: Dworkin, *Law's Empire*.
251. On the opposition of formal and substantive conceptions of the Rule of Law, claiming the importance of a third, procedural understanding: Waldron, 'The Rule of Law and the Importance of Procedure'; also Hildebrandt, 'Radbruch's Rechtsstaat and Schmitt's legal order'.
252. 'Infrastructure', Merriam-Webster.com: http://www.merriam-webster.com/dictionary/infrastructure
253. Wesel, *Frühformen Des Rechts in Vorstaatlichen Gesellschaften*; Salas, *Du Procès Pénal*; Hoebel, 'Feud: Concept, Reality and Method in the Study of Primitive Law'; Roberts, *Order and Dispute*; Geertz, 'Local Knowledge: Fact and Law in Comparative Perspective'.
254. Glenn, *Legal Traditions of the World*, Chapter 3, on the Chthonic legal tradition.
255. Ibid.
256. Ong, *Orality and Literacy: The Technologizing of the Word*; Eisenstein, *The Printing Revolution in Early Modern Europe*; Goody and Watt, 'The Consequences of Literacy'; Ihde, *Technology and the Lifeworld: From Garden to Earth*; Lévy, *Les Technologies de L'intelligence*; Stiegler, 'Die Aufklärung in the Age of Philosophical Engineering'.
257. See, however, Collins and Skover, 'Paratexts'; and Katsh, *The Electronic Media and the Transformation of Law*; Katsh, *Law in a Digital World*. Their focus is, however, rather narrow and their writing dates from before the widespread and ground-breaking employment of AI.
258. Hildebrandt, 'A Vision of Ambient Law'.
259. On the historical function of Islamic law as a buffer between ruler and ruled: An-Na'im, 'Human Rights in the Muslim World'.
260. Sir Edward Coke, conference between King James I and the Judges of England in 1608, 12 Coke's Reports 63, 65, 77, English Reports 1342, 1343 (King's Bench, 1608). Quoted by Posner, 'The Decline of Law as an Autonomous Discipline' at 762, note 1.
261. Mouffe, *The Democractic Paradox*.
262. Barlow, 'A Declaration of Independence of Cyberspace'; Grosheide, 'Being Unexceptionalist or Exceptionalist – That is the Question'; Goldsmith and Wu, *Who Controls the Internet?*
263. Hoffman, 'Reading Pain in a Human Face'.
264. Ofri, 'A Powerful Tool in the Doctor's Toolkit'.
265. Art. 7 and 8 CFREU. See De Hert and Gutwirth, 'Privacy, Data Protection and Law Enforcement. Opacity of the Individual and Transparency of Power'; Gonzalez Fuster, *The Emergence of Personal Data Protection as a Fundamental Right of the EU*.
266. Court of first instance in the Netherlands, Rechtbank Oost-Brabant, 26 November 2013, ECLI:NL:RBOBR:2013:6553 (in Dutch). Helas, the court of appeal, Hof Den Bosch, 19 August 2014, ECLI:NL:GHSHE:2014:2803, has struck down this reasoning, suggesting there is no disproportionality in checking the near-totality of all parking behaviours. Recent case law of the CJEU 8 April 2014, C-293/12 and C-594/12, provides arguments, however, that confirm that such unlimited inquisitiveness is out of bounds in a constitutional democracy, finding the imposition of indiscriminate retention of traffic data on telecom providers a disproportional infringement of the rights to privacy and data protection.
267. On rights as correlating with a duty of non-interference see Edmundson, *An Introduction to Rights*.
268. Cf. Kerr, 'The Case of the Third-Party Doctrine'; Murphy, 'The Case against the Case for Third-Party Doctrine'.
269. Gutwirth, *Privacy and the Information Age*.
270. Edmundson, *An Introduction to Rights*.
271. Schauer, *Profiles, Probabilities and Stereotypes*.

272. On contingency management as a means of reducing complexity in the works of Lubbe, Luhmann and Habermas, see Kött, *Systemtheorie und Religion*.
273. http://www.etymonline.com/index.php?term=category&allowed_in_frame=0
274. Though, to be precise, the DPD being a directive and not a regulation, it imposes the duty to create a legal framework compliant with the DPD. Once the pGDPR is in force, it will have direct effect in all member states.
275. Swan, 'The Quantified Self'; Neff, 'Why Big Data Won't Cure Us'.
276. Neff, 'Why Big Data Won't Cure Us' at 117.
277. Gleick, *The Information*.
278. On cross-contextual recombination, see Kallinikos, *The Consequences of Information: Institutional Implications of Technological Change*.
279. Robinson, 'Epiphenomenalism'.
280. Floridi has defined semantic information as well formed, meaningful and truthful data: Floridi, *The Blackwell Guide to the Philosophy of Computing and Information* at 106.
281. Some have attributed this to Nils Bohr, others claim it is a Danish proverb, see http://quoteinvestigator.com/2013/10/20/no-predict/
282. Again, we can find many attributions: http://quoteinvestigator.com/2012/09/27/invent-the-future/
283. Merton, 'The Self-Fulfilling Prophecy'.
284. Hildebrandt, 'The Rule of Law in Cyberspace' at 9.
285. I am quoting the pGDPR as voted in the European Parliament on 12 March 2014. The definition is in Art. 4 (3a), the prohibition is in Art. 20 (5).
286. Masiello and Whitten, 'Engineering Privacy in an Age of Information Abundance'.
287. boyd and Crawford, *Six Provocations for Big Data*.
288. Cate, Cullen and Mayer-Schönberger, *Data Protection Principles for the 21st Century: Revising the 1980 OECD Guidelines* at 3.
289. Waldron, 'Security and Liberty'.
290. Spiekermann, Korunovska, and Bauer, 'Psychology of Ownership and Asset Defense'.
291. Acquisti, 'Privacy in Electronic Commerce and the Economics of Immediate Gratification'.
292. Cate, Cullen and Mayer-Schönberger, *Data Protection Principles for the 21st Century: Revising the 1980 OECD Guidelines*.
293. Cavoukian, *The Unintended Consequences of Privacy Paternalism*.
294. Ibid.
295. Hildebrandt, 'Profiles and Correlatable Humans'.
296. Koning, Korenhof, Alpár, Hoepman, 'The ABC of ABC: An Analysis of Attribute-based Credentials in the Light of Data Protection, Privacy and Identity'.
297. Hardy, 'The Era of Cloud Computing'.
298. Bradford, 'The Brussels Effect' at 3 and 4.
299. Ibid at 3.
300. Goldsmith and Wu, *Who Controls the Internet?*
301. CJEU, 13 May 2014, C-131/12 Google v Gonzalez. Cf. Rosen, 'The Right to Be Forgotten'; Korenhof et al., *Timing the Right to Be Forgotten*.
302. Grosheide, 'Being Unexceptionalist or Exceptionalist – That is the Question'.
303. On the mutual constitution of science, technology and law: Jasanoff, *Science at the Bar: Law, Science, and Technology in America*.
304. Reidenberg, 'Yahoo and Democracy on the Internet'.
305. CJEU, 13 May 2014, C-131/12 Google v Gonzalez, 92 and 93.
306. Ibid 96.
307. Scott, 'Google Ready to Comply With "Right to Be Forgotten" Rules in Europe'.
308. Tung, 'Google May Highlight Search Results Dropped due to "Right to Be Forgotten" Demands'.
309. Cf. Moerel, *How to Make the Draft EU Regulation on Data Protection Future Proof*.
310. Hildebrandt and Tielemans, 'Data Protection by Design and Technology Neutral Law'.

311. Though the Art. 29 WP finds that the term cookies should not be regarded as excluding similar technologies. Art. 29 WP, Opinion 4/2012 on Cookie Exemption, available at http://ec.europa.eu/justice/data-protection/article-29/documentation/opinion-recommendation/files/2012/wp194_en.pdf
312. Nissenbaum, *Privacy in Context: Technology, Policy, and the Integrity of Social Life*.
313. Diaz, Tene and Guerses, 'Hero or Villain'.
314. Voorhoof and Cannie, 'Freedom of Expression and Information in a Democratic Society: The Added but Fragile Value of the European Convention on Human Rights', e.g. at 410.
315. Schizer, 'Subsidizing the Press', though it is debatable whether such legal obligations are currently positive law.
316. See http://www.usemp-project.eu
317. Quote from the transcription of her address on *Beauty and Catastrophe* at the Crystal Bridges Museum of American Art Bentonville, Arkansas, see https://www.youtube.com/watch?v=QeVZVIkAcxM&feature=youtu.be
318. Jacobs, 'Select before you Collect'.
319. Salient on this point, discussing what he calls the introjection of information that has been externalized by means of script or databases, Stiegler, 'Die Aufklärung in the Age of Philosophical Engineering'.

References

Aarts, Emile and Frits Grotenhuis. 'Ambient Intelligence 2.0: Towards Synergetic Prosperity'. In Manfred Tscheligi, Boris De Ruyter, Panos Markopoulus, Reiner Wichert, Thomas Mirlacher, Alexander Meschtscherjakov and Wolfgang Reitberger (eds) *AmI 2009*. Berlin Heidelberg: Springer, 2009: 1–13.

Aarts, Emile and Stefano Marzano. *The New Everyday: Views on Ambient Intelligence*. Rotterdam: 010, 2003.

Acquisti, Alessandro. 'Privacy in Electronic Commerce and the Economics of Immediate Gratification'. In *Proceedings of the 5th ACM Conference on Electronic Commerce*, 21–29. EC '04. New York: ACM, 2004.

Acquisti, Alessandro, Leslie K. John and George Loewenstein. 'What Is Privacy Worth?' *The Journal of Legal Studies* 42, no. 2 (June 2013): 249–74.

Adams, A.A., K. Murata and Y. Orito. 'The Japanese Sense of Information Privacy'. *AI & Society* 24, no. 4 (2009): 327–41.

Agre, Philip E. and Marc Rotenberg. *Technology and Privacy: The New Landscape*. Cambridge MA: MIT, 2001.

Altman, Irwin. *The Environment and Social Behavior: Privacy, Personal Space, Territory, Crowding*. Monterey CA: Brooks/Cole, 1975.

Ambrose, S.H. 'Paeleolithic Technology and Human Evolution'. *Science* 291 (2001): 1748–53.

An-Na'im, Abdullahi Ahmed. 'Human Rights in the Muslim World: Socio-Political Conditions and Scriptural Imperatives – A Preliminary Inquiry'. *Harvard Human Rights Journal* 3 (1990): 13–52.

Anderson, Chris. 'The End of Theory: The Data Deluge Makes the Scientific Method Obsolete'. *Wired Magazine* 16, no. 7 (2008). http://archive.wired.com/science/discoveries/magazine/16-07/pb_theory

Arendt, Hannah. *The Human Condition*. Chicago and London: University Press of Chicago, 1958.

Arisaka, Yoko. 'The Ontological Co-Emergence of "Self and Other" in Japanese Philosophy'. In Evan Thompson (ed.) *Between Ourselves*. Charlottesville: Imprint Academic, 2001: 197–208.

Asimov, I. *I, Robot*. Greenwich, CT: Fawcett, 1970.

Austin, J.L. *How to Do Things with Words*, 2nd edn. Boston: Harvard University Press, 1975.

Austin, John. *The Province of Jurisprudence Determined*, edited by W.E. Rumble. Cambridge: Cambridge University Press, 1995.

Ayres, Ian. *Super Crunchers: Why Thinking-by-Numbers Is the New Way to Be Smart*. New York: Bantam Books, 2007.

Barlow, John Perry. 'A Declaration of Independence of Cyberspace', 1996. https://projects.eff.org/~barlow/Declaration-Final.html

Benedict, Ruth. *The Chrysanthemum and the Sword: Patterns of Japanese Culture*. Boston: Houghton Mifflin, 1989.

Bennett, Colin J. 'Privacy Advocacy from the Inside and the Outside: Implications for the Politics of Personal Data Protection in Networked Societies'. *Journal of Comparative Policy Analysis: Research and Practice* 13, no. 2 (2011): 125–41.

Berlin, Isaiah. 'Two Concepts of Liberty'. In *Four Essays on Liberty*. Oxford and New York: Oxford University Press, 1969: 118–73.

Berman, Harold. *Law and Revolution: The Formation of the Western Legal Tradition*. Cambridge MA and London: Harvard University Press, 1983.

Biever, Celeste. 'Roomba Creator: Robot Doubles Need More Charisma'. *New Scientist*, 19 March 2014.

Bijker, Wiebe E., Thomas Parke Hughes and T.J. Pinch. *The Social Construction of Technological Systems: New Directions in the Sociology and History of Technology*. Cambridge MA: MIT Press, 1989.

Black, J. 'Critical Reflections on Regulation'. *Australian Journal of Legal Philosophy* 27 (2002): 47–226.

boyd, danah and Kate Crawford. *Six Provocations for Big Data*. SSRN Scholarly Paper. Rochester, NY: Social Science Research Network, 21 September 2011. http://papers.ssrn.com/abstract=1926431

Bradford, Anu. 'The Brussels Effect'. *Northwestern University Law Review* 107, no. 1 (2012): 1–68.

Brakel, J. van. *Interculturele Communicatie En Multiculturalisme*. Wijsgerige Verkenningen. Leuven Assen: Universitaire Pers Leuven, Van Gorcum Assen, 1998.

Brooks, Rodney. 'Intelligence without Reason'. In *Proceedings of the Twelfth International Joint Conference on Artificial Intelligence*, 1991: 569–95.

Brooks, Rodney. 'Intelligence without Representation'. *Artificial Intelligence* 47 (1991).

Brown, Penelope and Stephen Levinson. *Politeness: Some Universals in Language Usage*. Cambridge: Cambridge University Press, 1987.

Butler, Judith. *Giving an Account of Oneself*, Vol. 1. New York: Fordham University Press, 2005.

Calabresi, G. and A.D. Melamed. 'Property Rules, Liability Rules and Inalienability: One View of the Cathedral'. *Harvard Law Review* 84 (1972): 1089–128.

Calhoun, Craig. *Habermas and the Public Sphere*. Cambridge MA: MIT Press, 1992.

Capurro, Rafael. 'Privacy: An Intercultural Perspective'. *Ethics and Information Technology* 7, no. 1 (2005): 37–47.

Carter, Robert. 'Watsuji Tetsuro'. In *The Stanford Encyclopedia of Philosophy*, edited by Edward Zalta. London: Routledge, 2009. http://plato.stanford.edu/entries/watsuji-tetsuro/

Cate, F.H., P. Cullen and V. Mayer-Schönberger. *Data Protection Principles for the 21st Century: Revising the 1980 OECD Guidelines*. Microsoft, 2014. http://www.oii.ox.ac.uk/news/?id=1013

Cavoukian, Ann. *The Unintended Consequences of Privacy Paternalism*, 5 March 2014. http://www.privacybydesign.ca/index.php/paper/unintended-consequences-privacy-paternalism/

Cep, Casey N. 'The Pointlessness of Unplugging'. *The New Yorker Blogs*, 19 March 2014. http://www.newyorker.com/online/blogs/culture/2014/03/the-pointlessness-of-unplugging.html?mobify=0

Cheung, T. 'The Language Monopoly: Plessner on Apes, Humans and Expressions'. *Language & Communication* 26 (2006): 316–30.

Chopra, Samir and Laurence F. White. *A Legal Theory for Autonomous Artificial Agents*. Ann Arbor: University of Michigan Press, 2011.

Clark, Andy. *Natural-Born Cyborgs: Minds, Technologies, and the Future of Human Intelligence*. Oxford: Oxford University Press, 2003.

Cohen, Julie E. *Configuring the Networked Self: Law, Code, and the Play of Everyday Practice*. New Haven CT: Yale University Press, 2012.

Collins, Ronald and David Skover. 'Paratexts'. *Stanford Law Review* 44 (1992): 509–52.

Comaroff, John. *Rules and Processes: The Cultural Logic of Dispute in an African Context*. Chicago and London: The University of Chicago Press, 1981.

Dale, Peter N. *The Myth of Japanese Uniqueness*. London: Routledge, 2012.

Damasio, Antonio R. *The Feeling of What Happens: Body and Emotion in the Making of Consciousness*. New York: Harcourt Inc, 2000.

Damasio, Antonio R. *Looking for Spinoza: Joy, Sorrow, and the Feeling Brain*. Orlando FL: Harcourt, 2003.

Davidson, D. 'Actions, Reasons, and Causes'. In *Essays on Actions and Events*. New York: Clarendon Press, 2001: 3–20.

Davies, Roger J. and Osamu Ikeno. *The Japanese Mind: Understanding Contemporary Japanese Culture*. Boston: Tuttle Publishing, 2002.

De Hert, P. and S. Gutwirth. 'Privacy, Data Protection and Law Enforcement: Opacity of the Individual and Transparency of Power'. In Erik Claes, Antony Duff and S. Gutwirth (eds) *Privacy and the Criminal Law*. Antwerpen and Oxford: Intersentia, 2006.

Dennett, D. 'Intentional Systems Theory'. In *The Oxford Handbook of Philosophy of Mind*. Oxford: Oxford University Press, 2009: 339–50.

DEO, Shekhar Kumar, Manoj Rajshekar and Thyagarajapuram S. Ramakrishnan. 'System and Method for Creating and Implementing Scalable and Effective Surveys and Testing Methods with Human Interaction Proof (HIP) Capabilities', 6 March 2014.

Derrida, Jacques. 'Force of Law: The "Mystical Foundation of Authority"'. *Cardozo Law Review* 11 (1990): 920–1045.

Descola, Philippe. *Beyond Nature and Culture*. Chicago: The University of Chicago Press, 2013.

Descola, Philippe and Gisli Palsson. *Nature and Society: Anthropological Perspectives*. London and New York: Routledge, 1996.

Diaz, Claudia, Omer Tene and Seda F. Guerses. 'Hero or Villain: The Data Controller in Privacy Law and Technologies'. *Ohio State Law Journal* 74, no. 6 (2013): 923–63.

Dobinson, Kathryn. 'Roundup: How to Use Big Data to Tackle Public Sector Fraud'. *The Guardian*, 4 February 2013, Public Leaders Network. http://www.theguardian.com/public-leaders-network/2013/feb/04/roundup-big-data-fraud-error

Dreyfus, Hubert L. *What Computers Can't Do: The Limits of Artificial Intelligence*. New York: Harper & Row, 1979.

Dreyfus, Hubert L. *What Computers Still Can't Do: A Critique of Artificial Reason*. Cambridge MA and London: MIT Press, 1992.

Duhigg, Charles. 'How Companies Learn Your Secrets'. *The New York Times*, 16 February 2012. http://www.nytimes.com/2012/02/19/magazine/shopping-habits.html

Dworkin, Ronald. *Law's Empire*. Glasgow: Fontana, 1991.

Dwyer, Catherine. 'The Inference Problem and Pervasive Computing'. In *Proceedings of Internet Research 10.0*. Milwaukee WI, 2009.

Edmundson, William A. *An Introduction to Rights*, Cambridge Introductions to Philosophy and Law. Cambridge and New York: Cambridge University Press, 2004

Eisenstein, Elisabeth. *The Printing Revolution in Early Modern Europe*. Cambridge and New York: Cambridge University Press, 2005.

Ellul, Jacques. *The Technological Society*. New York: Knopf, 1964.

ENISA. *Give and Take: Good Practice Guide for Addressing Network and Information Security Aspects of Cybercrime*, 2012.

Esposito, Elena. *The Future of Futures: The Time of Money in Financing and Society*, Cheltenham: Edward Elgar, 2011.

Fayyad, Usama M., Gregory Piatetsky-Shapiro, Padhraic Smyth and Ramasamy Uthurusamy. *Advances in Knowledge Discovery and Data Mining*. Meno Park CA, Cambridge MA and London: AAAI Press/ MIT Press, 1996.

Ferber, Jacques. *Multi-Agent System: An Introduction to Distributed Artificial Intelligence*. Harlow: Addison Wesley Longman, 1999.

Floridi, Luciano. 'A Look into the Future Impact of ICT on Our Lives'. *The Information Society* 23, no. 1 (2007): 59–64.

Floridi, Luciano. *The Blackwell Guide to the Philosophy of Computing and Information*. Blackwell Philosophy Guides. Malden MA: Blackwell Publishing, 2004.

Floridi, Luciano. *The Onlife Manifesto – Being Human in a Hyperconnected Era*. Springer, 2014. http://www.springer.com/philosophy/ epistemology+and+philosophy+of+science/book/978-3-319-04092-9

Floridi, Luciano and J.W. Sanders. 'On the Morality of Artificial Agents'. *Minds and Machines* 14, no. 3 (2004): 349–79.

Flynn, Bernard. *The Philosophy of Claude Lefort: Interpreting the Political*. Northwestern University Studies in Phenomenology & Existential Philosophy. Evanston IL: Northwestern University Press, 2005.

Foqué, R. and A.C. 't Hart. *Instrumentaliteit En Rechtsbescherming*. Arnhem Antwerpen: Gouda Quint Kluwer Rechtswetenschappen, 1990.

Fountain, Henry. 'Yes, Driverless Cars Know the Way to San Jose'. *The New York Times*, 26 October 2012. http://www.nytimes.com/2012/10/ 28/automobiles/yes-driverless-cars-know-the-way-to-san-jose.html

France, Anatole. *Le Lys Rouge*. Paris: Calmann-Lévy, 1894.

Frankfurt, Harry G. 'Freedom of the Will and the Concept of a Person'. *The Journal of Philosophy* 68, no. 1 (1971): 5–20.

Frantz, Roger. 'Herbert Simon. Artificial Intelligence as a Framework for Understanding Intuition'. *Journal of Economic Psychology* 24, no. 2 (April 2003): 265–77.

Füchslin, Rudolf M., Andrej Dzyakanchuk, Dandolo Flumini, Helmut Hauser, Kenneth J. Hunt, Rolf H. Luchsinger, Benedikt Reller, Stephan Scheidegger and Richard Walker. 'Morphological Computation and Morphological Control: Steps toward a Formal Theory and Applications'. *Artificial Life* 19, no. 1 (2013): 9–34.

Fuller, Lon L. *The Morality of Law: Revised Edition*. New Haven CT: Yale University Press, 1969.

Gallagher, Shaun and Dan Zahavi. *The Phenomenological Mind: An Introduction to Philosophy of Mind and Cognitive Science.* London and New York: Routledge, 2008.

Gallie, W.B. 'Essentially Contested Concepts'. *Proc. Aristotelian Soc'ty* 56 (1956): 167–98.

Garreau, Joel. *Radical Evolution: The Promise and Peril of Enhancing Our Minds, Our Bodies – and What It Means to Be Human.* New York: Doubleday, 2005.

Geertz, Clifford. 'Local Knowledge: Fact and Law in Comparative Perspective'. In Clifford Geertz (ed.) *Local Knowledge: Further Essays in Interpretive Anthropology.* New York: Basic Books, 1983.

Geraci, Robert M. 'Spiritual Robots: Religion and Our Scientific View of the Natural World'. *Theology and Science* 4, no. 3 (2006): 229–46.

Gibson, J. *The Ecological Approach to Visual Perception.* Hillsdale NJ: Lawrence Erlbaum Associates, 1986.

Gier, Nicholas F. *Wittgenstein and Phenomenology: A Comparative Study of the Later Wittgenstein, Husserl, Heidegger, and Merleau-Ponty.* Albany NY: State University of New York Press, 1981.

Gigerenzer, Gerd. *Gut Feelings: The Intelligence of the Unconscious.* New York: Viking, 2007.

Gigerenzer, Gerd. 'Why Heuristics Work'. *Perspectives on Psychological Science* 3, no. 1 (2008).

Gigerenzer, Gerd and Reinhard Selten. *Bounded Rationality: The Adaptive Toolbox.* Cambridge MA: MIT Press, 2001.

Gitelman, Lisa (ed.) *'Raw Data' Is an Oxymoron.* Cambridge MA and London: MIT Press, 2013.

Glastra van Loon, J.F.G. 'Rules and Commands'. *Mind* LXVII, no. 268 (1958): 1–9.

Gleick, James. *The Information: A History, a Theory, a Flood,* 1st edn. New York: Pantheon, 2011.

Glenn, H. Patrick. *Legal Traditions of the World.* Oxford: Oxford University Press, 2007.

Goel, Sharad, Jake M. Hofman, Sébastien Lahaie, David M. Pennock, and Duncan J. Watts. 'Predicting Consumer Behavior with Web Search'. *Proceedings of the National Academy of Sciences,* 27 September 2010.

Goel, Vindu. 'Facebook Tinkers with Users' Emotions in News Feed Experiment, Stirring Outcry'. *The New York Times,* 29 June 2014. http://www.nytimes.com/2014/06/30/technology/facebook-tinkers-with-users emotions-in-news-feed-experiment-stirring-outcry.html

Goffman, Erving. *The Presentation of Self in Everyday Life.* New York: Anchor Books, 1959.

Goldsmith, Jack and Tim Wu. *Who Controls the Internet? Illusions of a Borderless World.* New York: Oxford University Press, 2008.

Gonzalez Fuster, G. *The Emergence of Personal Data Protection as a Fundamental Right of the EU.* Dordrecht: Springer, 2014.

Goody, Jack. *The Logic of Writing and the Organization of Society.* Cambridge and New York: Cambridge University Press, 1986.

Goody, Jack and Ian Watt. 'The Consequences of Literacy'. *Comparative Studies in Society and History* 5, no. 3 (1963): 304–45.

Greenleaf, Graham. 'JAPAN'. In *Country Studies*, Vol. 2010. Comparative Study on Different Approaches to New Privacy Challenges, in Particular in the Light of Technological Developments B.5. European Commission, 2010.

Greenleaf, Graham, Kiyoshi Murata and Andrew A. Adams. *'My Number' Unlikely to Thaw Japan's Frozen Data Privacy Laws.* Privacy Laws & Business International Report. Rochester, NY: Social Science Research Network, December 2012. http://papers.ssrn.com/abstract=2207903

Grosheide, F. Willem. 'Being Unexceptionalist or Exceptionalist – That is the Question'. *SCRIPTed* 9, no. 3 (15 December 2012): 340–53.

Gurses, Seda and Bettina Berendt. 'The Social Web and Privacy: Practices, Reciprocity and Conflict Detection in Social Networks'. In Elena Ferrari and Francesco Bonchi (eds) *Privacy-Aware Knowledge Discovery: Novel Applications and New Techniques.* Florida: Chapman and Hall/CRC Data Mining and Knowledge Discovery Book Series, 2010.

Gutwirth, S. *Privacy and the Information Age*, translated by Raf Casert. Lanham, New York and Oxford: Rowman & Littlefield, 2002.

Gutwirth, S., P. De Hert, and L. De Sutter. 'The Trouble with Technology Regulation from a Legal Perspective: Why Lessig's "Optimal Mix" Will Not Work'. In Roger Brownsword and Karen Yeung (eds) *Regulating Technologies.* Oxford: Hart, 2008: 193–218.

Habermas, Jürgen. *Between Facts and Norms: Contributions to a Discourse Theory of Law and Democracy.* Studies in Contemporary German Social Thought. Cambridge MA: MIT Press, 1996.

Harcourt, Bernard E. *Against Prediction: Profiling, Policing, and Punishing in an Actuarial Age.* Chicago: University of Chicago Press, 2007.

Hardy, Quentin. 'The Era of Cloud Computing'. *New York Times*, 12 June 2014.

Hart, H.L.A. *The Concept of Law.* Oxford: Clarendon Press, 1994.

Haugh, Michael. 'The Importance of "Place" in Japanese Politeness: Implications for Cross-Cultural and Intercultural Analyses'. *Intercultural Pragmatics* 2, no. 1 (2005): 41–68.

Haugh, Michael and Yasuko Obana. 'Politeness in Japan'. In *Politeness in East Asia*. Cambridge University Press, 2011. http://dx.doi.org/10.1017/CBO9780511977886.009

Hayles, N. Katherine. *How We Became Posthuman: Virtual Bodies in Cybernetics, Literature, and Informatics*. Chicago: University of Chicago Press, 1999.

Hegel, Georg Wilhelm Friedrich, *Elements of the Philosophy of Right*, edited by Alan W. Wood, translated by H.B. Nisbet. Cambridge Texts in the History of Political Thought. Cambridge and New York: Cambridge University Press, 1991.

Heidegger, Martin. *Being and Time*. Reprint edition. New York: Harper Perennial Modern Classics, 2008.

Heidegger, Martin. *The Question Concerning Technology, and Other Essays*. New York: Garland, 1977.

Hildebrandt, M. 'Privacy and Identity'. In Erik Claes, Antony Duff and Serge Gutwirth (eds) *Privacy and the Criminal Law*. Antwerpen and Oxford: Intersentia, 2006: 43–58.

Hildebrandt, M. 'Ambient Intelligence, Criminal Liability and Democracy'. *Criminal Law and Philosophy*, 2008.

Hildebrandt, M. 'Profiles and Correlatable Humans'. In Nico Stehr and Bernd Weiler (eds) *Who Owns Knowledge? Knowledge and the Law*. New Brunswick NJ: Transaction, 2008.

Hildebrandt, M. 'A Vision of Ambient Law'. In Roger Brownsword and Karen Yeung (eds) *Regulating Technologies*. Oxford: Hart, 2008.

Hildebrandt, M. 'Autonomic and Autonomous "Thinking": Preconditions for Criminal Accountability'. In Mireille Hildebrandt and Antoinette Rouvroy (eds) *Law, Human Agency and Autonomic Computing: The Philosophy of Law Meets the Philosophy of Technology*. Abingdon: Routledge, 2011.

Hildebrandt, M. 'Proactive Forensic Profiling: Unbounded Criminalization?' In R.A. Duff et al. (eds) *The Boundaries of the Criminal Law*. Oxford: Oxford University Press, 2011.

Hildebrandt, M. 'Criminal Liability and "Smart" Environments'. In A. Duff and Stuart Green (eds) *Philosophical Foundations of Criminal Law*. Oxford University Press, 2011: 507–32.

Hildebrandt, M. 'The Rule of Law in Cyberspace', 2013. http://works.bepress.com/mireille_hildebrandt/48

Hildebrandt, M. 'Balance or Trade-off? Online Security Technologies and Fundamental Rights'. *Philosophy & Technology* 26, no. 4 (2013): 357–79.

Hildebrandt, M. 'Slaves to Big Data. Or Are We?' *IDP Revista de Internet Derecho Y Política*, no. 17 (2013): 7–44.

Hildebrandt, M. 'Location Data, Purpose Binding and Contextual Integrity. What's the Message?' In Luciano Floridi (ed.) *Protection of Information and the Right to Privacy – A New Equilibrium?*, Vol. 17. Law, Governance and Technology Series. Dordrecht: Springer, 2014.

Hildebrandt, M. 'Criminal Law and Technology in a Data-Driven Society'. In *The Oxford Handbook of Criminal Law*, Oxford Handbooks in Law. Oxford: Oxford University Press, 2014.

Hildebrandt, M. 'Radbruch's Rechtsstaat and Schmitt's Legal Order: Legalism, Legality and the Institution of Law'. *Critical Analysis of Law* 2, no. 1 (Spring 2015).

Hildebrandt, Mireille and Katja De Vries (eds) *Privacy, Due Process and the Computational Turn: The Philosophy of Law Meets the Philosophy of Technology.* Abingdon: Routledge, Taylor & Francis, 2013.

Hildebrandt, M. and Serge Gutwirth. *Profiling the European Citizen: Cross-Disciplinary Perspectives.* Dordrecht: Springer, 2008.

Hildebrandt, M., B.J. Koops and E. De Vries. *Where Idem-Identity Meets Ipse-Identity: Conceptual Explorations.* Brussels: Future of Identity in the Information Society (FIDIS), 2009. See report D7.14a. http://www.fidis.net/resources/fidis-deliverables/

Hildebrandt, Mireille and Laura Tielemans. 'Data Protection by Design and Technology Neutral Law'. *Computer Law & Security Review* 29, no. 5 (October 2013): 509–21.

Hoebel, E. Adamson. 'Feud: Concept, Reality and Method in the Study of Primitive Law'. In A.R. Desai (ed.) *Essays on Modernization of Underdeveloped Societies.* Bombay: Thacker & Co, 1971: 500–512.

Hoffman, Jan. 'Reading Pain in a Human Face'. *New York Times*, April 2014. http://well.blogs.nytimes.com/2014/04/28/reading-pain-in-a-human-face/

Holmes, Oliver Wendell. 'The Path of the Law'. *Harvard Law Review* 10 (1897): 457–78.

Hornyak, Timothy N. *Loving the Machine: The Art and Science of Japanese Robots.* Tokyo and New York: Kodansha International, 2006.

Hudson, Barbara. 'Secrets of Self: Punishment and the Right to Privacy'. In Erik Claes and Antony Duff (eds) *Privacy and the Criminal Law.* Antwerp and Oxford: Intersentia, 2005.

Husserl, Edmund. *The Crisis of European Sciences and Transcendental Phenomenology: An Introduction to Phenomenological Philosophy.* Evanston: Northwestern University Press, 1970.

Ihde, Don. *Technology and the Lifeworld: From Garden to Earth.* The Indiana Series in the Philosophy of Technology. Bloomington: Indiana University Press, 1990.

Ihde, Don. *Philosophy of Technology: An Introduction*, Vol. 1. Paragon Issues in Philosophy. New York: Paragon House, 1993.

Ihde, Don. *Ironic Technics*. Automatic Press/VIP, 2008.

Intel Corporation, *Improving Traffic Management with Big Data Analytics*. Case Study. Intel Distribution for Apache Hadoop Software, 2013. http://www.intel.nl/content/dam/www/public/us/en/documents/case-studies/big-data-xeon-e5-trustway-case-study.pdf

Jacobs, Bart. *De computer de wet gesteld*. UB Nijmegen, 2003.

Jacobs, Bart. 'Select before you Collect'. *Ars Aequi*, 54 (2005–12): 1006–9. English presentation available at http://www.cs.ru.nl/B.Jacobs/TALKS/govcert05.pdf

Jasanoff, Sheila. *Science at the Bar: Law, Science, and Technology in America*. Cambridge MA and London: Harvard University Press, 1995.

Johnson, Robert. 'Kant's Moral Philosophy'. In Edward N. Zalta (ed.) *The Stanford Encyclopedia of Philosophy*, Spring 2014. http://plato.stanford.edu/archives/spr2014/entries/kant-moral/

Kaiman, Jonathan. 'China Reacts Furiously to US Cyber-Espionage Charges'. *The Guardian*, 20 May 2014. http://www.theguardian.com/world/2014/may/20/china-reacts-furiously-us-cyber-espionage-charges

Kallinikos, Jannis. *The Consequences of Information: Institutional Implications of Technological Change*. Cheltenham and Northampton MA: Edward Elgar, 2006.

Karnow, C.E.A. 'Liability for Distributed Artificial Intelligences'. *Berkeley Technology Law Journal* 11 (1996): 148–204.

Kasulis, Thomas P. 'Japanese Philosophy'. In E. Craig (ed.) *Routledge Encyclopedia of Philosophy*. London: Routledge, 1998. http://www.rep.routledge.com/article/G100SECT6

Katsh, M. Ethan. *The Electronic Media and the Transformation of Law*. New York: Oxford University Press, 1989.

Katsh, M. Ethan. *Law in a Digital World*. New York and Oxford: Oxford University Press, 1995.

Kawano, Sutsuki. *Ritual Practice in Modern Japan*. Honolulu: University of Hawai'i Press, 2005.

Kelsen, Hans. *General Theory of Law and State*. Union NJ: Lawbook Exchange, 1999.

Kelsen, Hans. *General Theory of Norms*. Oxford and New York: Clarendon Press; Oxford University Press, 1991.

Kephart, Jeffrey O. and David M. Chess. 'The Vision of Autonomic Computing'. *Computer* (January 2003): 41–50.

Kerr, Orin S. 'The Case of the Third-Party Doctrine'. *Michigan Law Review* 107, no. 4 (2009): 561–602.

Koning, Merel, Paulan Korenhof, Gergely Alpár, Jaap-Henk Hoepman. 'The ABC of ABC: An Analysis of Attribute-based Credentials in the Light of Data Protection, Privacy and Identity'. In J. Balcells, A. Cerrillo i Martínez, M. Peguera, I. Peña-López, M.J. Pifarré de Moner, and M. Vilasau Solana (eds) *Internet, Law and Politics. A Decade of Transformations. Proceedings of the 10th International Conference on Internet, Law & Politics. Universitat Oberta de Catalunya, Barcelona 3–4 July, 2014.* Barcelona: UOC-Huygens Editorial, 2014: 357–74.

Korenhof, Paulan, Jef Ausloos, Ivan Szekely, Meg Leta Ambrose, Giovanni Sartor and Ronald E. Leenes. *Timing the Right to Be Forgotten: A Study into 'Time' as a Factor in Deciding About Retention or Erasure of Data.* SSRN Scholarly Paper. Rochester, NY: Social Science Research Network, 13 May 2014. http://papers.ssrn.com/abstract=2436436

Kosner, Antony Wing. 'The Appification of Everything Will Transform The World's 360 Million Web Sites'. *Forbes*, 16 December 2012. http://www.forbes.com/sites/anthonykosner/2012/12/16/forecast-2013-the-appification-of-everything-will-turn-the-web-into-an-app-o-verse/

Kött, Andreas. *Systemtheorie und Religion: Mit einer Religionstypologie im Anschluss an Niklas Luhmann.* Würzburg: Königshausen u. Neumann, 2003.

Kramer, Adam D.I, Jamie E. Guillory and Jeffrey T. Hancock. 'Experimental Evidence of Massive-Scale Emotional Contagion through Social Networks'. *Proceedings of the National Academy of Sciences* 111, no. 24 (25 March 2014): 8788–90.

Kranzberg, Melvin. 'Technology and History: "Kranzberg's Laws"'. *Technology and Culture* 27, no. 3 (1986): 544–60.

Kurzweil, Ray. *The Singularity Is Near: When Humans Transcend Biology.* New York: Viking, 2005.

Langheinrich, Marc. 'Privacy by Design – Principles of Privacy-Aware Ubiquitous Systems'. In *Proceedings of the 3rd International Conference on Ubiquitous Computing.* Springer, 2001: 273–91.

Latour, Bruno. *We Have Never Been Modern.* Cambridge MA: Harvard University Press, 1993.

Latour, Bruno. 'For Bloor and Beyond – a Reply to David Bloor's Anti-Latour'. *Studies in History and Philosophy of Science* 30, no. 1 (1998): 113–29.

Latour, B. 'The Berlin Key or How to Do Words with Things'. In P.M. Graves-Brown (ed.) *Matter, Materiality and Modern Culture.* London: Routledge, 2000: 10–21.

Latour, Bruno. *An Inquiry into Modes of Existence: An Anthropology of the Moderns*, translated by Catherine Porter. Cambridge MA: Harvard University Press, 2013.

Latour, Bruno. 'Biography of an Inquiry: On a Book about Modes of Existence'. *Social Studies of Science* 43, no. 2 (1 April 2013): 287–301.

Leawoods, Heather. 'Gustav Radbruch: An Extraordinary Legal Philosopher'. *Journal of Law and Policy* 2 (2000): 489–516.

Lessig, Lawrence. *Code Version 2.0* (2nd edition of *Code and Other Laws of Cyberspace*, which was published in 1999). New York: Basic Books, 2006. See also http://codev2.cc

Lévy, Pierre. *Les Technologies de L'intelligence. L'avenir de La Pensée À L'ère Informatique*. Paris: La Découverte, 1990.

Liptak, Adam. 'Supreme Court Says Phones Can't Be Searched Without a Warrant'. *The New York Times*, 25 June 2014. http://www.nytimes.com/2014/06/26/us/supreme-court-cellphones-search-privacy.html

Liu, Lydia H. *The Freudian Robot: Digital Media and the Future of the Unconscious*. Chicago: University Of Chicago Press, 2011.

Lohr, Steve. 'For Big-Data Scientists, "Janitor Work" Is Key Hurdle to Insights'. *The New York Times*, 17 August 2014. http://www.nytimes.com/2014/08/18/technology/for-big-data-scientists-hurdle-to-insights-is-janitor-work.html

Lugosi, Charles I. 'Rule of Law or Rule by Law: The Detention of Yaser Hamdi'. *American Journal of Criminal Law* 30 (2003): 225–78.

Luhmann, Niklas. *Social Systems*. Stanford: Stanford University Press, 1995.

MacCormick, Neil. *Institutions of Law: An Essay in Legal Theory*. Oxford: Oxford University Press, 2007.

Macfarlane, Alan. *Japan through the Looking Glass*. London: Profile, 2007.

Manovich, Lev. 'Database as a Symbolic Form'. *Millennium Film Journal* 34 (Fall 1999). http://www.mfj-online.org/journalPages/MFJ34/Manovich_Database_FrameSet.html

Markoff, John. 'On "Jeopardy!" Watson Win is All but Trivial'. *The New York Times*, 16 February 2011. http://www.nytimes.com/2011/02/17/science/17jeopardy-watson.html

Markoff, John. 'Police, Pedestrians and the Social Ballet of Merging: The Real Challenges for Self-Driving Cars'. *The New York Times Bits Blog*, 29 May 2014. http://bits.blogs.nytimes.com/2014/05/29/police-bicyclists-and pedestrians-the-real-challenges-for-self-driving-cars/

Markoff, John. 'IBM Develops a New Chip that Functions Like a Brain'. *The New York Times*, 7 August 2014. http://www.nytimes.com/2014/08/08/science/new-computer-chip-is-designed-to-work-like-the-brain.html

Masiello, Betsy and Alma Whitten. 'Engineering Privacy in an Age of Information Abundance'. In *2010 AAAI Spring Symposium Series*, 2010.

Maturana, H.R. and F.J. Varela. *Autopoiesis and Cognition: The Realization of the Living*. Dordrecht: Reidel, 1991.

Mayer-Schönberger, Viktor and Kenneth Cukier. *Big Data: A Revolution That Will Transform How We Live, Work, and Think*, 1st edn. New York: Houghton Mifflin Harcourt, 2013.

McLuhan, Marshall. *Understanding Media: The Extensions of Man*. Cambridge MA: MIT Press, 1964.

Merton, Robert K. 'The Self-Fulfilling Prophecy'. *The Antioch Review* 8, no. 2 (1948): 193–210.

Miike, Yoshitaka. 'Japanese Enryo-Sasshi Communication and the Psychology of Amae: Reconsideration and Reconceptualization'. *Keio Communication Review*, no. 25 (2003): 93–115.

Mitchell, Tom M. *Machine Learning*. Burr Ridge, IL: McGraw Hill, 1997.

Miyashita, Hiroshi. 'The Evolving Concept of Data Privacy in Japanese Law'. *International Data Privacy Law* 1, no. 4 (11 January 2011): 229–38.

Mizutani Masahiko, James Dorsey and James H. Moor. 'The Internet and Japanese Conception of Privacy'. *Ethics and Information Technology* 6, no. 2 (2004): 121–8.

Moerel, Lokke. *How to Make the Draft EU Regulation on Data Protection Future Proof*. Tilburg: Tilburg University, 2014. http://www.debrauw.com/wp-content/uploads/NEWS%20-%20PUBLICATIONS/Moerel_oratie.pdf

Moravec, Hans. 'Pigs in Cyberspace'. In Max More and Natasha Vita-More (eds) *The Transhumanist Reader*. Chichester: John Wiley & Sons, 2013: 177–81 (first published in 1992). https://www.frc.ri.cmu.edu/~hpm/project.archive/general.articles/1992/CyberPigs.html

Morozov, Evgeny. *To Save Everything, Click Here: The Folly of Technological Solutionism*. New York: Public Affairs, 2013.

Mouffe, Chantal. *The Democractic Paradox*. London and New York: Verso, 2000.

Mul, Jos de (ed.). *Plessner's Philosophical Anthropology. Perspectives and Prospects*. Amsterdam: Amsterdam University Press, 2014.

Müller, Wolf, Günter Haffelder, Angelika Schlotmann, Andrea T.U. Schaefers and Gertraud Teuchert-Noodt. 'Amelioration of Psychiatric

Symptoms through Exposure to Music Individually Adapted to Brain Rhythm Disorders – a Randomised Clinical Trial on the Basis of Fundamental Research'. *Cognitive Neuropsychiatry* 19, no. 5 (2014): 399–413.

Murphy, Erin. 'The Case against the Case for Third-Party Doctrine: A Response to Epstein and Kerr'. *Berkeley Technology Law Journal* 24 (2009): 1239–53.

Murphy-Shigematsu, S. 'Multiethinic Japan and the Monoethnic Myth'. *Melus* 18, no. 4 (1993): 63–81.

Nagel, Thomas. 'What is it like to be a Bat?' *The Philosophical Review* LXXXIII, October (1974): 435–50.

Nakada, Makoto and Takanori Tamura. 'Japanese Conceptions of Privacy: An Intercultural Perspective'. *Ethics and Information Technology* 7, no. 1 (2005): 27–36.

Nakayama, Shigeru. *Science, Technology and Society in Postwar Japan*. London and New York: Kegan Paul International, 1991.

Neff, Gina. 'Why Big Data Won't Cure Us'. *Big Data* 1, no. 3 (2013): 117–23.

Negroponte, Nicholas. *Being Digital*. New York: Vintage Books, 1996.

Nissenbaum, Helen. 'Towards an Approach to Privacy in Public: The Challenges of Information Technology'. *Ethics and Behavior* 7, no. 3 (1997): 207–19.

Nissenbaum, Helen Fay. *Privacy in Context: Technology, Policy, and the Integrity of Social Life*. Stanford CA: Stanford Law Books, 2010.

Nonet, P. and P. Selznick. *Law and Society in Transition: Toward Responsive Law*. New York: Octogon Books, 1978.

Norman, Donald A. 'Affordance, Conventions, and Design'. *Interactions* 6, no. 3 (1999): 38–43.

Norman, Donald. *The Design of Everyday Things: Revised and Expanded Edition*. New York: Basic Books, 2013.

Ofri, Danielle. 'A Powerful Tool in the Doctor's Toolkit'. *New York Times*, 15 August 2013. http://well.blogs.nytimes.com/2013/08/15/a-powerful-tool-in-the-doctors-toolkit/

Ong, Walter. *Orality and Literacy: The Technologizing of the Word*. London and New York: Methuen, 1982.

Orito, Yohko and Kiyoshi Murata. 'Privacy Protection in Japan: Cultural Influence on the Universal Value'. In *Proceedings of ETHICOMP 2005*, 2005.

Osaka, Naoyuki, Takashi Ikeda and Mariko Osaka. 'Effect of Intentional Bias on Agency Attribution of Animated Motion: An Event-Related fMRI Study'. *PLoS ONE* 7, no. 11 (14 November 2012): e49053.

Ost, François and Michel van de Kerchove. *De la pyramide au réseau? pour une théorie dialectique du droit*. Publications des Fac. St Louis, 2002.

Packer, Herbert L. 'Two Models of the Criminal Process'. In *The Limits of the Criminal Sanction*. Stanford: Stanford University Press, 1968: 149–74.

Pariser, Eli. *The Filter Bubble: What the Internet is Hiding from You*. London: Penguin Viking, 2011.

Parker, Christine, Colin Scott, Nicola Lacey and John Braithwaite. *Regulating Law*. Oxford and New York: Oxford University Press, 2004.

Parsons, Talcott, and Edward Shils. *Toward a General Theory of Action*. Cambridge MA: Harvard University Press, 1951.

Parvinen, Petri Maurits Kaptein and Essi Poyry. 'Data-Driven vs. Theory-Driven Approaches to E-Selling' 35 (2012): 103–8.

Paulson, Stanley L. 'Lon L. Fuller, Gustav Radbruch, and the "Positivist" Theses'. *Law and Philosophy* 13, no. 3 (1994): 313–59.

Peirce, Charles S. and Patricia Ann Turrisi. *Pragmatism as a Principle and Method of Right Thinking: The 1903 Harvard Lectures on Pragmatism*. Albany: State University of New York Press, 1997.

Petronio, Sandra Sporbert. *Boundaries of Privacy: Dialectics of Disclosure*. SUNY Series in Communication Studies. Albany: State University of New York Press, 2002.

Pew Research Center. *US Views of Technology and the Future: Science in the Next 50 Years*, 14 April 2014. http://www.pewinternet.org/2014/04/17/us-views-of-technology-and-the-future/

Pfeifer, Rolf and Josh Bongard. *How the Body Shapes the Way We Think: A New View of Intelligence*. Cambridge MA and London: MIT Press, 2007.

Picard, Rosalind. *Affective Computing*. Cambridge MA: MIT Press, 1995.

Plessner, Helmuth. *Die Stufen Des Organischen under Der Mensch. Einleitung in Die Philosophische Anthropologie*. Berlin: Walter de Gruyter, 1975.

Posner, Richard A. 'The Decline of Law as an Autonomous Discipline: 1962–1987'. *Harvard Law Review* 100, no. 4 (1 February 1987): 761–80.

Powers, Richard. 'How Will I Die?' *The Guardian*, 1 November 2008. http://www.theguardian.com/science/2008/nov/01/human-genome-sequencing-richard-powers

Radbruch, Gustav. 'Five Minutes of Legal Philosophy (1945)'. *Oxford Journal of Legal Studies* 26, no. 1 (Spring 2006): 13–15.

Radbruch, Gustav. 'Statutory Lawlessness and Supra-Statutory Law (1946)'. *Oxford Journal of Legal Studies* 26, no. 1 (20 March 2006): 1–11.

Radbruch, Gustav. 'Legal Philosophy', *The Legal Philosophies of Lask, Radbruch, and Dabin*, translated by Kurt Wilk (reprint). Boston: Harvard University Press, 2014: 43–224.

Ratliff, Ben. 'Popcast: Who Owns Your Taste in Music?' *New York Times*, *ArtsBeat*, blog, 14 March 2014. http://artsbeat.blogs.nytimes.com/2014/03/14/popcast-who-owns-your-taste-in-music/

Rawls, John. *A Theory of Justice*. Cambridge MA: Belknap Press, 2005.

Reidenberg, Joel R. 'Yahoo and Democracy on the Internet'. *Jurimetrics* 42 (2001–2002): 261–80.

Ricoeur, Paul. *Interpretation Theory*. Austin: Texas University Press, 1976.

Ricoeur, Paul. *Oneself as Another*. Chicago: The University of Chicago Press, 1992.

Ricoeur, Paul. 'The Model of the Text: Meaningful Action Considered as a Text'. *New Literary History* 5, no. 1 (1973): 91–117.

Rip, Arie. 'Constructing Expertise: In a Third Wave of Science Studies?' *Social Studies of Science* 33, no. 3 (2003): 419–34.

Roberts, Simon. *Order and Dispute*. Harmondsworth: Penguin, 1979.

Robinson, William. 'Epiphenomenalism'. In Edward N. Zalta (ed.) *The Stanford Encyclopedia of Philosophy*, Summer 2012. http://plato.stanford.edu/archives/sum2012/entries/epiphenomenalism/

Rosen, Jeffrey. 'The Right to be Forgotten'. *Stanford Law Review Online* 64 (13 February 2012): 88–92.

Rouvroy, Antoinette and Yves Poullet. 'The Right to Informational Self-Determination and the Value of Self-Development: Reassessing the Importance of Privacy for Democracy'. In S. Gutwirth, P. De Hert and Y. Poullet (ed.) *Reinventing Data Protection*. Dordrecht: Springer, 2009.

Russell, Stuart and Peter Norvig. *Artificial Intelligence: A Modern Approach*, 3rd edn. Upper Saddle River NJ: Prentice Hall, 2009.

Salas, Denis. *Du Procès Pénal. Eléments Pour Une Théorie Inter-disciplinaire Du Procès*. Paris: Presses Universitaires de France, 1992.

Salganik, M.J. and D.J. Watts. 'Leading the Herd Astray: An Experimental Study of Self-Fulfilling Prophecies in an Artificial Cultural Market'. *Social Psychology Quarterly* 71, no. 4 (2008): 338–55.

Sanger, David E. 'U.S. Accuses China's Military in Cyberattacks'. *The New York Times*, 6 May 2013. http://www.nytimes.com/2013/05/07/world/asia/us-accuses-chinas-military-in-cyberattacks.html

Schauer, Frederick. *Profiles, Probabilities and Stereotypes*. Cambridge MA and London: Harvard University Press, 2003.

Schizer, David M. 'Subsidizing the Press'. *Journal of Legal Analysis* 3, no. 1 (20 March 2011): 1–64.

Schmitt, Carl. *Political Theology: Four Chapters on the Concept of Sovereignty*. Chicago: University of Chicago Press, 2005.

Schodt, Frederik L. *Inside the Robot Kingdom: Japan, Mechatronics, and the Coming Robotopia*, Vol. 1. Tokyo and New York: Kodansha International, 1988.

Schoenfeld, K.M. 'Rex, Lex et Judex: Montesquieu and La Bouche de La Loi Revisted'. *European Constitutional Law Review* 4 (2008): 274–301.

Schwartz, Barry. *The Paradox of Choice: Why More Is Less*. New York: HarperCollins, 2003.

Schwartz, Paul M. 'Internet Privacy and the State'. *Connecticut Law Review* 32, Spring (2000): 815–59. http://papers.ssrn.com/abstract= 229388

Scott, James C. *Seeing Like a State: How Certain Schemes to Improve the Human Condition Have Failed*. New Haven and London: Yale University Press, 1998.

Scott, Mark. 'Google Ready to Comply With "Right to Be Forgotten" Rules in Europe'. *New York Times, Bits Blog*, 18 June 2014. http:// bits.blogs.nytimes.com/2014/06/18/google-ready-to-comply-with-right-to-be-forgotten-rules-in-europe/

Searle, John. *The Construction of Social Reality*. New York: The Free Press, 1995.

Searle, John R. *Speech Acts: An Essay in the Philosophy of Language*. Cambridge: Cambridge University Press, 1969.

Shinohara, Kazuko. *Robotics Research in Japan*. The National Science Foundation, Tokyo Regional Office, 2006. http://www.nsf.gov/od/iia/ise/tokyo/reports/trm/rm06-06.pdf

Simon, Herbert A. *The Sciences of the Artificial*. Cambridge MA: MIT Press, 1996.

Smith, Patrick L. *Japan: A Reinterpretation*. New York: Vintage Books, 1998.

Solove, Daniel J. 'Conceptualizing Privacy'. *California Law Review* 90 (2002): 1087–156.

Solove, Daniel J. *The Digital Person: Technology and Privacy in the Information Age*. New York: New York University Press, 2004.

Solum, Lawrence B. 'Legal Personhood for Artificial Intelligences'. *North Carolina Law Review* 70, no. 2 (1992): 1231–87.

Sontag, Susan. *A Susan Sontag Reader*, Vol. 1. New York: Vintage Books, 1983.

Souriau, Étienne. *Les différents modes d'existence*. Paris: Presses Universitaires de France (PUF), 2009.

Spiekermann, Sarah, Jana Korunovska and Christine Bauer. 'Psychology of Ownership and Asset Defense: Why People Value Their Personal Information Beyond Privacy'. In: *International Conference on Information Systems (ICIS 2012)*, Orlando FL: AIS, 2012.

Stahl, Bernd Carsten. 'Can a Computer Adhere to the Categorical Imperative? A Contemplation of the Limits of Transcendental Ethics in IT'. In I. Smit and G.E. Lasker (eds) *Cognitive, Emotive and Ethical Aspects of Decision Making and Human Action*. Windsor, Ontario: IIAS, 2002: 13–18.

Stengers, Isabelle. 'Reclaiming Animism | E-Flux'. *E-Flux* no. 7 (2012). http://www.e-flux.com/journal/reclaiming-animism/

Stiegler, Bernhard. 'Die Aufklärung in the Age of Philosophical Engineering'. In *Digital Enlightenment Yearbook 2013: The Value of Personal Data*. Amsterdam: IOS Press, 2013: 29–39.

Stirling, Andy. 'Science, Precaution, and the Politics of Technological Risk'. *Annals of the New York Academy of Sciences* 1128, Strategies for Risk Communication Evolution, Evidence, Experience (2008): 95–110.

Sunstein, Cass. *Republic.com*. Princeton and Oxford: Princeton University Press, 2001.

Swan, Melanie. 'The Quantified Self: Fundamental Disruption in Big Data Science and Biological Discovery'. *Big Data* 1, no. 2 (1 June 2013): 85–99.

Tamura, Takanori. 'Japanese Feeling for Privacy'. *Manusya Journal of Humanities* no. 8 (2004): 121–39.

Tapscott, Don. *Grown up Digital: How the Net Generation is Changing Your World*. New York: McGraw-Hill, 2009.

Taylor, Charles. *Philosophical Arguments*. Cambridge MA: Harvard University Press, 1995.

Teubner, Günther. *Rights of Non-Humans? Electronic Agents and Animals as New Actors in Politics and Law*. European University Institute, MWP Lecture Series, 2007, '04, http://cadmus.eui.eu/handle/1814/6960.

Thaler, Richard H. and Cass R. Sunstein. *Nudge: Improving Decisions about Health, Wealth, and Happiness*. New Haven: Yale University Press, 2008.

The Economist, 'Data-Driven Finance. Go Figure. A New Class of Internet Start-Ups is Trying to Turn Data into Money'. *The Economist*, 17 March 2011.

Thomas, W.I. and D.S. Thomas. *The Child in America*. New York: Knopf, 1928.

Thompson, Evan. *Between Ourselves: Second-Person Issues in the Study of Consciousness*. Charlottesville: Imprint Academic, 2001.

Tung, Liam. 'Google May Highlight Search Results Dropped Due to "Right to Be Forgotten" Demands'. *ZDNet*, 9 June 2014. http://www.zdnet.com/google-may-highlight-search-results-dropped-due-to-right-to-be-forgotten-demands-7000030320/

Vallverdu, Jordi and David Casacuberta. 'The Panic Room: On Synthetic Emotions'. In Adam Briggle, Katinka Waelbers and Philip Brey (eds) *Current Issues in Computing and Philosophy*. Amsterdam: IOS Press, 2008: 103–15.

Vanderstraeten, Raf. 'Parsons, Luhmann and the Theorem of Double Contingency'. *Journal of Classical Sociology* 2, no. 1 (2007): 77–92.

Varela, F.J., Evan Thompson and Eleanor Rosch. *The Embodied Mind: Cognitive Science and Human Experience*. Cambridge MA: MIT Press, 1991.

Verbeek, Peter-Paul. *What Things Do: Philosophical Reflections on Technology, Agency and Design*. University Park PA: Pennsylvania State University Press, 2005.

Vinx, Lars. 'Carl Schmitt'. In Edward N. Zalta (ed.) *The Stanford Encyclopedia of Philosophy*, Winter 2013. http://plato.stanford.edu/archives/win2013/entries/schmitt/

Voorhoof, Dirk and Hannes Cannie. 'Freedom of Expression and Information in a Democratic Society: The Added but Fragile Value of the European Convention on Human Rights'. *International Communication Gazette* 72, no. 4–5 (6 January 2010): 407–23.

Waal, Frans de, Stephen Macedo and Josiah Ober. *Primates and Philosophers: How Morality Evolved*. Princeton: Princeton University Press, 2009.

Waldron, Jeremy. 'Security and Liberty: The Image of Balance'. *Journal of Political Philosophy* 11, no. 2 (1 June 2003): 191–210.

Waldron, Jeremy. 'The Concept and Rule of Law'. *Georgia Law Review* 43, no. 1 (2008): 1–42.

Waldron, Jeremy. 'The Rule of Law and the Importance of Procedure'. New York University Public Law and Legal Theory Working Papers, 1 October 2010. http://lsr.nellco.org/nyu_plltwp/234

Wallop, Harry. 'Spritz: Read War and Peace at 1,000 Words a Minute? No Thanks'. *Telegraph.co.uk*, 20: 18. http://www.telegraph.co.uk/technology/10687918/Spritz-Read-War-and-Peace-at-1000-words-a-minute-No-thanks.html

Weiser, Mark. 'The Computer for the 21st Century'. *Scientific American* 265, no. 3 (1991): 94–104.

Wesel, Uwe. *Frühformen Des Rechts in Vorstaatlichen Gesellschaften. Umrisse Einer Frühgeschichte Des Rechts Bei Sammlern Und Jägern Und Akephalen Ackerbauern Und Hirten.* Frankfurt am Main: Suhrkamp, 1985.

Westin, Alan. *Privacy and Freedom.* New York: Atheneum, 1967.

White, E.B. *Here Is New York.* New York: The Little Bookroom, 1949.

White, Thomas. *In Defense of Dolphins: The New Moral Frontier.* Malden MA: Wiley-Blackwell, 2007.

Wiener, Norbert. *Cybernetics: Or Control and Communication in the Animal and the Machine.* Cambridge MA: MIT Press, 1948.

Winch, Peter. *The Idea of a Social Science.* London and Henley: Routledge & Kegan Paul, 1958.

Wittgenstein, Ludwig, G.E.M. Anscombe, P.M.S. Hacker and Joachim Schulte. *Philosophical Investigations*, revised 4th edn. Malden MA: Wiley-Blackwell, 2009.

Wolf, Maryanne. *Proust and the Squid: The Story and Science of the Reading Brain.* Cambridge: Icon Books Ltd, 2008.

Wolpert, David H. and William G. Macready. 'No Free Lunch Theorems for Optimization'. *IEEE Transactions on Evolutionary Computation* 1, no. 1 (1997).

Wright, Bradley. 'What's a Spurious Correlation?' *Everyday Sociology Blog*, 28 April 2008. http://nortonbooks.typepad.com/everyday sociology/2008/04/whats-a-spuriou.html

Wu, Jeffrey. 'The Philosophy of As-Is: The Ethics of Watsuji Tetsuro'. *Stanford Journal of East Asian Affairs* 1 (Spring 2001): 96–101.

Wynne, Brian. 'Uncertainty and Environmental Learning'. *Global Environmental Change*, (June 1992): 111–27.

Yamamoto, Yutaka. 'A Morality Based on Trust: Some Reflections on Japanese Morality'. *Philosophy East & West* 40 (1990): 451–69.

Young, Alyson Leigh and Anabel Quan-Haase. 'Privacy Protection Strategies on Facebook'. *Information, Communication & Society* 16, no. 4 (2013): 479–500.

Zarsky, Tal Z. '"Mine Your Own Business!": Making the Case for the Implications of the Data Mining of Personal Information in the Forum of Public Opinion'. *Yale Journal of Law & Technology* 5, no. 4 (2002–2003): 17–47.

Zittrain, Jonathan. 'The Generative Internet'. *Harvard Law Review* 119 (May 2006): 1974–2014.

Zittrain, Jonathan. *The Future of the Internet: And How to Stop It.* New Haven CT: Yale University Press, 2008.

Abbreviations and glossary

AB research   A research design that enables one to track the impact of minor and major changes on the users of a service. For example, visitors of a website are divided in two; one half is directed to the current site (A), the other to the same site with a slight change in its appearance or behaviour (site B). Based on tracking **cookies** the behaviour of the users is measured and compared. This usually results in opting for either version A or B, after which the same procedure is followed for another change in the site. Online, such research can be performed automatically and with great speed, involving massive amounts of users. See also **herding behaviours**.

action/ behaviour   Action can be defined as meaningful behaviour; action implies a self-conscious subject capable of reflecting upon her own behaviours and developing intentions about them. Action can also be defined in terms of having beliefs and reasons. Behaviour is described from an observer's position and need not refer to an agent (even stones, the weather and the sun 'behave' in certain ways). See also **agent, (human) agency, 'agential'**.

affective computing   Computing that is capable of recognizing and/or influencing emotional states in humans. See also **synthetic emotions**.

affordance   The types of behaviours that a specific environment makes possible for an organism. In this book: the types of behaviours that a specific socio-technical infrastructure (STI) 'affords', i.e. makes possible or impossible for the agents that employ it.

agent, (human) agency, 'agential'   An agent is an entity that behaves in a way that responds to perceived consequences of its own behaviour; this does not imply consciousness or self-consciousness (it does not necessarily imply **action**). Agency is what characterizes an agent as compared to a non-agent, i.e. an entity that does not perceive its environment in relation to its own behaviours. The adjective 'agential' refers to whatever has the characteristics of agency. Human agency assumes the capability to act, based on beliefs and reasons, which both imply the use of human language. Human agency can also be defined as the capability to develop secondary reasons, i.e. reasons to act or not to act upon one's primary (initial) reasons. See also **action/behaviour**.

AI   artificial intelligence

avatar In Hinduism an avatar is an incarnation of a deity on earth; in computing it is a graphical representation or alter ego used by gamers to navigate virtual worlds.

behaviour/action See under **action/behaviour**

Big Data Space The heterogeneous, decentred, distributed timespace where exponential amounts of data are stored and processed, while access is distributed and accuracy is contingent upon a number of mostly invisible factors; as such, Big Data Space constitutes the **digital unconscious** of the **onli*f*e world**.

CFREU Charter of Fundamental Rights of the European Union

compliant robotics A branch of robotic research, also called soft robotics, that works with flexible (compliant) material instead of the metallic mechanics of conventional robotics.

cookie A small text file posted on the terminal equipment of a web user, which enables websites and many other partners to re-recognize a user. Cookies are used to enable identification, authentication, shopping, cross-domain tracing and tracking, behavioural advertising, **AB research**, and web analytics in general.

digital unconscious The largely invisible **Big Data Space** on which the **onli*f*e world** and its **ICI** of **pre-emptive computing** depend, where inferences are drawn and applied, largely beyond the ambit of conscious reflection.

DOF Degrees of freedom, a term used in robotics to indicate the range of potential movements of, e.g., a robot arm. In conventional robotics the DOF are kept low to reduce the computational requirements. In soft or **compliant robotics** there is no need to think in terms of DOF.

double contingency This refers to the fact that human beings have to anticipate how others anticipate them in order to make sense of their world. Since one can never be sure of how one's words and actions will be interpreted, our shared world hinges on a foundational uncertainty. This uncertainty is highly productive and helps to generate creative interaction as well as institutional artefacts that stabilize mutual expectations.

DPD European Union Data Protection Directive D 95/6/EC

DPbD Data Protection by Design, or, Data Protection by Default. The latter is a subset of the former, focused on designing for data minimization. The **pGDPR** attributes a legal obligation to implement DPbD on all data controllers. In this volume it is seen as an example of **LPbD**.

enaction A notion that refers to the entanglement of **action** and perception in living organisms, meaning that perception anticipates the consequences of 'own' potential actions for the organism; the feedback loop between **action** and perception is also critical for the concept of artificial **agency**.

extended mind   This notion expresses the idea that our mind is not contained in our 'skinbag', that cognition operates via various extensions outside the human body, notably extending our perception, navigation manipulation, memory and anticipations; e.g. bicycles, the script, musical instruments, mobile phones and search engines become cognitive resources that extend our mind.

FIPs   Fair information principles, i.e. the principles formulated in the 1980 OECD Guidelines.

herding behaviours   Based on insights from behavioural economics, cognitive psychology and the science of networks, measurable behaviours of web users (websurf, 'liking', purchasing and posting behaviours) are captured, stored and searched to detect imitation and threshold behaviours in very large groups of Internet users.

HMI   Human machine interfacing (refers to the technological mediation between a human person and the computer system she is using, e.g. a screen or touch pad) and/or Human Machine Interaction (refers to the interaction between human persons and the machines they operate).

hyperconnectivity   Refers to the type of connectivity enabled in a network architecture that enables people, devices and things to connect with the connections of the connections (etc.) of their connections, thus evoking a so-called network effect, meaning that the consequences of sharing behaviours through ever broadening circles of connections of connections are hard to foresee. Connecting with others over large distances in no time, at no cost has consequences for the experience of time, distance and space. This is exacerbated by the scale of connections, the distributed nature of networks and the automation of communication.

ICI   Information and communication infrastructure, e.g. the script, the printing press, mass media, the Internet, the world wide web.

institution   An identifiable part of the *Welt* that is brought about by human practices that depend on the use of human language and on persistent patterns of human interaction. Institutions are not given, not cast in stone and require hard work to be sustained. They *generate* and are *generated by* the conditions of felicity for human action to count as, for instance, a valid agreement or a valid act of worship, graduation, etc. Examples are: law, religion, education, marriage, employment, a market economy, government, the game of chess, freedom to contract, money.

ITU   International Telecommunications Union

KDD   Knowledge discovery in databases

legalism   A strict adherence to rule-based government or rule *by* law. It is either focused on legislation (codes and statutes, as with 19th-century continental law) or on strict interpretation of rules derived from case law (stare decisis in the 19th-century UK and legal formalism in the 19th-century USA).

legality   A requirement of the substantive conception of the Rule of Law, meaning that governments are bound to uphold and sustain the integrity of the legal system, including the protection it offers against the government to those under its rule. This entails that neither the legislator nor the administration can be judge in their own case, thus relating to the system of checks and balances that is typical for constitutional democratic government.

LPbD   Legal protection by design, which entails that legal conditions are translated into a technical requirement to sustain the force of law. The bottom line is that where computational infrastructures implicate the substance of fundamental rights they must: (1) engage democratic participation as to the defaults they constitute; (2) be engineered and designed in a way that makes them 'resistable'; and (3) be made 'contestible' in a court of law.

ML   Machine learning

onli*fe* world   The hybrid life world composed of and constituted by combinations of software and hardware that determine information flows and the capability to perceive and cognize one's environment, which is run by means of an **ICI** capable of pre-emptive computing, based on its tapping into the digital unconscious of **Big Data Space**.

ORP   Optimal reading point

PDA   Personal digital assistant

pGDPR   Proposed General Data Protection Regulation

pre-emptive computing   A type of computing that combines predictive analytics with computational interventions that are meant to replace human action, cater to it or overrule it before the human had a chance to even form a conscious intention.

RFID   Radio frequency identification, i.e. tiny tags attached to a thing or a person, thus enabling identification via RFID reader systems.

robot   A machine capable of performing specific tasks automatically, usually distinguished as industrial robotics, companion robots and virtual bots. Some robots are designed as lookalike human beings (androids, **avatars**), but this is not necessary.

smart grid   An energy supply system that is based on demand-response, on two-way communication between consumers, on data-driven network management and energy supply, and on remote control over household supply. It is usually meant to enable the integration of renewable energy that is uploaded to the network by individual households. It is hoped that the system will also integrate a regular power supply for massive amounts of electrical vehicles, and flexible pricing mechanisms are often seen as an indispensable tool to attune demand and supply. Artificial intelligence is used for load balancing and for enabling an efficient demand-response architecture.

SNS   social networking site

synthetic emotions   Based on the idea that human reason and decision-making is contingent upon emotional skills, computing systems are upgraded with engineered emotional states. See also **affective computing**.

Ubicomp   Ubiquitous computing

Umwelt   The environment that we can reference by pointing to it (called ostensive reference). More specifically, the immediate surroundings of a specific organism that is capable of navigating its surroundings based on reiterant loops of perception and action. What constitutes an *Umwelt* depends on how the organism perceives and interacts with its *Umwelt*, which is also contingent on what the environment affords (makes possible) in relation to the organism. See also *Welt*.

webbot   A software agent capable of searching the web, predicting future events based on tracking key words used on the Internet or conducting other specific operations on the web.

Welt   The experience of the world in which we find ourselves, beyond the *Umwelt*, thus including what we cannot point to. More specifically, the *Welt* is the meaningful environment that is constituted by human language, which enables us to present what is not present here or now, thus also enabling us to remember our past and to imagine our future. It enables us to point out what cannot be pointed at. Our environment is thus extended in time and space, especially after the introduction of written and printed text. Being dependent on human language, the *Welt* is contingent on how words and idioms refer to our extended environment by referring to each other (combining the intrasystematic meaning of terms with their external reference). The *Welt* thus generates and is generated by **institutions**.

Index

Aarts, Emile 60
AB research/ testing 87, 260
absolutism 164
abstract thought 162–3
accountability
  data controllers, of 189, 212
  government, of 155–8, 189
  harm approach 202
  human agency 53, 56, 58–9
  purpose binding 155–8, 202–3, 212
action *vs.* behaviours 86, 185, 260
actor network theory (ANT) 169
advertising, and consumer manipulation
    89–91
affective computing 70–71, 184–5, 260
affordances 260
  definition 47–50, 170–71
  onlife world, of 47–50, 183–5
  printing press, of 180–81
  script, of 177–81
agency
  affordances, and 47–50
  animism 128–30
  autonomy, and 22–3
  complete agents 27–30
  definition 22–3, 30, 260
  deterministic algorithms, and 23–4,
    185
  enaction 28, 40, 57, 225, 261
  global agency 26
  machine learning, and 24–6
  mindless agency *vs.* 'mindness' 22–3
  multi-agent systems (MAS) 26–7
  perception, role of 28, 47
  relational nature of 47–8
  self-organization 26–7
  smart agents *vs.* smart environments
    27

see also artificial agency; data-driven
    agency; human agency;
    smartness
Agre, Philip E. 80, 118
aida (inbetween) 114–15
algorithms
  agency, and 23–6, 185
  bias 34
  Big Data Space, and 30
  data mining 24–5
  definition 23–6
  deterministic algorithms 23–6, 185
  knowledge discovery in databases
    (KDD) 33–4
  machine learning 24
  training sets 24–5
  unpredictable outcomes, impact of
    23–4, 26
Altman, Irwin 79–80, 103, 105
amae (indulgence, dependence) 121–2
ambient intelligence (AmI) 7–8, 27,
    46–7, 60
  see also ubicomp
ambiguity 67, 142–3, 149, 188
analytics, benefits of 196–7
Anderson, Chris 25, 37–8
Animism 112–13, 128–30
'anyware' 9
Arendt, Hannah 85–6, 114
Aristotle 150
artificial agency
  action and perception 28
  autonomous computing, and 55–7
  cognitive resources, and 28
  definition 22–3, 260
  legal personhood, and 73
  legal subjectivity, and 12–13
  liability of 73
  machine learning, and 24–6

Between the covers

While meandering through San Francisco's *de Young* Museum of modern art, I encountered a large cast-glass statue of a woman. The statue shows the form and inclination of her body by the folds and draping of her dress. Upon inspection, the woman herself has evaporated into thin air; there is only the dress that traces the imprint of her delicate and lush bodily appearance, thus highlighting her disappearance. The dress is an empty mould that stands around the empty space of the woman, drawing the contours of her physical absence, thus preserving the memory of her evanescent being in the flesh. Like any work of art, Karin LaMonte's *Dress 3* invites onlookers to muse about the meaning of the work.[1] Its opacity and robustness disrupt the association of glass with transparency and fragility, confronting the spectator with the materiality of absence and the tangibility of memory. Some have suggested that the statue reminds us of the decay of the flesh and the loss of youth and beauty;[2] the dress has thickened into a relic of what the absent woman once looked like, highlighting the merciless process of aging and death.

For me *Dress 3* evokes the materiality of the immaterial, the contours of what cannot be defined, the casting of a person of flesh and blood in the costume that covers her role. It relates to privacy, to the hiding of the body, but also to the freedom to display and accentuate the curves of a woman who dresses up to show her self. It relates to role-playing, to the projection of an image, to staging a persona, while still masking the living body that breathes life into the mould. Like legal personhood, the dress enables a person to act her role while also protecting her from overexposure. In evoking elegance and the luscious enjoyment of being alive the statue – a contrario – reminds me of the rigidity of conventional robots, caught up in the limited degrees of freedom (DOF) that restrict their motoric skills to mechanical iterations. It raises the question of whether compliant robots will soon persuade us into taking an intentional stance, guessing there is something like a living entity on the inside, expressing itself in the embraceable softness of its approach.

The link with privacy, identity and persona became even more evident when I discovered LaMonte's *kinstugi* sculptures of Japanese kimonos.[3] They confirm the idea that privacy can be designed into an environment up to the point where one's clothes form an environment that helps to protect against the gaze of the other; against being read by significant others whose proximity makes impossible to *not-read* whatever one's body gives away. Different kimonos are used for different situations, during the course of a lifetime, depending on one's status, rank or community. A kimono therefore carries a message, projects a role, situates the person it envelops; it hides curves and movement, it suppresses enjoyment and spontaneity, requiring training to drape the garment and to move with dignity while keeping the folds in place. The affordances of the kimono differ from those of the lush dress typified by *Dress 3*. They are part of another tradition where politeness, rank and groupism keep people in check while requiring them to respect each other's privacy without necessarily translating this into a right to privacy.

If the technological landscape changes course, we cannot assume that the protection it affords remains unchanged. A dress is a technology; a tool used for a specific function, incorporating and generating a web of meaning. To preserve privacy, non-discrimination, due process and the presumption of innocence, we may have to 'dress up' differently, reconsidering the affordances of the covers we need to present *and* to shelter ourselves in view of the intrusions of hot and cold weather – and impertinent surveillance.

NOTES

1. See <http://www.karenlamonte.com/>.
2. Arthur Danto, *Karen LaMonte: Absence Adorned*, Tacoma, WA, Museum of Glass International Center for Contemporary Art, 2005.
3. Laura Addision en Karen LaMonte, *Karen LaMonte Floating World*, Los Angelos, Art Works Publishing, 2013. Kinstugi is the Japanese technique of repairing broken ceramics while using gold. It entails that fractures are repaired by emphasizing rather than hiding their faultlines. See e.g. Chana Bloch. 'The Joins' *Southern Review* 50.1 (2014): 1-1, available at http://muse.jhu.edu/login?auth=0&type=summary&url=/journals/southern_review/v050/50.1.bloch.pdf.

Printed and bound by CPI Group (UK) Ltd, Croydon, CR0 4YY

27/10/2024

14580410-0002